Major Psychological Assessment Instruments

Major Psychological Assessment Instruments

Volume II

CHARLES S. NEWMARK, *Editor*

Chapel Hill, North Carolina

Allyn and Bacon
Boston   London   Sydney   Toronto

Copyright © 1989 by Allyn and Bacon
A Division of Simon & Schuster
160 Gould Street
Needham Heights, Massachusetts 02194-2310

Series Editor: John-Paul Lenney
Series Editorial Assistant: Susan S. Brody
Production Administrator: Annette Joseph
Production Coordinator: Susan Freese
Editorial-Production Service: Total Concept Associates
Cover Administrator: Linda K. Dickinson
Manufacturing Buyer: Bill Alberti

Library of Congress Cataloging-in-Publication Data
(Revised for volume 2)

Major psychological assessment instruments.

   Includes bibliographies and index.
   1. Psychological tests.   I. Newmark, Charles S.
[DNLM: 1. Psychological Tests.   WM 145 M233]
BF176.M35   1985   150′.28′7   85–753
ISBN 0–205–08457–5 (v. 1)
ISBN 0–205–11923–9 (v. 2)

Printed in the United States of America

10 9 8 7 6 5 4 3 2 1   94 93 92 91 90 89

Dedicated with love to: *Steven Douglas Newmark*
Beth Michelle Newmark
Erica Lynn Newmark

For long life, health, and happiness!

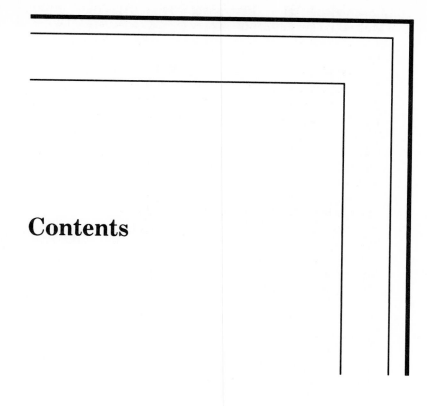

Contents

Contributors and Their Affiliations

Leopold Bellak   Professor of Psychiatry, Albert Einstein College of Medicine/Montefiore Medical Center, Bronx, New York

Domenic V. Cicchetti   Senior Research Psychologist and Biostatistician, V.A. Medical Center, West Haven, Connecticut

Charles J. Golden   Professor of Neuropsychology and Director of the Neuropsychology Laboratory, Drexel University, Philadelphia, Pennsylvania

Harrison G. Gough   Institute of Personality Assessment and Research, Pebble Beach, California

Catherine Green   Professor, Department of Psychology, University of Miami, Coral Gables, Florida

Samuel Karson   Professor and Director of Clinical Training, School of Psychology, Florida Institute of Technology, Melbourne, Florida

Michael I. Lah   Office of Student Mental Health, Wesleyan University, Middletown, Connecticut

Theodore Millon   Professor and Director of Graduate Clinical Training, Department of Psychology, University of Miami, Coral Gables, Florida

Charles S. Newmark   Diplomate in Clinical Psychology, Private Practice in Chapel Hill, North Carolina

Jerry W. O'Dell   Professor, Department of Psychology, Eastern Michigan University, Ypsilanti, Michigan

Victoria Shea   Department of Psychiatry, University of North Carolina School of Medicine, Chapel Hill, North Carolina

Helen Siegel   Research and Editorial Assistant, Department of Psychiatry, Albert Einstein College of Medicine, Bronx, New York

Sara S. Sparrow   Professor of Psychology and Chief Psychologist, Child Study Center, Yale University, New Haven, Connecticut

Patricia O'Brien Towle   Training and Research Psychologist, Mental Retardation Institute, Westchester County Medical Center, Valhalla, New York

Gary S. Wilkinson   Vice President, Jastak Assessment Systems, Jastak Associates, Wilmington, Delaware

Preface

Volume I of *Major Psychological Assessment Instruments* was published in 1985 in order to provide in a single source an in-depth examination of the most widely used tests in current psychological assessment practices. More than just a compilation of how-to manuals, this book gave the reader easy access to information concerning the introduction, construction, administration, interpretation, and status of these major tests. The intent was to present the core clinical knowledge and foundation necessary for the competent use of these instruments.

Extremely favorable book reviews; positive feedback from colleagues, students, and other readers; and the relatively high sales volume substantiated the need and provided the impetus for a second volume. Volume II adheres to the same style and format but deals with ten other widely used instruments in current psychological assessment practice: the Millon Clinical Multiaxial Inventory—II, the 16 PF, the California Psychological Inventory, the Children's Apperception Test, the Rotter Incomplete Sentences Blank and other sentence completion tests, the Luria Nebraska Neuropsychological Battery, the Vineland Adaptive Behavior Scales, the Wide Range Achievement Test—Revised, the Wechsler Preschool and Primary Scales of Intelligence, and the Peabody Picture Vocabulary Test—Revised. These tests are discussed in terms of their basic underlying assumptions, strategies, and issues, and each is accompanied by an illustrative case example. This work should serve as an invaluable reference for school, clinical, and counseling psychologists.

I am extremely appreciative of the authors' significant contributions. Working with such a dedicated, responsible, and reliable group of professionals has been a rewarding experience. All of the authors have published extensively and are nationally recognized authorities in their respective areas.

Appreciation must be extended to Georgye Woody and Linda Gottesman for their assistance in typing and proofreading the manuscript, and to James R. Council of North Dakota State University, Harrison Voigt of the California Institute of Integral Studies, and Mary M. Wellman of Rhode Island College for their review of the manuscript. Additionally, I am especially indebted to John-Paul Lenney, editor at Allyn and Bacon. His flexibility and support facilitated the development of Volume II.

Finally, I am thankful for the many comments and criticisms of Volume I that have been offered by students and colleagues, and I hope that Volume II has benefited from their input in the way it was intended.

Major
Psychological
Assessment
Instruments

1

Introduction to Volume II

Charles S. Newmark

In her Introduction to Volume I, Shea (1985) provides an articulate and lucid overview of the assessment process. She discusses such relevant issues as evaluating referral questions, selecting assessment procedures, adhering to standardized directions and scoring procedures, and interpreting and communicating the results within the context of the referral question. In conclusion, Shea notes that psychologists, in attempting to measure and predict human behaviors through the use of psychological tests, must assume a major professional and ethical responsibility. They must be cognizant of both the limitations of their assessment instruments and the pervasive influence of chance and error.

Psychologists always must incorporate a variety of crucial demographic variables into the interpretation process. These variables include age, sex, socioeconomic status, religious background, cultural background, education, occupation, race, and reason for the evaluation. Age, for example, affects responses on most assessment instruments; children, adolescents, adults, and the elderly differ normatively on many tests and also in their empirical correlates, although in some cases the discrepancy is not so great that another set of interpretive materials is needed. Although a discussion of the effects of these demographic variables on various assessment instruments often is presented in the test manual, little information usually is provided concerning how "the reason for the evaluation" should be integrated into the interpretive process. Parents involved in a custody case, malingering work compensation claimants, job applicants, parents being evaluated as a result of child abuse charges—all have sufficient motivation to present themselves as psychologically well adjusted. This motivation no doubt results in some distortion in their responses to personality tests. In contrast, an accused murderer attempting to receive a reduced sentence through the use of the insanity defense has sufficient motivation to provide responses that suggest significant psychopathology. Garb (1984) provides a cogent and concise discussion of the incremental validity of using demographic data in personality assessment. It is essential that psychologists be aware of the effects of such commonly ignored variables on their clients'/patients' responses to assessment instruments.

In addition to the appropriate didactic experiences obtained in an approved graduate program, and the accompanying practicum experiences, it is essential that professionals who administer and interpret psychological tests become familiar with "Ethical Principles of Psychologists" (American Psychological Association, 1981) and the recently revised *Standards for Educational and Psychological Testing* (American Education Research Association, 1985). The former pamphlet was developed by the American Psychological Association (APA), and the latter manual was a joint venture involving the APA, the American Educational Research Association, and the National Counsel on Measurement in Education. That these professional guidelines require periodic revision demonstrates that ethical practice in psychology is not governed by rigid rules, but must adapt and respond to changes in the needs and interests of those served by psychologists. Although the "Ethical Principles" are beyond the scope of this chapter, the newly revised *Standards* deserve some attention. These *Standards* address major current uses of tests, technical issues related to a broad range of social and legal concerns, and the varied needs of all participants in the testing process. These *Standards* were formulated with the intent of being consistent with the "Ethical Principles."

To give the reader the flavor of the *Standards,* a few brief examples will be presented. Standard 6.11 states: "In school, clinical and counseling applications, a test taker's score should not be accepted as a reflection of lack of ability with respect to the characteristic being tested for without consideration of alternate explanations for the test taker's inability to perform on that test at that time."* This suggests that although most

*From *Standards for Educational and Psychological Testing* by the American Education Research Association, the American Psychological Association, and the National Council on Measurement in Education, 1985. Washington, DC: Author. Copyright 1985 by the American Psychological Association. Reprinted by permission of the publisher and author.

psychological testing manuals emphasize the importance of considering demographic variables in interpreting test scores, a few other variables also should be considered, including medications; visual, auditory, or motor impairments; or other handicapping conditions that may adversely affect a test taker's performance. It is incumbent on the test interpreter to integrate all of this information into the interpretive process. Otherwise, the final report could be seriously flawed, as alternative explanations will be ignored.

Standard 7.3 states: "When differential diagnosis is needed, the user should choose, if possible, a test for which there is evidence of the test's ability to distinguish between two or more diagnostic groups of concern rather than merely to distinguish abnormal cases from the general population."* Thus, it is important that validity information as well as a table indicating the degree of overlap of predictor distributions among different criterion groups be provided. For example, although the original intent of the authors of the Minnesota Multiphasic Personality Inventory (MMPI) was differential psychiatric diagnosis, this has not proved particularly successful. In fact, Meyer (1983) provides at least seventeen possible diagnoses for the common 2-7 two-point code, nine possible diagnoses for the 8-9 two-point code, and eight possible diagnoses for the 4-6 two-point code. Almost every two-point code has at least several possible diagnoses. Therefore, if a differential diagnosis is needed, the MMPI should be used only in conjunction with other psychological tests. This is no doubt the case for many psychological assessment instruments. The test interpreter thus must become aware of how well a particular test can distinguish not only between psychiatric cases and the general population, but also among psychiatric cases.

As another example, Standard 13.1 states: "For non-native English speakers or for speakers of some dialects of English, testing should be designed to minimize threats to test reliability and validity that may arise from language differences."* Some tests, therefore, are inappropriate for use with linguistic minority members whose knowledge of the testing language is questionable. In contrast, tests such as the MMPI, the most widely used objective personality assessment instrument and the most widely researched of all psychological tests, have been translated into numerous languages, and the cross-national validity of this test for psychiatric classification has been well documented (Butcher & Pancheri, 1976). Unfortunately, however, the wealth of cross-national research on the MMPI is not available for many other tests. Hence, caution is urged in such circumstances, and these concerns should be documented in the report. Additionally, when evaluating an individual from a linguistic

*From *Standards for Educational and Psychological Testing* by the American Education Research Association, the American Psychological Association, and the National Council on Measurement in Education, 1985. Washington, DC: Author. Copyright 1985 by the American Psychological Association. Reprinted by permission of the publisher and author.

minority, it is often helpful if the test administrator has some special training in how to interact with these individuals. Linguistic differences are an often overlooked variable in the administration and interpretation of psychological assessment instruments.

These are just three examples of the approximately 180 *Standards* recently adopted to serve as technical guidelines for individuals administering and interpreting psychological assessment instruments. Before any qualified professional attempts to administer and interpret tests, it is imperative that he or she become familiar with all of these *Standards,* keeping in mind the continuing need for monitoring and revising this manual as new developments occur.

REFERENCES

American Education Research Association, American Psychological Association, National Counsel on Measurement in Education. (1985). *Standards for educational and psychological testing*. Washington, DC: Author.

American Psychological Association. (1981). Ethical principles of psychologists. *American Psychologist, 36,* 633–638.

Butcher, J. N., & Pancheri, P. (1976). *Cross-national MMPI research*. Minneapolis: University of Minnesota Press.

Garb, H. N. (1984). The incremental validity of information used in personality assessment. *Clinical Psychology Review, 4,* 641–655.

Meyer, R. G. (1983). *The clinician's handbook*. Boston: Allyn and Bacon.

Shea, V. (1985). Overview of the assessment process. In C. S. Newmark (Ed.), *Major psychological assessment instruments* (pp. 1–10). Boston: Allyn and Bacon.

2

Interpretive Guide to the Millon Clinical Multiaxial Inventory (MCMI-II)

Theodore Millon
Catherine Green

      The revised Millon Clinical Multiaxial Inventory (MCMI-II) (Millon, 1987) is an objective psychodiagnostic instrument designed for use with psychiatric patients who are undergoing clinical evaluation or are involved in psychotherapy. A relatively brief self-report inventory, it is composed of 175 items to which patients respond either "true" or "false." Scores for twenty-two clinical scales and three validity scales are derived from these responses; thirteen of these scales are coordinated with the personality disorders making up Axis II of the *Diagnostic and Statistical Manual of Mental Disorders* (DSM-III) (American Psychiatric Association, 1987), and nine serve to represent the more common clinical syndromes of Axis I. This chapter describes the development of the MCMI-II, how it has been developed from and beyond the MCMI, procedures for its administration and scoring, and the rationale and theory used in scale selection. It also provides some interpretive information on each of the clinical scales, viewed both individually and in high-point profile codes.

NATURE AND DEVELOPMENT OF THE MCMI AND MCMI-II

Psychodiagnostic instruments appear to be most useful if they are linked systematically to a comprehensive clinical theory. Unfortunately, as many have noted (Butcher, 1972), personality and clinical assessment techniques have developed almost independently. The MCMI-II is different. Each of its twenty-two clinical scales was constructed as an operational measure of a prototype derived from a comprehensive theory of personality and psychopathology (Millon, 1969, 1981, 1986a, 1986b). Its coordination with the official diagnostic system and its prototypic categories further enhance its utility. With the advent of the DSM-III and DSM-III-R (American Psychiatric Association, 1980, 1987), diagnostic categories and labels have been specified precisely and defined operationally. Few self-report instruments currently available are as fully consonant with the nosological format and conceptual terminology of the DSM-III-R as is the MCMI-II.

Separate MCMI-II scales have been constructed in line with the DSM-III-R model; notable here is the division between the more enduring personality characteristics of patients (Axis II) and the more acute clinical disorders they display (Axis I), a distinction judged to be of considerable value by test developers, theorists, and clinicians (Dahlstrom, Welsh, & Dahlstrom, 1975). This distinction allows the clinician to separate ongoing and pervasive features of psychopathological functioning from features that are transient or circumscribed. Similarly, the scales distinguish between various levels of severity; for example, a patient's premorbid personality style is assessed independently of its degree of pathology.

During test construction, all item selections were based on data in which target diagnostic groups were contrasted with a population of representative but undifferentiated psychiatric patients. This shift to a general psychiatric rather than a normal comparison population allows greater discrimination efficiency of scales and, consequently, heightens differential diagnostic accuracy. Actuarial base-rate data, rather than normalized standard score transformations, were employed both in calculation and in quantifying scale measures. These data not only provided a basis for selecting the best differential diagnostic cutting lines, but also increased the probability that the frequency of MCMI-II generated diagnoses and profile patterns would be roughly equivalent to representative clinical prevalence rates.

Item selection and scale development progressed through a sequence of three validation steps: (1) theoretical-substantive, (2) internal-structural, and (3) external-criterion (Jackson, 1970; Loevinger, 1957). By using each of these three traditional validation strategies, the MCMI and then the MCMI-II sought to uphold the standards of test developers committed to diverse methods of construction and validation (Hase & Goldberg, 1967). Furthermore, each successive validation stage included only those items that had survived preceding validation stages. Thus, rather than a product of compromise, the final items and scales of the MCMI-II met, through sequential refinement, the basic criteria of each construction method.

A major goal of the MCMI was to keep the total number of items small enough to encourage use of the inventory in a wide variety of diagnostic and treatment settings, yet large enough to permit the assessment of a broad range of clinically relevant behaviors. At 175 items, the MCMI-II appears to meet this goal.

Cross-validation data have been gathered with a number of independent samples and support the generalizability, dependability, and accuracy of diagnostic scale cutting lines and profile interpretations (Green, 1982). Large and diverse samples have been studied (Millon, 1987) since the introduction of the MCMI, but local base rates and cutting lines may still be useful for special settings. Nevertheless, the cross-validation data available at this time suggest that the MCMI-II can be employed with a reasonable level of confidence in diverse clinical settings.

Reliability and validity data on the MCMI-II, as well as information on the rationale and methodology employed throughout test construction and subsequent cross-validation, can be found in detail in the test manual (Millon, 1987). As noted earlier, validation was an ongoing process involved in all phases of test development, rather than a procedure to verify the MCMI-II's effectiveness following its completion; in effect, validation of the MCMI-II was an integral element at each step of construction and cross-validation, rather than an afterthought. In addition, a substantial number of studies, condensed and summarized in the test manual, were carried out before the publication of the MCMI; follow-up studies are reported in the MCMI-II manual (Millon, 1987) and in a recent conference (Green, 1987); each provides considerable information on the reliability and the cross-validation of both the MCMI and the MCMI-II. Current ongoing research from many clinical settings should result in a growing body of literature in the near future (Godfrey, 1987).

The revision of the MCMI was undertaken as a result of changes in its underlying theory, changes that led to two "new" personality disorders as well as modifications in several others. Where justified, the content of the MCMI was modified to accord maximally to the new DSM-III-R. MCMI and tentative MCMI-II items that failed to show consistency and robustness across various populations were deleted. In addition, a polythetic system of differential item weights was instituted. Items were assigned weights of 3, 2, or 1 depending on their prototypic centrality; these differential weights were introduced to optimize diagnostic accuracy and to diminish interscale correlations. The same three-stage validation procedure that had been utilized in the development of the MCMI was employed in the MCMI-II revision.

Although diagnoses may be completed by clinicians reviewing scale and profile evaluations, computer-generated assessments and interpretive reports may be obtained from the publisher, the Professional Assessment Services division of National Computer Systems. Each computer report synthesizes data from score elevations and profile configurations drawing from both empirical research and MCMI-II theory-based references (Millon, 1969, 1981, 1986a, 1986b). Following current psychodiagnostic thinking, the interpretive report focuses on a multiaxial framework of assessment.

The MCMI-II should not be employed as a general instrument, that is, used with normal populations or for any purposes other than psychodiagnostic screening or clinical assessment. Normative data and transformation scores are based solely on clinical samples. Although the MCMI-II's use as an operational measure of relevant theoretical constructs is fully justified, the samples employed for such purposes should be drawn only from comparable clinical populations. To administer the MCMI-II to a wider range of problems or class of subjects is to apply the instrument to circumstances and populations for which it is not appropriate.

ADMINISTRATION, SCORING, AND NORMS

Administration of the MCMI-II follows a procedure similar to that of most self-report inventories. Test directions, patient information chart, identification grid, and special coding sections for clinicians are printed on the front page. Answer choices (*true* and *false*) are printed next to each of the 175 item statements. This increases the accuracy of patient markings and allows the clinician to scan individual item responses.

Machine scoring is clearly the best method for obtaining MCMI-II results. Computer scoring rarely makes recording or quantification errors, regardless of the complexity of the steps involved. The item weights and the extended series of validity modifications, as well as the calculation of twenty-five separate clinical scales, make hand scoring rather problematic. Hand-scoring templates for the MCMI-II are not available at this time but may be developed once final scoring adjustments have been refined.

MCMI Test Construction Sample

Norms for the MCMI were based primarily on samples of clinical patients involved in psychological assessment or psychotherapy (Millon, 1987). It consisted of 1,591 subjects, 58 percent male and 42 percent female, ranging in age from eighteen to sixty-six. An additional 256 patients, 57 percent male and 43 percent female, were involved in the first major cross-validation study. Clinicians in 108 hospitals and outpatient centers (223 participating clinicians) and in private practice (39 clinicians) from 27 states and Great Britain provided patient test protocols. Although entirely random or precise probability sampling was not feasible, an effort was made to produce a high degree of diversity and representativeness for both the construction and the cross-validation populations.

A balance of the major syndrome categories for which the instrument was designed was created by selecting several groups of patients: newly admitted hospital patients, patients hospitalized between three and six months, and patients ready for hospital discharge; patients or clients at family service agencies, psychiatric clinics, community mental health centers, college counseling or guidance centers, and alcohol and drug abuse clinics and hospitals; and, finally, patients seen in private practice. Of those making up the test construction population for the MCMI, 1,125 (71 percent) were outpatients and 466 (29 percent) were inpatients. The cross-validation clinical group was composed of 179 (70 percent) outpatients and 77 (30 percent) inpatients.

Subsequent MCMI data on over 43,000 patients were reviewed in 1981 to evaluate their score and profile distribution, as well as to examine the utility of various adjustment and correction scores. This population was 46 percent male and 54 percent female; approximately 84 percent were outpatients and 16 percent inpatients. Selected subsamples of these data were drawn to recalculate transformation scores and assess various indexes of reliability and validity. In general, it appears that the MCMI is most useful and demonstrates greatest diagnostic validity with patients during the early phases of clinical assessment or psychotherapy.

MCMI-II Test Construction Sample

The MCMI-II norms involved data drawn from two samples. A nationally representative sample of 519 clinicians administered both the MCMI and the MCMI-II to their patients, as well as providing DSM-III-R diagnoses on a total of 825 patients. The second sample included 93 clinicians from 70 settings, notable by the fact that they were very familiar with both the MCMI and its underlying theory. They administered the MCMI-II to 467 of their patients, and also provided DSM-III-R diagnoses.

Base-Rate Scores

The traditional procedure of transforming raw scores into standard scores is inappropriate under certain circumstances. Standard scores assume normal distributions or frequency spreads that are equivalent for the traits or dimensions being measured. This assumption is not met when a set of scales is designed to represent personality or clinical syndromes, since neither is normally distributed or of equal prevalence in populations of patients. In addition, a clinical instrument is not designed to place a patient at a point on a frequency distribution but, rather, is intended to indicate whether the patient belongs in a particular diagnostic category. Transformation scores for such instruments that are more directly meaningful and useful than conventional standard scores need to be constructed (Meehl & Rosen, 1955).

For the MCMI-II, raw scores have been transformed into base-rate scores, a conversion determined by known personality and diagnostic prevalence data. Moreover, cutting lines were chosen to maximize correct diagnostic classifications, that is, calculated in terms of optimal sensitivity, specificity, positive predictive power, and negative predictive power statistics. Prevalence base-rate data for each MCMI personality and syndrome scale were obtained for the MCMI-II with data obtained from the 1,292 patients making up the MCMI-II normative population.

In these studies, clinicians were asked to diagnose their patients with reference to the DSM-III-R criteria for each MCMI-II related personality disorder and clinical syndrome. These investigations produced two sets of prevalence data, which were transformed from raw scores into base-rate scores. The first set of transformations represented the total prevalence of characteristics of each personality or clinical prototype. The second set represented the proportion of the total patient population represented by each personality or clinical prototype when judged to be the most prominent or salient within its subgroup. This was obtained by tabulating the percentage of each subset of personalities and symptom disorders rated the most salient or pervasive by the judging clinicians. For example, 21 percent of the total patient sample were judged as presenting some narcissistic personality features, but only 8 percent were judged to be predominantly or most distinctly narcissistic personalities.

Two arbitrary numbers were selected to denote the two base-rate cutting lines drawn from the prevalence studies. Base-rate (BR) scores of 75 were set for all scales as the cutting line at which scale percentages would correspond to the clinically judged prevalence rate for presence of a personality disorder or clinical syndrome's symptom features. In the example noted in the preceding paragraph, 21 percent of a representative group of MCMI-II respondents would score at BR 75 or above on the Narcissistic Personality scale. Similarly, the BR score of 85 was selected on all scales to represent the cutting line where scale percentages would correspond to the clinically judged prevalence rate for the highest or most salient personality disorder or clinical syndrome. In the foregoing example, 8 percent of a representative group of MCMI-II respondents would score at BR 85 or above on the Narcissistic Personality scale.

Percentages at or above the BR 75 and BR 85 cutting lines differ for different personality disorders and clinical syndromes because the prevalence of these syndromes and disorders differs. Thus, 12 percent of the MCMI-II male respondents score at BR 75 or above on the Antisocial scale, and 6 percent of males will score at BR 85 or above—figures that are lower than those for the Narcissistic scale, since the prevalence of the antisocial disorder is less than that of the narcissistic disorder. Through this procedure BR cutting lines and scores were established to ensure that the frequency of MCMI-II single-scale diagnoses and profile patterns would correspond as closely as possible to the prevalence base rates generated in the nationally representative norms obtained in the clinical judgment studies.

THEORETICAL BASIS FOR SCALE SELECTION

As previously stated, it is extremely useful to have a consistent theoretical system on which to base a logical classification of syndromes and a framework for developing a parallel set of inventory scales.

Three features considered essential to a good classification system of psychological tests guided the development of the MCMI-II, namely severity, diversity, and heterogeneity. Scales should be differentiated according to severity. Most instruments gauge severity in terms of scale elevation alone, yet type and degree of pathology are difficult to determine with this approach. To facilitate these distinctions, the MCMI-II differentiates ten basic personality scales of mild severity from three more severe personality pathology scales. Similarly, six clinical syndrome scales identify disorders of moderate severity, and three other scales gauge disorders of marked severity. Three validity scales further clarify the diagnostic picture. At the same time, the MCMI-II recognizes that similar disorders share commonalities, though differing in their degree of severity; the more serious impairments are appraised as separate but still related variants of their less severe correlates.

In line with the preceding, scales were arranged to reflect a clinical picture of several covarying traits and symptoms; instruments that focus on one, often dramatic, behavioral sign fail to recognize the complexity of these relationships. When each MCMI-II scale was constructed, a number of different clinical features were included to tap the diversity and complexity of personality styles and symptom syndromes.

The features of each MCMI-II diagnostic scale may overlap, where appropriate, with those of other clinical scales, rather than the scale standing on its own as a discrete entity. For example, in both the MCMI-II theory and the inventory, all clinical syndromes of Axis I are viewed as disruptions in a patient's basic personality pattern (Axis II) that emerge when an individual is under stress. In this way clinical syndromes are seen not as discrete diagnoses but as necessary elements of a larger complex of clinical features within which they are embedded.

As previously stated, it is extremely useful to have a consistent theoretical system on which to base a classification of syndromes and a framework for developing a coordinated set of inventory scales. The guiding texts of the MCMI-II, *Modern Psychopathology* (Millon, 1969) and

Disorders of Personality (Millon, 1981), as well as Millon's more recent writings (1986a, 1986b), describe such a theoretical system. Despite its wide range of applicability, the theory is based on derivations from a simple combination of a few variables. Essentially, it presents ten basic styles of personality functioning that can be formed logically from a 5 × 2 matrix consisting of two basic dimensions.

The first dimension relates to the primary source from which individuals gain comfort and satisfaction (positive reinforcements or pleasure) or attempt to avoid emotional pain and distress (negative reinforcements). Patients who experience few rewards or satisfactions in life, whether from self or others, are referred to as *detached* types. When patients reverse positive and negative reinforcements, or substitute pain for pleasure, they are termed *discordant* personalities. Those who measure their satisfactions or discomforts by how others react to or feel about them are described as *dependent*. Where gratification is measured primarily in terms of one's own values and wishes, with little attention to the concerns or needs of others, the patient is said to exhibit an *independent* personality style. Finally, those who experience conflict over whether to be guided by what others say and wish or to follow their own desires and needs are referred to as *ambivalent* personalities.

The second dimension of the theoretical matrix reflects the basic pattern of coping behavior the individual generally employs to maximize rewards and to minimize pain. Those patients who seem aroused and attentive, altering life events to achieve gratification and avoid discomfort, display an *active* pattern; in contrast, those who appear apathetic, restrained, yielding, resigned, or seemingly content to allow events to take their own course, without personal regulation or control, possess a *passive* pattern.

PERSONALITY STYLES AND PATHOLOGIES

Combining the five sources of primary reinforcement with the two instrumental or coping patterns results in ten basic personality styles: active- and passive-detached; active- and passive-discordant; active- and passive-dependent; active- and passive-independent; active- and passive-ambivalent. These patterns and their DSM-III-R counterparts are listed in Table 2–1.

Three more decompensated patterns of personality pathology in the DSM-III-R are perceived in the theory as elaborations of one of the ten more basic personality styles that display severe structural defects owing to the press of persistent or intense adversity. No matter how severe or maladaptive these structural defects may be, they are distortions in the underlying organization of personality that are consistent with one of the basic *styles* of personality. For example, the schizotypal personality, as-

Table 2–1 MCMI-II Scales, Theory-Derived Personality Patterns, and Their DSM-III-R Counterparts

MCMI Scale	Theoretical Pattern	DSM-III-R Classification
1	Passive-detached	Schizoid personality
2	Active-detached	Avoidant personality
3	Passive-dependent	Dependent personality
4	Active-dependent	Histrionic personality
5	Passive-independent	Narcissistic personality
6A	Active-independent	Antisocial personality
6B	Active-discordant	Aggressive (sadistic)
7	Passive-ambivalent	Compulsive personality
8A	Active-ambivalent	Passive-aggressive personality
8B	Passive-discordant	Self-defeating personality

sessed on MCMI-II Scale S, represents a structurally defective variant among patients characterized usually by one of the two basic detached personality styles, the schizoid or the avoidant. Similarly, the DSM-III-R borderline personality, assessed on Scale C, is seen as a structurally disturbed variant of several personality styles, for example, the ambivalent patterns, such as the passive-aggressive and self-defeating styles. The paranoid personality, noted on Scale P, is a structurally problematic form, usually of the two independent personality styles, the narcissistic and the antisocial.

Axis I clinical syndromes are seen as embedded within a patient's personality pattern. Although occasionally relatively distinct and largely transient states, waxing and waning over time, their presence depends on the impact of stressful situations. Most typically they caricature or exaggerate a patient's more enduring personality style. Regardless of how distinct they may appear, however, they are judged as meaningful only in the context of the patient's personality, and are appraised with reference to that pattern.

A variety of clinical categories are included on Axis I of the DSM-III-R. Typical of those of moderate severity that are assessed on the MCMI-II are: anxiety, somatoform, bipolar-manic, dysthymia, alcohol abuse, and drug abuse; three more severe disorders—psychotic thinking, major depression, and delusion disorders—are tapped as well. Although certain clinical syndromes arise most frequently among particular personality styles, each of these symptom conditions occurs in several patterns. For example, dysthymia (Scale D) occurs most often among avoidant, dependent, passive-aggressive, and self-defeating personalities, whereas drug dependence (Scale T) is found primarily among histrionic, narcissistic, and antisocial styles.

Numerous covariations are possible between Axis I clinical syndromes and Axis II personality disorders, and the MCMI-II seeks to exhibit these interrelationships. Although syndrome and personality scales are assessed independently, each syndrome can readily be interpreted in the context of the specific personality in which it is embedded.

The major personality characteristics and symptom pictures tapped by MCMI-II scales will be briefly described, along with their symbols and the number of items scored on each scale. A more complete description of these prototypical categories is available elsewhere (Millon, 1969, 1981, 1986a, 1986b). The most salient features commonly found among high scorers in an adult psychiatric population who evidence the personality disorder and clinical syndrome are portrayed. The twenty-two clinical scales are organized into four broad categories to differentiate enduring personality patterns (traits) from clinical symptom syndromes, as well as between moderate and marked levels of psychological severity.

Basic Personality Patterns (Axis II)

The following descriptions of high scale scorers focus on ways of functioning that are characteristic of these patients even under normal circumstances. They reflect those enduring and pervasive traits that represent patient styles of behaving, perceiving, thinking, feeling, and relating to others. Although patients in crisis exhibit more distinctive pathological symptoms, the features noted refer to their premorbid characterological pattern. The descriptions correspond closely to the characterizations that clinicians employed in the previously discussed MCMI prevalence studies (Millon, 1987). Typical profile patterns that derive from combinations of high scores will be described in a later section.

Scale 1 (35 Items)   The passive-detached orientation is similar to the DSM-III-R schizoid personality disorder. These patients are noted by their lack of desire and their inability to experience deeply either pleasure or pain. They tend to be apathetic, listless, distant, and asocial. Needs for affection as well as emotional feelings are minimal, and the individual is typically a passive observer, detached from the rewards as well as from the demands of human relationships.

Scale 2 (40 Items)   The active-detached orientation is comparable to the DSM-III-R avoidant personality disorder. These patients experience few positive reinforcements from either self or others, are perennially on guard, and are disposed to distance themselves from what they feel will be life's painful experiences. Their adaptive strategy reflects a deeply ingrained fear and mistrust of others. Despite desires to relate, they have learned that it is best to deny these feelings and maintain a good measure of interpersonal distance.

Scale 3 (37 Items)   The theoretically generated passive-dependent orientation is equivalent to the DSM-III-R dependent personality disorder. Such individuals have learned not only to turn to others as their source of nurturance and security but also to wait passively for others to take the initiative. They are typified by a search for relationships in which they can lean on others for affection, security, and guidance. As a function of life's experiences, they have simply learned the comforts of assuming a passive role in interpersonal relations, accepting what kindness and support they may find, and willingly submitting to the wishes of others in order to maintain their affection and support.

Scale 4 (40 Items)   The active-dependent orientation corresponds to the DSM-III-R histrionic personality disorder. Although, like passive-dependents, they turn toward others, these individuals appear on the surface to be quite unlike their passive counterparts. This difference owes to the active-dependent's facile and enterprising manipulations to maximize the attention and favor of others, as well as to avoid their indifference. They often show an insatiable, if not indiscriminate, search for stimulation and affection. Beneath a guise of confidence and self-assurance lies a fear of genuine independence and a constant need for signs of acceptance and approval.

Scale 5 (49 Items)   The passive-independent orientation parallels the DSM-III-R narcissistic personality disorder. These individuals are noted for their egotistic self-involvement, in which they experience significant pleasure by simply focusing on themselves. Early experience has taught them to have a high degree of self-esteem, but this confidence may be founded on false premises. Nevertheless, they assume that others will recognize their special qualities, and they benignly exploit others for their own advantage. Although the tributes of others are both welcome and encouraged, their sense of superiority requires little confirmation through genuine accomplishments or social approval. The belief that things simply will work out well for them undermines what little incentive they may have to engage in the reciprocal give-and-take of social life.

Scale 6A (45 Items)   The active-independent orientation most resembles the outlook, temperament, and life-style of the DSM-III-R antisocial personality disorder. These individuals anticipate pain and suffering at the hands of others and act forcefully to counteract it through duplicitous and illegal behaviors designed to exploit others for self-gain. They are skeptical concerning the motives of others, have a strong desire to maintain their autonomy, and wish revenge for what they judge the injustices of the past. Often irresponsible and impulsive, they see their behaviors as justified because others are considered harmful and untrustworthy; their own ruthlessness is only a means to head off abuse and victimization.

Scale 6B (45 Items)   The active-discordant orientation incorporates the sadistic personality disorder listed in the DSM-III-R appendix. It recognizes the clinical features of individuals who are not publicly antisocial, but whose behaviors abuse and humiliate others, no less violate their rights and feelings. Termed *aggressive* personalities in the theory (Millon, 1986a, 1986b), they are generally hostile and combative, and are indifferent to, if not pleased by, the negative consequences of their abusive and brutal behaviors. Although they may cloak or sublimate their more malicious and power-oriented tendencies in socially approved vocations, they are seen in private as dominating and antagonistic persons.

Scale 7 (38 Items)   The passive-ambivalent orientation coincides with the DSM-III-R obsessive-compulsive personality disorder. These individuals have been shaped into accepting the reinforcements imposed on them by others. Their prudent and perfectionistic ways derive from a conflict between hostility toward others and a strong fear of social disapproval. They resolve this ambivalence by overconforming behaviors that suppress their strong resentments, and by placing high demands on themselves. Self-restraint serves to control their intense oppositional feelings, resulting in an overt passivity and public compliance. Lurking behind this front of propriety and constraint, however, are intense oppositional feelings that occasionally break through their controls.

Scale 8A (41 Items)   The active-ambivalent orientation approximates a more extensive variant of the DSM-III-R passive-aggressive personality disorder. These individuals struggle between following the rewards offered by others as opposed to those desired by themselves. This dilemma represents an inability to resolve struggles similar to those of passive-ambivalents (compulsives); however, the conflicts of the active-ambivalent personality remain on the surface and intrude into everyday life. These patients get themselves caught up in endless wrangles and disappointments as they vacillate between deferential behavior and obedience one time, and defiance and negativism the next. They display an erratic pattern of explosive anger or stubbornness intermingled with periods of guilt and contrition.

Scale 8B (40 Items)   The passive-discordant orientation corresponds to the newly introduced DSM-III-R self-defeating personality disorder, a type well described in the early literature on the so-called masochistic personality. Relating to others in a self-sacrificing manner, these persons allow, if not encourage, others to take advantage of them. Focusing on their very worst features, many feel that they deserve being shamed and humbled. To compound their pain and anguish, states they experience as familiar, they actively and repetitively recall their past misfortunes, and transform otherwise fortunate circumstances into potentially problematic ones. Typically acting in an unassuming and self-denigrating way, they will often magnify their flaws and place themselves in an inferior light or abject position.

Scale S (44 Items)   The DSM-III-R schizotypal personality disorder represents a poorly integrated and dysfunctionally detached individual. These patients prefer social isolation, with few, if any, personal attachments and obligations. Inclined to be either autistic or cognitively confused, they think tangentially and often seem self-absorbed and ruminative. Behavioral eccentricities are notable, and the patient is often seen as strange or different. Depending on whether their pattern has basically been active or passive, there will be either an anxious wariness and hypersensitivity or an emotional flattening and lack of affect.

Scale C (62 Items)   The DSM-III-R borderline personality disorder can occur with a wide number of the theory's milder personality styles. Structurally defective, borderlines experience extreme endogenous moods, with recurring periods of dejection and apathy, often interspersed with spells of anger, anxiety, or euphoria. What distinguishes them most clearly from the two other more severe personalities, the schizotypal and the paranoid, is the constant shifting of moods, seen most clearly in the instability and lability of their affect. Many share recurring self-mutilating and suicidal thoughts, appear overly preoccupied with securing affection, have difficulty maintaining a sense of identity, and display a cognitive-affective ambivalence.

Scale P (44 Items)   The DSM-III-R paranoid personality disorder covaries most frequently with three of the theory's personality styles, the narcissistic, antisocial, and aggressive-sadistic types. Here one sees a vigilant mistrust of others and a defensiveness against imagined or anticipated criticism and deception. There is an abrasive irritability and a tendency to precipitate exasperation and anger in others. There is a fear of losing independence, leading these patients to resist external influence and control vigorously.

In contrast to the personality disorders (Axis II), the clinical syndrome disorders making up Axis I are best seen as extensions or distortions of patients' basic personality patterns. These Axis I clinical syndromes tend to stand out distinctly or to be transient states, waxing and waning over time, depending on the impact of stressful situations. Typically, they are exaggerations of the patient's basic personality.

Most of the clinical syndromes described in this section are of the reactive kind and are of briefer duration than the personality disorders. They usually represent states in which an active pathological process is clearly manifested. Many of these symptoms are precipitated by external events. Typically, they appear in somewhat striking or dramatic form, often accentuating or intensifying the patients' more routine features. During periods of active pathology, it is not uncommon for several symptoms to covary at any time and to change over time in their degrees of prominence. Scales A, H, N, D, B, and T represent disorders of moderate severity; Scales SS, CC, and PP reflect disorders of marked severity.

Scale A: Anxiety (25 Items)   Patients achieving high scores often report feeling either apprehensive or specifically phobic; they are typically tense, indecisive, and restless and often complain of a variety of physical discomforts, such as tightness, excessive perspiration, ill-defined muscular aches, and nausea. A review of the specific items on the scale will aid in determining whether the patient is primarily phobic. Most, however, give evidence of a generalized state of tension, manifested by an inability to relax, a fidgety quality to movements, and a readiness to overreact and be easily startled. Somatic discomforts—for example, clammy hands or upset stomach—are also characteristic. Also notable are an apprehensive sense that problems are imminent, a hyperalertness to one's environment, an edginess, and a generalized touchiness.

Scale H: Somatoform (31 Items)   Here we see psychological difficulties expressed through somatic channels, persistent periods of fatigue and weakness, and a preoccupation with ill health and a variety of often dramatic but largely nonspecific pains in different and unrelated regions of the body. Some patients demonstrate a primary somatization disorder that is manifested by recurrent, multiple somatic complaints, often presented in a dramatic, vague, or exaggerated way. Others have a history that may be best considered hypochondriacal, since they interpret minor physical discomforts or sensations as signifying a serious ailment. If diseases are factually present, they tend to be overinterpreted, despite medical reassurance. Typically, these somatic complaints are employed to gain attention.

Scale N: Bipolar-Manic (37 Items)   This high-scoring patient evidences periods of restless overactivity and distractibility, pressured speech, impulsiveness, and irritability. Also evident may be an unselective enthusiasm; planning for unrealistic goals; an intrusive, if not pressured and demanding quality to interpersonal relations; decreased need for sleep; flights of ideas; and rapid and labile shifts of mood. Very high scores may signify psychotic processes, including delusions or hallucinations.

Scale D: Dysthymia (36 Items)   The high-scoring patient remains involved in everyday life but has been concerned over a period of two or more years with feelings of discouragement or guilt, a lack of initiative and behavioral apathy, low self-esteem, and frequently voiced futility and self-deprecatory comments. During these periods of dejection, there may be a tearfulness, suicidal ideation, a pessimistic outlook toward the future, social withdrawal, poor appetite or overeating, chronic fatigue, poor concentration, a loss of interest in pleasurable activities, and a decreased effectiveness in fulfilling ordinary and routine life tasks. Unless Scale CC (Major Depression) is also elevated, there is little likelihood that psychotic features will be evident. Close examination of the specific components of the patient's high score should enable the clinician to discern the nature of the dysthymic mood (e.g., low self-esteem or hopelessness).

Scale B: Alcohol Dependence (46 Items)   The high-scoring patient probably has a history of alcoholism; may have made efforts to overcome the difficulty, with minimal success; and, as a consequence, experiences considerable discomfort in both family and work settings. What is of value in this and the subsequent scale (Drug Dependence) is the opportunity to understand the problem within the context of the patient's overall personality style.

Scale T: Drug Dependence (58 Items)   The high-scoring individual is likely to have had a recurrent or recent history of drug abuse. There is likely to be difficulty in restraining impulses or keeping them within conventional social limits, as well as an inability to manage the personal consequences of these behaviors. Comprising many subtle and indirect items, this scale may be helpful in identifying those with problems of drug abuse who are not readily disposed to admit their difficulties.

Scale SS: Thought Disorder (33 Items)   Depending on the length and course of the problem, these patients are usually classified as schizophrenic, schizophreniform, or brief reactive psychosis. They may periodically exhibit incongruous, disorganized, or regressive behavior; often appear confused and disoriented; and occasionally display inappropriate affect, scattered hallucinations, and unsystematic delusions. Their thinking may be fragmented or bizarre, their feelings may be blunted, and they may have a pervasive sense of being isolated and misunderstood by others. Withdrawn, seclusive, and secretive behavior may be notable.

Scale CC: Major Depression (24 Items)   These patients are usually incapable of functioning within their normal environment; they are severely depressed and express a dread of the future, suicidal ideation, and a sense of hopeless resignation. Some exhibit marked motor retardation, whereas others display an agitated quality, incessantly pacing about and bemoaning their sorry state. Several somatic processes are often disturbed during these periods—notably, there may be a decreased or increased appetite, fatigue, weight loss or gain, insomnia, or early rising. Problems of concentration are common, as are feelings of worthlessness and/or guilt. Repetitive fearfulness and brooding are frequently in evidence. Depending on the underlying personality style, there may be a shy, introverted, and seclusive pattern; a sluggish immobility; or an irritable, complaining, and whining tone.

Scale PP: Delusional Disorder (23 Items)   This high-scoring patient, often considered acutely paranoid, may become intermittently belligerent, voicing irrational but interconnected sets of delusions of a jealous, persecutory, or grandiose nature. Depending on the constellation of other concurrent syndromes, there may be clear-cut signs of disturbed thinking and ideas of reference. Moods usually are hostile, and feelings of being picked on and mistreated are expressed. A tense undercurrent of suspiciousness, vigilance, and an alertness of possible betrayal are typical concomitants.

Modifier and Correction Indices

The literature is replete with studies suggesting factors that may distort the results of various self-report inventories. These distortions may produce test data that either require adjustments to increase their validity or are so awry that they are totally unusable for either measurement or interpretive purposes. However, evidence for the importance of these confounding factors is mixed. Deliberate misrepresentation or random responding on personality or clinical inventories is much less common than often thought. Similarly, the role of response styles as a source of distortion seems to be a minor factor in comparison to the content of substantive scales. Inventories whose scoring is substantially determined by external-criterion research are only minimally affected by problems of stylistic or intentional distortion; potentially confounding items either fail to correlate with external criteria and are thereby removed, or prove to be predictive of these criteria.

As evident from our efforts to appraise and control for these factors, the preceding argument has not been interpreted as a rationale for dismissing the potential impact of problematic test-taking attitudes. Six modifiers and corrections were developed for the MCMI-II; each of them can serve both as a sign of potential stylistic, situational, or personologic tendencies in its own right, or as an index of complications that may bring the reliability or validity of the MCMI-II scores into question. It is this latter function of evaluating potentially problematic results to which our attention will be briefly directed in this section.

The first of the gauges to be appraised are the four highly unusual items that make up the *validity index.* On the machine-scored profile printout, records with index scores of 2 or more are identified as invalid; a score of 0 is recorded as valid; and a score of 1 on the index is noted by the statement "questionable validity." The automated interpretive report advises readers to be cautious in accepting the interpretations of protocols with a validity index score of 1; it records protocols as invalid and terminates the report when two or more index items are marked. Despite its brevity, the validity index has proved to be highly sensitive to careless, confused, or random responding.

The *disclosure level,* labeled *Scale X,* is the second of the indices that may signify problematic response behaviors, notably whether the patient was inclined to freely reveal self, on the one hand, or to be reticent and secretive, on the other.

Calculated by the degree of positive or negative deviation from the mid-range of an adjusted composite raw score total of ten basic personality scales, it is further transformed into a base-rate (BR) score equivalent. Corrections are made only if the adjusted composite raw score is greater than 400 or less than 250. If the composite sum is less than 145 or greater than 590, however, the results should be considered invalid, and are so indicated on the profile page of the interpretive report. Viewed on its own as a single measure, a low BR score on Scale X indicates either a general hesitancy and reserve, or a broad unwillingness to be candid about one's psychological feelings and problems; conversely, a high BR score on Scale X suggests an unusually open and self-revealing attitude, not only while completing the inventory, but probably also in discussing one's emotional difficulties with others.

The *desirability gauge,* referred to as *Scale Y,* seeks to identify the degree to which the results may have been affected by the patient's inclination to appear socially attractive, morally virtuous, and/or emotionally well composed. High BR scores on Scale Y signify the tendency to place oneself in a favorable light; the higher the score, the greater the care that must be given to discovering what the patient may be concealing about his or her psychological or interpersonal difficulties.

Scale Z, the *debasement measure,* reflects tendencies opposite to those of Scale Y, although on occasion both indexes are high, especially among patients who are unusually self-disclosing (Scale X). In general, high BR scores on Scale Z suggest inclinations to depreciate or devalue oneself by presenting emotional and personal difficulties in stronger terms than are likely to be uncovered upon objective review. Especially high scores deserve closer examination than usual, not only for purposes of gaining a more accurate assessment of what might prove to be a distorted level of psychological severity, but also to inquire whether the responses signify a call for help—a drawing of attention by a patient experiencing an especially distressing degree of emotional turmoil.

Corrections are introduced on Scales S, C, A, H, and D to represent the degree to which the BR scores on the desirability gauge (Scale Y) and the debasement measure (Scale Z) differ. Positive scores (where Y is greater than Z) result in adding the correction to the aforementioned scales; negative scores (Z greater than Y) result in subtracting the correction from these scales.

The computer-based interpretive report provides an analysis of the likely meaning of the configuration of Scales X, Y, and Z. For example, a low BR on Scales X and Y, with a high score on Scale Z, suggests a moderate exaggeration of current emotional problems that is likely to have been sufficiently corrected so as to retain the MCMI-II's interpretive validity.

The *denial/compliant adjustment* correction represents the need to build in an additional BR modification for psychological defensiveness among respondents whose highest personality scales were either compulsive (Scale 7), narcissistic (Scale 5), or histrionic (Scale 4); the desirability adjustment is insufficient to bring their personality pathology and clinical syndrome scale scores up to clinically judged levels of disturbance. When the consequences of various adjustments were checked empirically, it was found that diagnostic accuracy could be increased, albeit modestly, by raising certain personality pathology and clinical disorder BR scores among these three personality types. Ongoing research has shown also that diagnostic accuracy is increased if the BR scores of certain personality pathology and clinical syndrome scales are reduced when the highest personality scale is either avoidant (Scale 2) or self-defeating (Scale 8B). Here, the adjustment seeks to counteract the tendency to overreport psychological symptomatology. Scales affected are S, C, P, A, H, and D.

Finally, scores obtained on measures of personality characteristics may be distorted when patients are experiencing acute or intense emotional stress (Hirschfeld et al., 1983). In what has been termed the *high depression/anxiety adjustment,* corrections are made in the three personality scales most frequently impacted by concurrent psychic turmoil, that is, Scales 2 (avoidant), 8B (self-defeating), and C (borderline). The signals for these adjustments are BR scores on Scales A (anxiety) and/or D (dysthymia) of 85 or higher. Varying combinations of the preceding Axis I scores, outpatient versus inpatient status, and duration of inpatient status determine the extent to which the BR scores of Scales 2, 8B, and C are reduced.

Moderator Variables

Some argue that an increase in clinical accuracy can be achieved by introducing relevant moderator variables (e.g., biographical, observational, and demographic data) into the interpretive process. Moreover, failure to recognize their impact may result in highly distorted results. For this reason, the MCMI-II should be limited to populations that are not notably different in background from the sample employed to develop the instrument's base-rate norms. The problem of population deviance should be minimal with the MCMI-II, however, because of the diverse settings and nationally representative character of the original normative sample. Nevertheless, there may be special circumstances that justify developing separate base-rate norms, such as special ethnic or racial groups, unusual geographic regions, or extreme educational and age levels.

Research to date on the MCMI-II has been limited to developing normative distinctions only along the parameters of sex and ethnicity. Although efforts were made to sample as representative a national distribution as possible in terms of other potentially significant moderator variables—age, geographic region, marital status, and socioeconomic class—there do not appear to be appreciable distinctions based on these data. Studies of the relationship between these so-called moderator variables and BR scores indicate some differences in scale elevations and profile configurations. It is not clear, however, whether these differences reflect sampling distributions or whether they represent "true" characteristics that differentiate these subpopulations. Where data have been analyzed, the differences are generally consistent with clinically judged prevalence base rates. For the present, distinctive base-rate norms have been drawn on the MCMI-II to select male and female respondents for each of three ethnic/racial groups—whites, blacks, and Hispanics.

UNDERTAKING CLINICAL PROFILE ASSESSMENTS

Although the clinical meaning of each scale may be grasped by referring to the descriptive sections presented earlier in this chapter, more extensive discussions may be found in *Modern Psychopathology* (Millon, 1969) and *Disorders of Personality* (Millon, 1981). Further, no matter how useful individual scales may be in identifying specific clinical traits or syndromes, their interpretive value can be greatly enhanced if they are analyzed within the context of a profile of several scales. This practice of appraising the total configuration or pattern of scale elevations has grown significantly in recent years.

Fortunately, the theoretical framework and clinical characterizations associated with the MCMI-II are available in comprehensive publications (Millon, 1969, 1981, 1986a, 1986b). Similarly, an extensive body of empirical data, some of it directly related to the external validation of MCMI-II profiles, is reported in the MCMI-II manual (Millon, 1987).

The quality of the information that can be deduced by the profile analysis of a particular case results from several factors: the overall empirical validity of the inventory, the adequacy of the theory that provides the logic and hypotheses underlying the separate scales, the skill of the clinician, and the interpreter's experience in employing the inventory with comparable populations.

The following paragraphs outline the recommended steps to be followed for configural interpretation.

First, the personality and clinical features characterizing each of the separate scales should be thoroughly reviewed before undertaking an analysis of profile configurations, since the clinical accuracy of such interpretations is dependent, not only on the validity, but also on the meaning and significance of the individual scales making up the profile.

Second, as is true with all diagnostic or personality tests, if interpretations are to be accurate, they should be made within the context of each patient's demographic background, biography, and other clinical features. So-called blind interpretations may be useful during graduate training, but are unwise in professional clinical settings. Thus, information concerning sex, age, socioeconomic class, mental status observations, and interviews should all be used to provide a perspective for assessing the MCMI-II profile.

Third, a basic separation should be made in the initial phase of interpretation between those scales pertaining to the basic clinical personality pattern (1 through 8B), those pointing to the presence of severe personality pathology (S, C, and P), those signifying moderate clinical syndromes (A through T), and those indicating a severe clinical state (SS, CC, and PP). As described earlier in this chapter, each section of the profiles reflects different and important dimensions of the clinical picture. For this reason, then, the clinician should begin by dividing the profile into a series of subsections, focusing first on the significance of scale elevations and profile patterns within each section.

Once this is completed, the major step of integrating these subsections of the profile can proceed. This synthesizing process is twofold: (1) interweaving all the personality scales into an interpretive synthesis that blends the more central features that characterize the basic personality scales (1 through 8B) with those reflected in the severe personality pathology scales (S, C, and P), should they exceed the BR 75 cutting line; and (2) bringing into account not only the presence of identified clinical syndromes (Scales A through PP), but also the distinctive character they are likely to possess given the particular personality style.

The value of this interpretive procedure is that it breaks the pattern of labeling patients and fitting them into discrete and rigid categories. By stressing the complex network of personality traits and clinical symptoms, configural analysis allows the clinician to mold a picture that gives a dimension of interrelatedness to otherwise fixed diagnostic categories, and thus more clearly reflects each patient's individuality.

Procedures for Interpretations

The three basic steps to be followed are outlined here as a starting point from which clinicians may wish to develop alternative techniques:

1. *Scale elevations:* The greater the BR score magnitude on a scale, the greater the probability that the patient possesses the personality or clinical characteristics measured by the scale. BR cutting lines at 75 and 85 may be used to identify "presence" and "prominence." Furthermore, the higher the score elevation, the greater the probable intensity or severity of the trait or syndrome tapped by the scale.

Scales that achieve the highest score elevation in a profile subsection serve as an anchor point for modifying and integrating other, subsidiary high scores in that section.

2. *Sectional profile analysis:* The following guidelines may be helpful in assessing each of the four major subsections of the profile and extracting the essential features they contain.

a. *Clinical personality Axis II patterns* (Scales 1 through 8B): A configuration comprising the highest two or three scales may be used in a clinically logical manner to identify and synthesize the various dimensions of the patient's interpersonal pattern, affectivity, cognitive style, and behavior tendencies. Scales included in these analyses should be limited, however, to only the highest two or three scales, especially if they exceed the 75 BR score level; exceptions can be made to this rule among profiles with overall low BR scores. Where distinct salients occur (one scale above 85 BR and no other attaining 75 or above), interpretations may closely follow the personality characteristics outlined in the scale descriptions section of this chapter.

b. *Severe personality Axis II pathologies* (Scales S, C, and P): Each scale should first be viewed separately. BR scores falling below 60 do not usually provide specific diagnostic information. BR scores from 75 to 84, inclusive, suggest a chronic and moderately severe level of personality functioning (schizotypal, borderline, paranoid): scores of 85 and above often are indicative of a more decompensated personality pattern.

Formulating a profile interpretation of these three scales involves two steps. First, the relative height of the scales should be noted to gauge the pathological personality pattern, for example, schizotypal (S)85, borderline (C)35, paranoid (P)75; this profile would support a prominent schizotypal pattern with subsidiary, yet significant paranoid features. Second, both the basic clinical personality pattern and the pathological personality disorder profile may be integrated to provide a more complex synthesis of the patient's basic personality structure and the level and character of his or her pathological features, for example, a basic passive-aggressive personality at the borderline level.

c. *Moderately severe (Axis I) clinical syndromes* (Scales A through T): These six scales should first be viewed separately. BR scores between 60 and 74 are suggestive but not sufficiently indicative of the scale's symptom pathology, unless they are the highest scores of this segment of the profile; scores from 75 through 84 suggest the presence of the scale's disorder; scores of 85 and above provide strong support for the presence of the pathological symptom.

d. *Markedly severe (Axis I) clinical syndromes* (Scales SS, CC, and PP): These three scales may indicate a psychotic level of disturbance when scores exceed BR 74; scores of 85 or above provide strong support for this influence, whereas scores from 75 through 84 are highly suggestive. Although each scale should be approached separately to pinpoint the particular character of the disorder, mixed pictures are not uncommon. Clinicians must draw on their interpretive background to integrate these data within the overall profile of personality and symptom scales.

Certain patterns are likely to appear with substantially greater frequency than others in settings that service particular populations, such as drug addicts, or upper-middle-class "neurotics," or long-term Veterans Administration outpatients. In such settings, clinicians develop a special expertise that enables them to spot and quickly assess minor score variations.

Empirical research indicates that the frequency of certain MCMI profiles is greater than others when the test is administered in a broad and representative clinical population. With the first subsection of the profile, that pertaining to basic personality pattern, clinicians are likely to find a higher proportion of the two- and three-point combinations that are listed in Table 2–2. These combinations may make up nearly 70 percent of all MCMI-II profiles in a diverse patient population.

Frequent covariations within the DSM-III, Axis II clinical, and more severe pathological personality scales (S, C, and P) are listed in Table 2–3. These can serve as a guide to the most common relationships that occur between these profile sections. Of equal value is Table 2–4, which lists the most frequent covariations between the Axis II personality code combinations and high BR scores on the nine Axis I clinical syndrome scales (A through PP).

Table 2–2 Frequent Clinical Personality Pattern (Scales 1 through 8B) and High-Point Configural Combinations

High-Point Scale	Frequent Clinical Personality Pattern Configural Combinations
1	123, 126B, 128A, 13
2	213, 218B, 238B, 28A8B, 28B1, 28B3, 28B8A
3	317, 321, 328B, 345, 357, 348B, 371, 374, 38B2, 38B7
4	435, 437, 453, 456A, 456B, 458A, 46B5, 48A6B
5	543, 546B, 547, 56A4, 56AB4
6A	6A6B5, 6A8A5, 6A8A6B
6B	6B54, 6B56A, 6B8A2, 6B8A5, 6B8A6A
7	71, 731, 734, 74, 754, 756B, 76B5
8A	8A2, 8A28B, 8A38B, 8A4, 8A6B6A, 8A8B2
8B	8B23, 8B32, 8B8A2, 8B8A3

Table 2–3 Covariation of Basic Clinical Personality Pattern Configurations (Scales 1 through 8B) and High BR Severe Personality Pathology Scales (S, C, and P)

High Severe Personality Pathology Scales: One- and Two-Point Combinations	Frequent Covariant Two-Point Basic Clinical Personality Configurations
S	12, 23, 28A, 8A2
C	28A, 28B, 34, 38B, 43, 45, 48A, 6A6B, 6A8A, 6B8A, 8A2, 8A4, 8A6A, 8A8B, 8B8A
P	54, 6B5, 6B8A
SC	12, 13, 18A, 23, 28A, 28B
SP	21, 58A, 75
CP	46A, 56A, 56B, 58A, 6A6B, 75

Fairly common covariations are worth noting here. For example, the high-point pairs 28A, 48A, 648A, and 8A8B with C are quite common as a basis for identifying the currently popular borderline personality designation. The 12 and 23 combination with a high S scale is quite characteristic of the new schizotypal pattern. High 37 and 73 pairs are

Table 2–4 Covariation of Basic Clinical Personality High-Point Configurations (Scales 1 through 8B) and High BR Clinical Syndrome Scales (A through PP)

High-BR Clinical Syndrome Scales	Frequent Covariant Two-Point Basic Clinical Personality Configurations
A	12, 21, 23, 28A, 28B, 31, 32, 38A, 38B, 48A, 8A2, 8A3, 8B2, 8B3
H	32, 43, 48A, 8A2, 8B2
N	34, 43, 45, 54
D	12, 23, 28A, 28B, 31, 32, 38A, 38B, 48A, 8A2, 8B2
B	12, 21, 23, 28A, 28B, 43, 45, 46A, 46B, 54, 56A, 56B, 6A4, 6A5, 6A6B, 6B5, 6B6A, 6B8A
T	12, 45, 46A, 46B, 54, 56A, 56B, 6A4, 6A5, 6A6B, 6A8A, 6B6A, 6B8A
SS	12, 21, 23, 28B, 32, 38B, 8B2
CC	28A, 28B, 32, 38A, 38B, 8A2, 8A3, 8B2, 8B3
PP	56A, 56B, 6A2, 6A6B, 6B6A, 8A6A, 8A6B

frequently seen in psychosomatic clinics. The 45 and 54 combinations
have been highly prevalent among another recently popular diagnosis,
the narcissistic personality. The 56A and 645 pair is often associated with
traditional sociopathic types and current antisocial personality diagnoses,
as well as a high percentage of drug abusers.

In the following sections, a number of interpretive features of five
of the more typical MCMI-II two-point codes will be presented. These are
only a small number of the interpretive possibilities for the MCMI-II.
Important differences may be deduced and demonstrated empirically between a matched pair of high-point codes, depending on which of the pair
is higher. For example, a significant difference may be shown to exist
between a 32 and a 23 high-point code. In the former case, patients are
likely to control their social aversiveness sufficiently to become comfort-
ably dependent on institutional, if not personal, sources of support; in the
latter example, distrust is likely to overtake the individual, and needed
sources of support may be tolerated, but only tentatively and with much
discomfort. It is often clinically useful also to record the third highest in
a profile code series. This reflects the fact that certain scales are notably
"penetrant" and/or "expressive" even when ranking somewhat down in
the profile configuration. For example, Scales 6A and 8A frequently alter
the clinical meaning of a profile when they are the third highest scale.
Thus, a 321 code suggests a pattern substantively different from a 328A.
In the former case, the patient is likely to have become accustomed to an
inadequate and dependent state with chronic flattening of affect; in patients with the latter profile, however, we often see displays of stubbornness, passive-aggressive behavior, and periodic irritable outbursts.

As with the single-scale interpretive guidelines presented previously, the two-point code descriptions furnished in the following sections
represent prototypes. Because of the effects of moderator variables, the
uniqueness of each case, and the inevitable limitations of any psychometric technique, what follows is by no means infallible as a guide to
depicting every patient who exhibits a particular profile code.

Code 28B: Avoidant and Self-Defeating   The behavior of these patients is characterized by a pervasive apprehensiveness and the expec-
tancy that people will be rejecting and disparaging. Despite a long-
suppressed desire to relate and be accepted by others, they often feel it
is best to maintain a safe distance. Recurrent anxieties and a pervasive
sadness typify their emotional lives. A surface apathy may be exhibited
in their efforts to damp down or conceal an excess of sensitivity and
anticipation of rebuke. Behind their façade of restraint are intensely
painful feelings that occasionally break through. The peace and security
that they need, however, are threatened when they express any resentments, and they constantly seek to minimize the hostility they expect.

These patients frequently display a mournful irritability. Their downcast moods are frequently interspersed with expressions of guilt and contrition. Many feel misunderstood, unappreciated, and demeaned by others; they are characteristically pessimistic and disillusioned about life, and feel entitled to the derogation they seem to experience. Their resulting low self-esteem is further compounded by tendencies toward extreme introspection and self-derogation. The alienation that they feel from others is paralleled by feelings of alienation from themselves.

Not only are these patients hypersensitive and apprehensively ill at ease; in addition, they experience a constant and confusing undercurrent of tension and sadness. Moreover, they frequently turn against themselves, feeling remorseful and self-condemnatory. They vacillate between their desire for acceptance, their fears, and a general numbness of feeling.

These patients appear to have learned to be on guard against anticipated ridicule and contempt. Detecting the most minute traces of annoyance expressed by others, they often make the molehill of a minor slight into a mountain of personal derision and condemnation. Moreover, they have learned that good things do not last and that support and friendship end in disappointment and rejection. Anticipating disillusionment, they often jump the gun and withdraw.

Code 34: Dependent and Histrionic   The behavior of these patients is best characterized by their submissiveness, dependency, and deficits in competent assertiveness. Fears of losing emotional support often lead them to be overcompliant and obliging. Behaving in a superficially charming manner, they may seek attention through self-dramatizing behaviors. Many are quite naive about worldly matters and avoid taking everyday positions of responsibility. Their thinking is often unreflective and scattered. When faced with interpersonal tensions, they attempt to maintain an air of buoyancy and to deny disturbing thoughts or acknowledge inner tensions.

These patients are likely to be highly accommodating and responsive to the needs of others. Having learned to accept an inferior role, they allow others to assume the role of being more competent than themselves. An active soliciting of praise, a marketing of appeal, and a tendency to be entertaining are also apparent. They seek harmony with others, often without regard to their own values and beliefs. Unassertive and lacking in confidence, they avoid situations that may involve personal conflict.

Despite their efforts to control any oppositional feelings, their repressed angers and frustrations may break out into the open at times. Their resentments stem in part from their awareness that they have little or no identity apart from others. Instead of valuing themselves, they submerge in favor of others. However, they no longer believe that these relationships will fulfill their needs or even protect them against loss. Despite their growing disillusion with others, they are still alert to signs of potential hostility and rejection and seek to minimize the dangers of indifference and disapproval. By paying close attention to the desires of others, they are able to shape their behaviors to conform to others' wishes and needs.

Despite a growing desire to assert their independence, these patients feel helpless when faced with responsibilities that demand assertiveness and initiative. The loss of the central source of emotional support and guidance often prompts severe dejection, and they may begin openly to solicit signs of reassurance. Guilt, illness, anxiety, and depression are used to deflect serious criticism and to transform threats of disapproval into expressions of support and empathy. More extreme reactions, such as a severe depression or a brief manic period or even a most uncharacteristic hostility, may spill forth when the security of their dependency is genuinely threatened.

Code 56A: Narcissistic and Antisocial   These patients characteristically display an overbearing and arrogant sense of self-worth, an indifference to the welfare of others, and an intimidating interpersonal manner. Tendencies to exploit others and to expect special recognition and consideration without assuming reciprocal responsibility are notable. Actions that raise questions of personal integrity may indicate a deficient social conscience, as they show little regard for the rights of others.

These patients attempt to maintain an image of cool strength, arrogance, fearlessness, self-reliance, unsentimentality, and hard-boiled competitiveness. They also may display a rash willingness to risk harm, and are notably fearless in the face of threats and even punitive action. Indeed, punishment may only reinforce their rebellious and hostile feelings. Malicious tendencies seen in others are used to justify their own aggressive inclinations and may lead to frequent personal and family difficulties, as well as to occasional legal entanglements. Antisocial behavior and alcohol or drug problems may be prominent reasons for referral.

When matters are well under control, these patients may be skilled in the ways of social influence and adept at exploiting the good will of others. More commonly, they are envious of others, are wary of their motives, feel unfairly treated, and are easily provoked to anger. Their thin façade of sociability can quickly give way to angry or caustic comments. A marked suspicion of those in authority leads these patients to feel secure only when they possess power.

Lacking deep feelings of loyalty and displaying an indifference to truth, they may successfully scheme beneath a veneer of civility. Their guiding principle is that one must outwit others, controlling and exploiting them before they gain control. Displaying a chip-on-the-shoulder attitude, they often exhibit a readiness to attack those whom they distrust. If they are unsuccessful in channeling their ever-present aggressive impulses, resentment may mount into acts of brutal hostility.

Code 48A-C: Histrionic, Passive-Aggressive, and Borderline

These patients' behavior is typified by a thin veneer of sociability and maturity. Beneath this façade, however, lies an intense fear of true autonomy, a need to present a favorable public front, and a pained submission to the expectancies of others. These individuals' front of social propriety and self-assurance covers deep and increasingly intense, but generally suppressed, antagonisms and feelings of worthlessness. There is a struggle to control these oppositional tendencies through discipline and a socially agreeable affability, with moments of dramatic conviviality. These patients engage in a wide variety of interpersonal maneuvers designed to elicit favorable attention and social approval. There is a long-standing pattern of being deferential and ingratiating with superiors, going to great lengths to demonstrate efficiency and serious-mindedness while completing all tasks regardless of the fairness of the demands.

Recent failures to evoke this approval may have led to depressive periods and chronic anxiety. At this point patients are high-strung and moody, seeking to express attitudes contrary to inner feelings of tension, anger, and dejection. In an effort to avoid these discomforts, these individuals have become increasingly sensitive to the moods and expectations of others. The extreme other-directedness used in achieving approval has resulted in a life-style characterized by its high adaptability. These patients have also learned to be alert to signs of potential hostility and rejection, and usually avoid disapproval by adapting their behaviors to conform to the desires of others. This preoccupation with external approval, however, has resulted in a growing sense of personal impotence and social dependency.

These patients deny awareness of inner deficiencies, since awareness would point up the discrepancy between the overt impressions created and the patient's inner feelings of sterility and emotional poverty, coupled with an unwillingness to accept blame. This tendency to seal off and deny the elements of inner life further intensifies dependence on others. Increasingly, deep resentments have begun to emerge toward those to whom these patients conform and on whom they depend. These antagonisms have periodically broken through surface constraints to erupt in outbursts of guilt and contrition. These vacillations in behavior between periods of submissive compliance and sullen negativism compound discomforts. Such public displays of inconsistency and impulse expression contrast markedly with self-image. There are bitter complaints about being treated unfairly; about expecting to be disappointed and disapproved of by others; and about no longer being appreciated for one's diligence, sociability, and respectability. With the persistence of these ambivalent feelings, these patients have begun to suffer somatic discomforts, and voice growing distress about a wide range of physical symptoms.

Code 23S: Avoidant, Dependent, and Schizotypal

As with their pure avoidant counterparts, these personalities are restrained, isolated, apprehensive, guarded, and shrinking. Protectively, they seek to "kill" their feelings and desires, bind their impulses, and withdraw from social encounters, thereby defending themselves from the pain and anguish of interpersonal relationships. The surface apathy and seeming indifference of these patients is not, as it is in the schizotypal-schizoid, owing to an intrinsic lack of sensitivity, but rather is due to their attempt to restrain, damp down, or deaden excessive sensitivity and awareness of their dependency needs. In addition to their social isolation, they depreciate their self-worth. There is an abandonment of self and a disowning and remoteness from feeling and desire. The "real" selves of these personalities have been devalued and demeaned, split off, and rejected as humiliating or valueless. Not only are these schizotypals alienated from others, then, but they also find no refuge and comfort in turning to themselves. Their isolation is twofold: little is gained from others, and only a despairing sense of shame is found within themselves. Without the rewards of self or others to spur them, they drift into personal apathy and social isolation. Having little hope of gaining affection and security, these patients learn that it is best to deny real feelings and aspirations. Cognitive processes are intentionally confused in an effort to disqualify and discredit rational thinking.

Disharmonious affects, irrelevant and tangential thoughts, and an increasingly severe social bankruptcy develop as these patients are forced to build an ever-tighter armor around themselves. Their characteristic eccentricities derive from this wall of isolation and insularity that they have constructed. By insulating themselves, shrinking their world, and deadening their sensitivities, they have laid the groundwork for feelings of emptiness and unreality. To counter the anxieties of depersonalization and derealization, they may exhibit excited and bizarre behaviors, contrive peculiar and hallucinatory images, and shout utterly unintelligible sounds, all in an effort to attract attention and affirm themselves. Failing, as is likely, in these efforts to quiet their anxieties, they may turn to a make-believe world of superstitions, magic, and telepathy—anything they can fashion from their imagination that will provide them a pseudocommunity of fantasied persons and objects to which they can safely relate.

These patients are most likely to be precipitated into a frank psychotic disorder when confronted with painful humiliation and derogation from others. Although they have sought by active withdrawal and isolation to minimize social contact, this coping defense is not impenetrable. Should their armor be pierced and their protective detachment assaulted and encroached on, they will not only experience the anguish of the present but also have reactivated within them the painful memories of past assaults. Fearful lest they be further humiliated and injured, and unable to govern the onrush of previously repressed anxieties and angers, these patients may lose all control and be drowned in a wave of chaotic and primitive impulses. Thus, at the moment their external world inundates them, their inner world erupts.

Selection of Noteworthy Responses

The use of "critical items" as a supplement to the formal scales of a self-report inventory is well established, although some controversy remains concerning their primary purpose and how best to select them (Caldwell, 1969; Grayson, 1951; Koss, Butcher, & Hoffman, 1976; Lachar & Wrobel, 1979). Both Caldwell and Grayson, for example, chose their items on rational grounds with the thought of identifying potential psychotic states; Koss and colleagues sought empirical indicators that would distinguish different crisis conditions in the lives of patients; Lachar and Wrobel attempted to locate and confirm face valid descriptors that corresponded to specific areas of psychological concern. The approach taken to select and verify the utility of what are termed "noteworthy responses" in the MCMI differed as well.

Twenty-four clinicians (16 Ph.D.'s and 8 M.S.W.'s) completed a brief one-page form asking them to identify "noteworthy realms"—that is, psychological events or characteristics, not directly appraised by scales on an early form of the MCMI, about which they would like to see some gauge or index. Eight realms were chosen for further study on the basis of having been proposed by 12 or more clinicians. The names they were assigned summarized their essential content: alcohol abuse, drug abuse, emotional dyscontrol, self-destructive potential, health preoccupation, neurological dysfunction, manic behavior, and interpersonal alienation.

The fact that 20 or more of the 24 clinicians recorded the alcohol abuse, drug abuse, and manic behavior realms was a major factor in leading us to develop formal scales for each of these syndromes, hence their presence on MCMI and MCMI-II. Only five themes remained, therefore, as potential "noteworthy response" realms.

Eleven clinicians were then asked to select MCMI development items that they judged as reflecting the content of the five noteworthy areas. A high degree of consensus was achieved in four of the five realms, with the neurological dysfunction theme failing to generate agreement on a sufficient number of items to justify its continued use. Empirical support for the validity of the noteworthy items was also obtained.

Seven of the MCMI noteworthy items were deleted in the construction phases of MCMI-II; five new items introduced into MCMI-II were selected to replace them. Their content similarity to extant items served as the basis of their selection; they are supportable, therefore, on rational/substantive grounds only. It is this final set of items that serve as the noteworthy responses of the MCMI-II.

An Illustrative Narrative Report

The five axes that have been selected for the MCMI-II correspond, in the main, to the major axes pertaining to psychosocial processes in the DSM-III-R format:

1. *clinical syndrome (Axis I),* summarizing the patient's current primary complaints and behavioral signs;
2. *personality disorder (Axis II),* describing the patient's long-standing and deeply ingrained style of interpersonal behavior;
3. *course of disorder,* referring to the duration and variability of the major clinical symptoms;
4. *psychosocial stressors (Axis IV),* reflecting situational variables that underlie or contribute to impaired functioning; and
5. *prognostic and therapeutic implications,* detailing considerations worthy of note in appraising future progress, and in planning and executing treatment.

The organization of the recently updated MCMI-II interpretive report is arranged in the following sequence:

1. an introductory set of paragraphs noting the limitations and restrictions of use;
2. a judgment on the probable validity and reliability of the test data on which the report is based;
3. a paragraph stating several basic demographic characteristics of the patient, the nature of reported complaints, and the period of time associated with the present disorder;
4. a series of paragraphs describing the major features of the patient's personality pattern (Axis II) and level of impairment;
5. a descriptive and interpretive summary of current clinical syndromes (Axis I), presented in their order of relative significance or salience;
6. a listing of "noteworthy responses" signifying problem areas deserving further evaluation, grouped into four categories: (a) health preoccupations, (b) interpersonal alienation, (c) emotional dyscontrol, and (d) self-destructive potential; and
7. a summary section organized in a multiaxial diagnostic format, including subsections on each of the five axes described previously.

The MCMI-II printout, shown in the appendix to this chapter, illustrates a typical interpretive report.

CONCLUSIONS

Although this interpretive guide has encompassed a wide range of themes and topics, it must be considered but a brief introduction to the MCMI-II. New though the instrument may be, it was developed by employing the most modern of psychometric principles and the most up-to-date thought in psychopathology. Nevertheless, those who use the instrument and its associated interpretive reports should have a strong background in psychometric methods, test logic, and clinical practice and theory in order to be able to utilize the instrument fully.

It is important to reiterate that normative data and interpretive deductions made from the MCMI-II are based entirely on clinical samples; hence, the test should be administered exclusively to persons who exhibit psychological symptoms or are actively involved in programs of professional psychodiagnosis or psychotherapy. It is inappropriate to employ and interpret MCMI-II results with other problems or subjects. Data are now being gathered and will soon be available for patients and at settings other than the original normative population (e.g., patients with marital difficulties).

Despite a relative paucity of research data currently published on the MCMI-II, a substantial number of projects are in progress. Given its youth, many more years of both research evaluation and clinical utility will have to pass for the MCMI-II to become one of the standard tools in the clinician's assessment kit. Evaluations of this sort will ensure that the MCMI-II continues to improve on its auspicious beginnings.

REFERENCES

American Psychiatric Association. (1980). *Diagnostic and statistical manual of mental disorders* (3rd ed.). Washington, DC: Author.

American Psychiatric Association. (1987). *Diagnostic and statistical manual of mental disorders* (3rd ed., revised). Washington, DC: Author.

Butcher, J. N. (Ed.). (1972). *Objective personality assessment.* New York: Academic Press.

Caldwell, A. B. (1969). *MMPI critical items: Unpublished mimeo.* Los Angeles: Caldwell Reports.

Dahlstrom, W. G., Welsh, G. S., & Dahlstrom, L. E. (1975). *An MMPI handbook* (Vol. 2) (rev. ed.). Minneapolis: University of Minnesota Press.

Godfrey, J. (1987). *Noteworthy Responses, 3, 4–5.*

Grayson, H. M. (1951). *Psychological admissions testing program and manual.* Los Angeles: Veterans Administration Medical Center.

Green, C. (1982). The diagnostic accuracy and utility of MMPI and MCMI computer interpretive reports. *Journal of Personality Assessment, 46,* 359–365.

Green, C. (1987). *Proceedings of the conference on the Millon Inventories.* Minneapolis: National Computer Systems.

Hase, H. D., & Goldberg, L. R. (1967). The comparative validity of different strategies of deriving personality inventory scales. *Psychological Bulletin, 67,* 231–248.

Hirschfeld, R. M. A., Klerman, G. L., Clayton, P. S., Keller, M. B., MacDonald Scott, M. A., & Larkin, B. H. (1983). Assessing personality: Effects of the depressed state on trait measurement. *American Journal of Psychiatry, 140,* 695–699.

Jackson, D. N. (1970). A sequential system for personality scale development. In C. D. Spielberger (Ed.), *Current topics in clinical and community psychology* (Vol. 2). New York: Academic Press.

Koss, M. P., Butcher, J. N., & Hoffman, N. G. (1976). The MMPI critical items: How well do they work? *Journal of Consulting and Clinical Psychology, 44,* 921–928.

Lachar, D., & Wrobel, T. A. (1979). Validating clinical hunches: Construction of a new MMPI critical item set. *Journal of Consulting and Clinical Psychology, 47,* 277–284.

Loevinger, J. (1957). Objective tests as instruments of psychological theory. *Psychological Reports, 3,* 635–694.

Meehl, P. E., & Rosen, A. (1955). Antecedent probability and the efficiency of psychometric signs, patterns, or cutting scores. *Psychological Bulletin, 55,* 194–216.

Millon, T. (1969). *Modern psychopathology.* Philadelphia: Saunders.

Millon, T. (1981). *Disorders of personality: DSM-III, Axis II.* New York: John Wiley & Sons.

Millon, T. (1983). *Toward the complementary use of the MMPI and the MCMI.* Paper presented at the Eighth International Conference on Personality Assessment, Copenhagen.

Millon, T. (1986a). Personality prototypes and their diagnostic criteria. In T. Millon & G. L. Klerman (Eds.), *Contemporary directions in psychopathology: Toward the DSM-IV.* New York: Guilford Press.

Millon, T. (1986b). A theoretical derivation of pathological personalities. In T. Millon & G. L. Klerman (Eds.), *Contemporary directions in psychopathology: Toward the DSM-IV.* New York: Guilford Press.

Millon, T. (1987). *Millon Clinical Multiaxial Inventory II manual.* Minneapolis: National Computer Systems.

Appendix:
Millon Clinical Multiaxial Inventory II

ID NUMBER: 168424   DATE: 14-SEP-87   PAGE: 1

MCMI reports are normed on patients who were in the early phases of assessment or psychotherapy because of emotional discomforts or social difficulties. Respondents who do not fit this normative population or who have inappropriately taken the MCMI for nonclinical purposes may have distorted reports. To optimize clinical utility, the report highlights pathological characteristics and dynamics rather than strengths and positive attributes. This focus should be kept in mind by the referring clinician reading the report.

Based on theoretical inferences and probabilistic data from actuarial research, the MCMI report cannot be judged definitive. It must be viewed as only one facet of a comprehensive psychological assessment, and should be evaluated in conjunction with additional clinical data (e.g., current life circumstances, observed behavior, biographic history, interview responses, and information from other tests). To avoid its misconstrual or misuse, the report should be evaluated by mental health clinicians trained in recognizing the strengths and limitations of psychological test data. Given its limited data base and pathologic focus, the report should not be shown to patients or their relatives.

INTERPRETIVE CONSIDERATIONS

In addition to the preceding considerations, the interpretive narrative should be evaluated in light of the following demographic and situational factors. This 25 year old single white woman with a technical school education, currently seen professionally as an outpatient, reports her most recent problems as sexual problems and loneliness; difficulties appear to have taken the form of an Axis I disorder within a period of three to twelve months.

The response style of this patient showed no unusual test-taking attitude that would distort MCMI results.

AXIS II: PERSONALITY PATTERNS

The following pertains to those enduring and pervasive characterological traits that underlie this woman's personal and interpersonal difficulties. Rather than

ID NUMBER = 168424   VALID REPORT
PERSONALITY CODE = - ✳ ✳ 2 3 8B * 1 + 6A 7 4 " 8A 6B 5   // - ✳ - ✳ //
SYNDROME CODE = ✳ ✳ S C ✳ // - ✳ ✳ - ✳ //
DEMOGRAPHIC = 00001228/ON/F/25/W/N/ T2/P/SX/LO/30928/03/09/30182/ 920 0020

CATEGORY		SCORE RAW	SCORE BR	PROFILE OF BR SCORES	DIAGNOSTIC SCALES
MODIFIER INDICES	X	292	45		DISCLOSURE
MODIFIER INDICES	Y	5	24		DESIRABILITY
MODIFIER INDICES	Z	21	67		DEBASEMENT
CLINICAL PERSONALITY PATTERN	1	21	67		SCHIZOID
CLINICAL PERSONALITY PATTERN	2	31	81		AVOIDANT
CLINICAL PERSONALITY PATTERN	3	34	81		DEPENDENT
CLINICAL PERSONALITY PATTERN	4	17	36		HISTRIONIC
CLINICAL PERSONALITY PATTERN	5	14	0		NARCISSISTIC
CLINICAL PERSONALITY PATTERN	6A	14	42		ANTISOCIAL
CLINICAL PERSONALITY PATTERN	6B	8	0		AGGRESSIVE/SADISTIC
CLINICAL PERSONALITY PATTERN	7	27	41		COMPULSIVE
CLINICAL PERSONALITY PATTERN	8A	13	24		PASSIVE-AGGRESSIVE
CLINICAL PERSONALITY PATTERN	8B	29	77		SELF-DEFEATING
SEVERE PERSONALITY PATHOLOGY	S	20	55		SCHIZOTYPAL
SEVERE PERSONALITY PATHOLOGY	C	29	46		BORDERLINE
SEVERE PERSONALITY PATHOLOGY	P	10	36		PARANOID
CLINICAL SYNDROME	A	26	77		ANXIETY DISORDER
CLINICAL SYNDROME	H	20	53		SOMATOFORM DISORDER
CLINICAL SYNDROME	N	10	25		BIPOLAR: MANIC DISORDER
CLINICAL SYNDROME	D	38	81		DYSTHYMIC DISORDER
CLINICAL SYNDROME	B	22	59		ALCHOHOL DEPENDENCE
CLINICAL SYNDROME	T	11	20		DRUG DEPENDENCE
SEVERE SYNDROME	SS	13	60		THOUGHT DISORDER
SEVERE SYNDROME	CC	21	60		MAJOR DEPRESSION
SEVERE SYNDROME	PP	5	37		DELUSIONAL DISORDER

Profile of BR Scores scale markers: 35 60 75 85 100

focus on her more marked but essentially transitory symptoms, this section concentrates on her habitual, maladaptive methods of relating, behaving, thinking, and feeling.

The behavior of this woman may be characterized as fearful, dependent, socially shy, and self-effacing. Hesitant about self-assertion, she has learned to lean on others for security, and she assumes the role of a submissive and self-sacrificing partner in close relationships. Exceedingly insecure and vulnerable if separated from those who provide support, she willingly places herself in inferior or demeaning positions, permitting others to be exploitive and abusive. In fact, she may seek out relationships in which she will suffer. She resents those who fail to appreciate her intense needs for affection and nurturance; however, since her security is threatened when these resentments are expressed, she hesitates discharging any negative feelings and only does so in a passive-aggressive manner. Ever fearful of rebuff, she would rather withdraw voluntarily from painful social relationships or try to convince herself that martyrdom is a worthy state, all in an effort to prevent herself from venting her anger directly.

Depressive feelings, loneliness, and isolation are increasingly experienced. Her underlying tension and emotional dysphoria are present in disturbing mixtures of anxiety, sadness, and guilt. Her insecurity and her fear of abandonment account for what may appear at times to be a quiet, submissive, and benign attitude. Aside from her occasional expressions of resentment, she is extremely conciliatory, placating, even ingratiating. By acting weak, expressing self-doubt, being self-depriving, communicating a need for assurance and direction, and displaying a desire to submit and comply, she hopes to evoke nurturance and protection. By submerging her individuality, focusing on her worst features and lowly status, subordinating her personal desires, and submitting at times to abuse and intimidation, she hopes to avoid total abandonment.

Frequent complaints of inadequacy, fatigability, and illness may reflect her underlying mood of depression. Under these circumstances, simple responsibilities demand more energy than she can muster. Life may be referred to as empty with constant feelings of weariness and apathy. By withdrawing, being dependent and self-abnegating, or restricting her social involvements to situations in which she is exploited or abused, she precludes new, potentially favorable experiences from redirecting her life.

AXIS I: CLINICAL SYNDROMES

The features and dynamics of the following distinctive Axis I clinical syndromes are worthy of description and analysis. They may arise in response to external

ID NUMBER: 168424   DATE: 14-SEP-87   PAGE: 4

precipitants, but are likely to reflect and accentuate enduring and pervasive aspects of this woman's basic personality makeup.

Clinical features of dysthymia are an integral part of this depressed woman's characterological makeup. Not only when she is notably downhearted and blue is her sorrowful and disconsolate demeanor apparent, for her feelings of dejection and self-defeating attitudes are intrinsic to her life. She routinely voices concerns over her social adequacy and personal worthiness, makes repeated self-deprecatory and guilt-ridden comments about her failures and unattractiveness, and regularly complains about her inability to do things right. Although she reports being aggrieved and mistreated by others, she also claims to deserve the anguish and abuse she receives, an admittance consistent with her self-image as an unworthy and undeserving person. In consonance with her unconscious dynamics, she not only may tolerate relationships that aggravate her misery but also may precipitate conditions and events that perpetuate it.

Consistent with her general downhearted style, this aggrieved and unhappy woman records the symptomatology of an anxiety disorder. Discontent and anguished in most spheres of her life, she reports a steady stream of psychological tensions that give rise to a general anxiety syndrome, which includes fearful presentiments, an inability to think or concentrate, and physical fatigue. Also possible are several of the syndrome's specific variants, such as panic attacks and agoraphobia. Plagued by doubts, expecting the worst, and repeatedly undermining opportunities to better her circumstances, she likely sets in motion self-defeating stressors that further promote her concerns and difficulties.

NOTEWORTHY RESPONSES

The following statements were answered by the patient in the direction noted in the parentheses. These items suggest specific problem areas that may deserve further inquiry on the part of the clinician.

HEALTH PREOCCUPATION
18. Lately, I get butterflies in my stomach and break out in cold sweats (T).
33. I feel weak and tired much of the time (T).
96. In recent weeks I feel worn out for no special reason (T).

INTERPERSONAL ALIENATION
32. I protect myself from trouble by never letting people know much about me (T).
49. I am a quiet and fearful person (T).
141. I am very ill-at-ease with members of the opposite sex (T).

EMOTIONAL DYSCONTROL
   167. Lately, I have gone all to pieces (T).

SELF-DESTRUCTIVE POTENTIAL
   54. I began to feel like a failure some years ago (T).
   76. I feel terribly depressed and sad much of the time now (T).
   79. Serious thoughts of suicide have occurred to me for many years (T).

PARALLEL DSM-III-R MULTIAXIAL DIAGNOSES

Although the diagnostic criteria utilized in the MCMI-II differ somewhat from those in the DSM-III-R, there are sufficient parallels to recommend consideration of the following assignments. More definitive judgments should draw on biographic, observation, and interview data in addition to self-report inventories such as the MCMI-II.

AXIS I: CLINICAL SYNDROME
The major complaints and behaviors of the patient parallel the following Axis I diagnoses, listed in order of their clinical significance and salience.

   300.40 Dysthymic Disorder
   300.02 Generalized Anxiety Disorder

AXIS II: PERSONALITY DISORDERS
A deeply ingrained and pervasive pattern of maladaptive functioning underlies the Axis I clinical syndromal picture. The following personality diagnoses represent the most salient features that characterize this patient.

Personality configuration composed of the following:

   301.82 Avoidant Personality Disorder
   301.60 Dependent Personality Disorder
   301.89 Self-defeating Personality Disorder

Course: The major personality features described previously reflect long term or chronic traits that are likely to have persisted for several years prior to the present assessment.

The clinical syndromes described previously tend to be relatively transient, waxing and waning in their prominence and intensity depending on the presence of environmental stress.

ID NUMBER: 168424   DATE: 14-SEP-87   PAGE: 6

AXIS IV: PSYCHOSOCIAL STRESSORS STATEMENTS
In completing the MCMI-II, this individual identified the following factors that
may be complicating or exacerbating her present emotional state. They are listed
in order of importance as indicated by the client. This information should be
viewed as a guide for further investigation by the clinician.

Social/Personal Difficulties.

PROGNOSTIC AND THERAPEUTIC IMPLICATIONS

Because she tends to demean her self-worth and to mistrust others, this woman
is unlikely to sustain a consistent therapeutic relationship. Maneuvers designed
to test the sincerity of the therapist will probably be evident. Since she fears
facing her feelings of unworthiness and senses that her coping defenses are weak,
she may withdraw from treatment before any real gains are made. Efforts to
explore the contradictions in her feelings and attitudes may result in a seesaw
struggle, with periods of temporary progress followed by retrogression. Genuine
gains will require slow, laborious work and a building of trust by enhancing her
shaky sense of self-worth.

The potential gains of therapy not only may fail to motivate this patient but also
may serve as a deterrent. Therapy may reawaken what she views as false hopes;
that is, it may remind her of the dangers and humiliations she experienced when
she tendered her affections to others but received rejection in return. Now that
she has found a modest level of comfort by distancing herself from others, she
would rather let matters stand and maintain the level of adjustment to which
she has become accustomed.

At the cognitive-behavioral level, therapeutic attention may be carefully directed
to her hesitancy, suspiciousness, and self-deprecating attitudes, behaviors that
evoked humiliation, contempt, and derogation in the past. Efforts to press her to
reduce her sensitivity to rebuff and her fearful style may only reinforce her
aversive inclinations.

Another realm worthy of attention is associated with her extensive scanning of
the environment, by which she actually increases the likelihood that she will
encounter what she wishes to avoid. Her exquisite antennae pick up and transform what most people overlook. In effect, her hypersensitivity backfires by becoming an instrument that brings to awareness, time and again, the very pain
she wishes to escape. Her vigilance and self-demeaning comments intensify rather
than diminish her anguish.

Analytic procedures can be useful in reconstructing unconscious anxieties and mechanisms that pervade all aspects of her behavior. Family techniques can be employed to moderate destructive patterns of communication that contribute to or intensify her social problems. In addition, group therapy may assist her in learning new attitudes and skills in a more benign and accepting social setting than she normally encounters.

3

The 16 PF

Samuel Karson
Jerry W. O'Dell

The Sixteen Personality Factor Questionnaire (16 PF) is a paper-and-pencil personality questionnaire, first developed in the 1940s by Raymond B. Cattell. Unlike many of the tests described in these volumes, the 16 PF was designed to measure the *normal* personality, as opposed to, say, the Minnesota Multiphase Personality Inventory (MMPI), which was developed to assess the presence and extent of psychopathology. The boundaries between normal and abnormal behavior, however, have never been clear, and we have found the 16 PF to be of great value in understanding both normal *and* abnormal behavior. In recent years, the practice of many clinicians has expanded to include assessment of persons with relatively intact personalities (in personnel selection, for example), and the 16 PF is especially helpful in such situations. In any event, the test has become, with the MMPI, one of the two most widely used objective personality assessment instruments, with well over a thousand research

We would like to thank the staff of IPAT for providing the artwork for this chapter, and also Dr. Philip Farber for his helpful and careful examination of the manuscript.

citations in the *Mental Measurements Yearbooks*. Part of the test's growing popularity can probably be attributed to the fact that the current 16
PF Forms A and B have been carefully constructed so as to contain
relatively few items that clients or patients find objectionable or regard
as an invasion of privacy.

CONSTRUCTION OF THE 16 PF

One cannot really comprehend the development of the 16 PF without
an understanding of the personality theory and research strategies of
Raymond Cattell. Unfortunately for the novice, or even for the average
clinician, Cattell's highly mathematical writings do not make easy reading.

Cattell set himself the task of measuring *all* important dimensions
of the normal personality. To accomplish this task, he somehow had to
obtain a complete set of categories describing the normal personality.
Such a list is not easy to find, but Cattell arrived at a clever solution. It
occurred to him that a compendium of all terms describing human personality could be found in the English language. Indeed, our language
must contain terms descriptive of all major components of human personality. To solve the problem, then, one would somehow have to reduce
the large number of terms in English that describe human personality
to the smallest number of underlying variables that would account for
the information in the original list.

Although our language contains an enormous number of words,
Allport and Odbert (1936) found that a list of about four thousand adjectives covered the human personality realm fairly completely. Still, four
thousand concepts are far too many to be comprehended readily by the
average psychologist. How could one reduce that number while still re-
taining the richness of the language?

Cattell accomplished this task through an extremely complex statistical process known as *factor analysis*. In simplest terms, this technique
allows one to reduce a large number of concepts, such as four thousand
English words, to the smallest number of underlying *factors* that will
still account for most of the original information. The details of the original construction of the 16 PF may be found in Cattell's 1946 book, *The
Description and Measurement of Personality*. Because there were no computers in general use at the time, Cattell had to make a great many
compromises in these early analyses.

Cattell's initial factor analyses seemed to indicate that the English
language could be reduced to about fifteen underlying factors that encompass human personality well. To these personality factors, Cattell
insightfully added a short measure of intelligence, thereby arriving at
the sixteen basic factors of the test. Cattell feels that he has found most
of these factors in several realms of human behavior, not only in paper-

and-pencil questionnaires, but in objective tests and miniature life situations as well. An awesome amount of research has been done by Cattell and others in validating this test. The long list of Cattell's writings may be found in *Multivariate Behavioral Research* (1984, pp. 344–369).

Cattell's claim that sixteen basic factors underlie human personality has not gone uncontested; other workers have found differing numbers of factors. But many of the factors developed by him make excellent sense, and appear to encompass the extent of normal personality fairly well. For example, his primary personality factors appear to be capable of predicting real-life behavior accurately in many practical and applied areas, as, for example, in foreign service personnel (Karson & O'Dell, 1987b).

Many choices are open to the researcher who is conducting a factor analysis. One option allows a decision as to whether the factors found are to be independent of one another, or whether they may be intercorrelated. Cattell chose to allow his factors to be correlated (as they are in real life) and, because of this, was able to develop a higher-order set of factors, the so-called second-order factors. That is, after the original sixteen factors were extracted, he then proceeded to factor-analyze the original factors! These second-order factors describe broader aspects of human personality; many seem to be found in almost all scientifically developed personality tests (Lorr, Nerviano, & Myhill, 1985).

This original factor-analytic research has produced five forms of the 16 PF, A through E, generally most recently revised in the late 1960s. Forms A and B are roughly equivalent forms for routine use with adults; we strongly urge that, to improve reliability, these two forms be used together as a single test. Forms C and D are shorter, less reliable forms, used for rougher screening. Finally, Form E was designed for persons with poor reading ability.

The reader who wishes to know precisely how the 16 PF was constructed would do well to read Cattell's 1946, 1957, and 1973 books, which describe the process in great detail. Our own book (Karson & O'Dell, 1976) presents an admittedly oversimplified version of the process.

ADMINISTRATION AND SCORING

Because the 16 PF is designed for persons aged sixteen and over, administration is relatively simple. The test can be given by persons without professional training. Clear, printed instructions for the test are given on the cover of the test booklet. The 16 PF *Manual* (IPAT, 1986) gives the administrator a number of hints and ways of establishing adequate rapport. Certainly, no clinician should have any difficulty in administering this test. Indeed, it is quite easy to train a capable secretary to perform this task well, as we have done for a number of years.

The 16 PF may be scored in a number of ways. The test may be readily hand scored with scoring stencils and norms tables provided by the Institute for Personality and Ability Testing (IPAT), the test publisher. We have had many relatively untrained assistants who were able to score the test, look up the norms, and plot the profile with little difficulty, although it is often found that calculation of the second-order factors can be tricky. In point of fact, we confess that in our work (other than research) we seldom calculate the values of the second-order factors when interpreting 16 PF profiles, when the test has been hand scored.

If a number of answer sheets are to be scored, IPAT provides inexpensive scoring services. Machine scoring is probably well worth the minimal cost, if the time available makes it feasible, for it is virtually error-free. In addition, the computer scoring programs accurately yield a number of scores that are bothersome to calculate by hand, namely the second-order factors. Also available, if desired, are a variety of computer interpretations of the test, such as the Karson Clinical Report (Karson & O'Dell, 1987a) and the recently developed Karson Personnel Report.* These reports seem most useful to professionals who already know how to interpret the 16 PF and thus also know when to qualify or ameliorate certain of the interpretive statements indicated.

THE SCALES OF THE 16 PF

In discussing the scales of the 16 PF, we are immediately faced with a problem. Cattell frequently gave the scales new and unusual names so that they would not be confused with older personality constructs that, though similar, might well be somewhat different from the 16 PF scales. Thus, Scale L, which contains items measuring suspiciousness, was called Protension, to give it a more precise meaning.

Because these terms can be confusing to a psychologist not familiar with the 16 PF literature, in this chapter we will use simpler names, taken from the 16 PF *Manual* or from our 1976 book. A good deal of precision may be lost in our approach, but, we hope, with the trade-off of increasing the reader's understanding.

Further, it should be noted that the 16 PF factors are *bipolar;* that is, both high *and* low scores on the factors have meaning. This fact may be a bit confusing to a clinician who has, over the years, become accustomed to tests like the MMPI, on which one typically assigns meaning only to high scores.

Moreover, the scales are listed roughly in order of their relative importance in human personality—or, as the psychometrician would say,

---

*The Karson Personnel Report, written by Samuel Karson and Michael Karson, is marketed by Dennis L. Johnson, Ph.D., 844 East Ocean Boulevard, Stuart, Florida 33494

in order of the variance they contribute. The careful reader will note that certain scales, for example D and J, are not used on the 16 PF. Cattell has not found these factors in the adult samples, but they do appear in children and adolescents.

Scores on the 16 PF scales are expressed in standard scores called *stens,* an abbreviation for *standard ten,* because the scores range from 1 to 10. Stens have a mean of 5.5 and a standard deviation of 2, for the technically minded.

Response Set Scales on the 16 PF

Unfortunately, persons taking personality tests often do not answer them honestly, or with proper care. Thus, it is essential to have scales available for determining such response sets. This is especially the case since the Institute for Personality and Ability Testing (IPAT) has developed ways of correcting the 16 PF first-order factors for response sets, much as the K correction is used on the MMPI.

Three such scales have been developed for Form A of the 16 PF. The derivation and scoring of the "motivational distortion" ("faking good"), "faking bad," and "random" scales are described in detail by Karson and O'Dell (1976, pp. 151–156).

The motivational distortion scale was constructed by asking subjects to fill out the 16 PF in such a way as to make the best possible impression. Items which differentiated between this group and normal subjects were used to construct the scale. Construction of the faking bad scale was similar; however, subjects were asked to fill out the 16 PF so as to make a very bad impression.

Initial work suggested that a raw score of 6 or greater on each scale might indicate faking. Subsequently, however, Krug (1978) has reported, on the basis of a sample of almost five thousand, that a sten score of 7 or more on motivational distortion and faking bad is a better choice (Karson & O'Dell, 1976, p. 153).

The random scale, constructed in much the same fashion as the MMPI F scale, consists of item responses that are made very infrequently by subjects. With this scale, a sten score of 7 or greater is generally taken as an indication of carelessness in answering.

The importance of this scale is further highlighted by the fact that the random scale was recently reported by Karson and O'Dell (1987b) to be the only scale on the 16 PF that loaded significantly on a psycho-pathology second-order factor, along with MMPI Scales F, 4, 6, and 8! Consequently, this scale merits serious consideration as one of the best indicators of psychopathology on the 16 PF, in addition to being a measure of the test-taking attitude for which it was originally designed (O'Dell, 1971). The relationship of the random scale to scale F on the MMPI is readily apparent and quite striking. Moreover, it is abundantly clear that the random scale should be routinely scored whenever Form A of the 16 PF is given. Unfortunately, at present IPAT does not always routinely score this very important scale.

It is urged that all three of these scales be scored and used in routine practice; the tendencies measured by these scales are all too prevalent in clinical and industrial practice.

The First-Order Factor Scales

Because of the limited space available here, we shall describe the 16 PF primaries briefly. It is important to remember that, in the search for significant variables in personality, the 16 PF has a decided edge over other tests, in that it is deeply embedded in a data-based multivariate personality theory which lends itself readily to both psychodynamic and behavioristic interpretations. The best single brief description of the primary factors can be found in the *Administrator's Manual for the 16 PF* (IPAT, 1986). For a more clinically oriented discussion of the factors in greater detail, we recommend our own book (Karson & O'Dell, 1976).

Scale A: Reserved versus Outgoing   Persons scoring at the low end of this scale (sten of 1 to 4) are seen by others as cold, formal, detached, reserved, and aloof. People at the other end (sten of 7 to 10) tend to be friendly, easygoing, cooperative, outgoing, warm, and adaptable.

Unquestionably, in our society, which lauds the socially outgoing person, a high score on this scale is preferable to a low one. The American's ego ideal is clearly not the cold, detached person described by a low score on Scale A. Clinically, however, an extreme deviation in either direction on this scale can be troublesome. The person who is unnecessarily outgoing and effusive can get on other people's nerves. The senior author is fond of noting that someone scoring at the low end of this scale is apt to be suffering from the well-known burnt-child reaction, especially if scale E is also low. Still, it is perfectly possible to be A– and still be in good mental health, although this may well be uncommon, at least in our society. This is because A+ persons tend to move toward people, and others in turn move toward them, whereas A– persons tend to move away from others and others tend to move away from them.

Scale B: Low versus High Intelligence   Clinical psychologists do not usually think of intelligence as an aspect of "personality," but it is obviously of great importance, second only to the concepts measured on Scale A. Therefore, a short intelligence scale was included on the 16 PF. It is important to keep in mind that this scale is *in no way* a substitute for a full intelligence test. Scale B is very short and has one of the lowest reliability coefficients of all of the scales on the 16 PF. Still, if a patient obtains a very low score on this scale, it is a fairly safe presumption that something is amiss. It may well be that the person taking the test is suffering from disabling anxiety, or only that he or she did not attend to the items as carefully as most people do.

Scale C: Emotional Instability versus High Ego Strength
Emotional stability is highly valued in our culture, and thus we find that it appears early in Cattell's list of basic dimensions of personality. Someone low on Scale C (sten of 1 to 4) is low in frustration tolerance, easily upset, and inappropriately emotional. A person high on this factor (sten of 7 to 10) strikes others as being emotionally mature and stable, is typically calm, and is consistently ready to face the exigencies of everyday life. It is advisable to inspect the faking good and faking bad scores carefully before interpreting this scale.

Clearly, this dimension is of paramount importance to the practicing clinician. High ego strength and maturity are important assets in any psychotherapeutic procedure. Any indication of low ego strength may have the gravest implications for a person's coping behavior and ability to deal effectively with stress on a sustained basis.

Scale E: Submissiveness versus Dominance
The need to dominate others is clearly one of the primary motives in human history. Someone high on Scale E is typically described as aggressive, assertive, angry, and probably controlling and stubborn. The E + person usually does not suffer from an anxiety disorder, but he or she might well have a dominating personality. Cattell (1957) makes the interesting observation that high dominance has been observed extensively in the animal realm.

A person very low on Scale E, on the other hand, may well have serious adjustment problems, especially if the score on Scale A is also very low. As mentioned earlier, the senior author sees the pattern of A − and E − as indicative of the well-known burnt-child reaction. In general, it is healthier to obtain a high score on Scale E than a low one. Still, the E + person might well be described as a troublesome person with whom to interact on a peer basis, because he or she needs to be in charge of others.

Scale F: Serious versus Fun-Loving
A person low on this scale is characterized by Cattell (1957) as dull, subdued, quiet, and pessimistic. On the other hand, someone who is high on Scale F is usually cheerful, energetic, effervescent, trustful, and quick.

As we have noted previously (Karson & O'Dell, 1976), Scale F measures concepts very similar to the idea of what DSM-III now calls a bipolar disorder, formerly called manic depression. We have found that a low score on F, coupled with high O (guilt-proneness) is often indicative of depression, and should be examined carefully.

In short, Scale F indicates the degree to which one takes life seriously. If one were hiring a salesman, one might want someone who was F+; if one were looking for a responsible, prudent person, F— might well be the ticket. As a flight companion on a long trip, however, we would prefer an F+ person.

Scale G: Expedient versus Conventional

A person low on Scale G is considered to be fickle, unscrupulous, self-indulgent, and unsteady. Someone high on G is typically persevering, conforming, moralistic, and ordered, as well as highly concerned about what others may think.

There is a great deal of similarity between the items of this scale and the MMPI L or Lie scale. A high G or high Lie scale score may point to a person who is naively trying to impress the examiner as an extremely pure, moral person.

As noted in our 1976 book, we believe that a G+ score indicates only that the respondent understands the importance of making a show of external morality, without necessarily having introjected the parental standards so necessary for successful adjustment in our society. Since we know that G+ does not measure guilt, we prefer the term *group conformity* for it. This implies that the person goes along with the group for societal reasons, without necessarily believing in its actions. Nazi Germany provides an excellent example of this important distinction.

Scale H: Shy versus Bold

As the scales of the 16 PF progress through their alphabetical order, we find that each scale takes in less of the total variance of the normal personality than do its predecessors. Since the scales are allowed to be correlated, the scales to be discussed may seem similar in some ways to previous scales. Scale H is a case in point. It has important similarities with Scales A, F, and H, and with Q2, but it retains a unique identity. The key word here is *boldness,* associated with the high end of the scale, or, as the 16 PF *Manual* calls it, *venturesomeness.* H+ implies a certain social boldness and directness, great interest in the opposite sex, and especially a strong need to be stimulated and challenged by the environment. In short, H+ people enjoy adventure, excitement, and change.

H—, the other extreme, is more likely to signal emotional problems. In his 1946 book, Cattell applied the term "withdrawn schizothymia" to H—. If we recall that "schizothymia" was at the same time applied to A—, it is clear that, at that time at least, H— was considered to be a more serious personality problem than A—. Although Cattell has tempered his views on these factors somewhat, one may still regard a low score on H as an indicator of strong dispositional timidity. In 1957 Cattell called H— "threctia," or "threat-sensitivity"; we still find this term to be apt.

Scale I: Tough-Minded versus Tender-Minded   This dichotomy goes back at least to the writings of William James. Although at first glance it may seem to be more of a character trait than an indication of psychopathology, we have found it useful in successfully distinguishing alcoholics from other psychiatric cases in the U.S. Foreign Service (Karson & O'Dell, 1987b). Scale I is one of the most fascinating of the primary factors because it gets at a person's ego ideal, value systems, and sense of identity. It is, among other things, the "macho" factor on the 16 PF.

Someone who answers these questions so as to obtain a score of I− can be described as self-reliant, tough-minded, practical, realistic, and (as the 16 PF *Manual* says) rough. A person at the other end, I+, may well be too vulnerably sensitive, aesthetic, and passive. Thus, an I+ person would usually not be comfortable in a job that required independent and hard decisions, whereas an I− person might easily feel out of place in one of the helping professions, such as clinical psychology or social work. This factor correlates highly with Scale 5 on the MMPI in many of the samples we have studied (Karson & O'Dell, 1987b).

Scale L: Trusting versus Suspicious   Although Scale L contributes a relatively small amount of variance, it is one of the more important indicators of psychopathology. A low score on Scale L may well point to positive mental health. A high score on this scale, however, is not good. According to Cattell's researches, the L+ person is suspicious, brooding, jealous, skeptical at best, and hard to fool.

Like the E+ person, someone high on L can well be troublesome when interaction is required. The L+ client will typically be anxiously insecure, resentful, and hostile, and will displace and project angry feelings. A high score on L warrants further inquiry.

Scale M: Practical versus Imaginative   As we come to this tenth scale, we are approaching scales of relatively little variance in the personality realm. These scales, however, may be of great importance in our understanding of psychopathology, especially psychosomatic cases. Indeed, it is rather difficult at times to discover precisely what is measured by this somewhat obscure factor, or to differentiate it easily from Scale I, with which it is strongly related.

Someone high on this scale usually has an active fantasy life and may well be narcissistic and self-absorbed, especially if also expedient (G−). He or she may well be potentially creative, if also high on intelligence (B) and self-control (C+ and Q3+). The M− person, on the other hand, is practical, steady, and conventional in his or her interests. Interestingly, Scale M was found to distinguish foreign service officers with psychological problems who had to be returned to the United States from those who could remain in their overseas jobs. In this situation, M+ was found to be an asset to successful coping and a valuable discriminator (Karson & O'Dell, 1987b).

Scale N: Naive versus Shrewd   The N− person is seen as too direct and forthright, somewhat clumsy in interpersonal relations, and perhaps too self-revealing. The N+ person might well be considered a sharp operator, someone very socially aware and even shrewd. Before considering someone high on Scale N as being sophisticated, however, one should make sure that he or she has sufficient intelligence (B+) to carry it off. In some male samples we have studied, N+ is related to good upbringing and positive character integration (Karson & O'Dell, 1974b).

In general, we have found Scale N to be less useful than most of the other scales in clinical personnel work.

Scale O: Assured versus Guilt-Prone   With Scale O, we arrive at an interesting paradox. Cattell has made it clear that this scale contributes only a small amount of variance to the total personality realm. Yet, this scale is the first on the 16 PF to concern itself with guilt and worry. Since such feelings are often prominent in persons seen by clinicians, we have invariably found this scale to be of great use.

The O− person is self-assured, unruffled, and secure. The person high on O, however, is apprehensive, feels guilty and insecure, and worries a great deal. It appears that O+ may also be a good indicator of depression, especially if F− also occurs. At the same time, someone with a severely low score on O may well have inadequate superego controls.

The importance of Scale O may be shown by its prominence on the second-order anxiety factor, to be discussed later. Any clinician would do well to inquire carefully into high scores on this scale.

Scale Q1: Conservative versus Radical   Scales Q1 through Q4 are unlike the previous twelve scales in that they have been found only in questionnaire data, and not in objective tests and life situations that Cattell has studied. Still, these scales are remarkably useful to the clinician making judgments about psychopathology.

Someone low on Q1 respects traditions, is conservative, and resists change. A person high on Q1 is critical, liberal, and intellectual, with a free-thinking point of view. Such a person is easily open to change but difficult to be around. Q1 sounds a good deal like E+ (dominance), but the Q1+ person is usually more intellectual and critical—a person who likes to attack the establishment. In our 1976 book, we mentioned Fidel Castro and George Bernard Shaw as examples of Q1. One is tempted to think of an unresolved oedipal conflict with Q1+. Certainly, such a person might well have difficulty in interacting with authority figures. Essentially, Q1+, which represents an intellectualized form of anger, keeps company with E+ and L+ on Cattell's second-order factor of independence, which we feel actually measures hostility (for more information on this topic, see Krug, 1981).

Scale Q2: Group-Dependent versus Self-Sufficient   This questionnaire factor is clearly a measure of extraversion. Someone low on Q2 needs group support, likes to work around other people, and is what the 16 PF *Manual* calls a "joiner." The Q2 + person, on the other hand, likes to make his or her own decisions, generally has good work habits (especially if also Q3 +), is independent without necessarily dominating others, and tends to be a loner.

Scale Q3: Lacking Control versus Able to Bind Anxiety   A person low on Q3 is aimless, undisciplined, and lax in interpreting society's proscriptions; not surprisingly, the Q3 − typically has not introjected an appropriate identity. Such a person will have great difficulty with work that requires precision and sustained, careful attention to detail. The Q3 + person, on the other hand, is controlled, precise, and even compulsive. Such a person knows what he or she is about and keeps a tight rein on all feelings.

We regard Q3 as a measure of how well a person can deal with, or "bind," anxiety. Someone with a compulsive approach to life can usually keep anxiety well under control. However, if Q3 + is combined with G + (group conformity) and L + (suspiciousness), we usually have a case of undue obsessiveness and rigidity, with limited spontaneity or humor.

Scale Q4: Relaxed versus Tense   Q4 is clearly the principal anxiety indicator among the primary 16 PF factors. Someone low on Q4 may well be low on anxiety (or faking it!), tranquil, and satisfied with his or her life. Examine the motivational distortion scale very carefully when Q4 is low, because people who fake good typically do so on all the anxiety scales (C, O, L, Q3, and Q4).

A very high score on Q4 always deserves careful attention. A person answering these somewhat obvious questions in the Q4 + direction may well be making a plea for help. Indeed, a very high score on this factor, which measures free-floating anxiety, may well indicate such an extreme degree of anxiety that it is often apparent to the clinician in the interview without having to administer a personality test. Typical accompaniments to Q4 + include feelings of frustration and irritability, as well as restlessness and insomnia.

The Second-Order Factors of the 16 PF

As mentioned earlier, during the development of the 16 PF, the scales were allowed to be intercorrelated. Because of this, it was possible to factor-analyze the primaries to yield second-order factors. These second-order factors are broad indicators of personality, which can be computed by hand when necessary with the help of a worksheet provided by IPAT. Of course, all computer scoring systems furnish the second-order factors.

Of the dozen or so second-order factors that have been found to date in Cattell's widely varied researches on personality, we shall briefly discuss the five most important. As we shall see, second-order factors are thought to be a good deal more general in nature than the original scales.

At the outset, we reiterate the fact that in our work in clinical, industrial, and governmental settings, we typically use only the first-order factors, A through Q4, in our interpretations. This is not to say that we are not fully cognizant of the second-order factors when interpreting the primaries, but only that we seldom actually calculate the higher-order factors, except for research purposes (Karson & O'Dell, 1976, p. 98).

Second-Order Factor QI: Extraversion versus Introversion   This scale reflects the famous Jungian concept of *introversion–extraversion*. Someone maximally high on QI is A+ (outgoing), F+ (fun-loving), H+ (bold), and Q2− (group-dependent).

A low score on this factor indicates that the person is shy, perhaps inhibited. Should the score be very low, one might perhaps expect an almost schizoid withdrawal. At the same time, the 16 PF *Manual* notes that a low score on this factor may well have positive characteristics; that is, such a person might well make a very precise worker.

A high score on the second-order factor of extraversion may also be an asset, since our society tolerates the extravert somewhat better than the introvert. A person high on extraversion is outgoing and good at interpersonal relations. Still, there are work situations in which too much extraversion could be troublesome.

On this, as on all second-order factors, it is important that the test interpreter look at the pattern of the underlying primary factors. One person might obtain a low score on this factor because of a very low score on Scale A, whereas another could get exactly the same second-order score because of a low score on Scale F. It is essential for the clinician to examine all such differences with great care.

Second-Order Factor QII: Anxiety versus Dynamic Integration This second-order factor is of exceptional importance in the determination of pathology. A person high on QII is C− (low in ego strength), L+ (suspicious), O+ (guilt-prone), Q3− (unable to bind anxiety), and Q4+ (high in free-floating anxiety). In general, these are not desirable traits for good adjustment or for positive mental health.

Obviously, having low anxiety is generally a much better sign for positive mental health than having high anxiety. Again, however, this depends to a large extent on the precise pattern of the primary scores. A person might have a high anxiety score, with a reasonably high score on

C (ego strength). Such a patient is usually considered better off than someone with a very low score on C, for the potential for improvement seems more likely. Similarly, a high score on Scale L (suspiciousness) would not be a good sign.

Second-Order Factor QIII: Tough Poise versus Sentimentality

Someone high on this factor is *low* on Scales A (reserved), I (tough-minded), and M (practical). A person with a low score on this second-order factor is too easily disrupted by his or her emotions, may be artistic, and may not be carefully controlled by reality. We have found that such persons, for example, are rarely found in jobs requiring attention to detail, such as air traffic control work (Karson & O'Dell, 1974b).

The person high on "cortertia" (Cattell's name for tough poise) is described as aloof, hard, decisive, realistic, and perhaps insensitive to the feelings of others. Such a person may well be a good decision maker but may also have difficulty in dealing with people's feelings. (One cannot help thinking, in this connection, of the character of Mr. Spock on "Star Trek.")

Second-Order Factor QIV: Independence (Hostility) versus Subduedness

As we reach this second-order factor, we begin to encounter factors that are less well defined. Someone high on independence is E+ (dominant), L+ (suspicious), M+ (imaginative), Q1+ (rebellious), and Q2+ (self-sufficient).

It should be obvious, from the pattern of scores just mentioned, that the person high on this second-order factor is usually hostile and difficult to get along with because of excessive anger. Still, he or she may get things done and may show a good deal of initiative. Someone low on this factor is described as dependent, subdued, and even passive.

We rarely refer to this second-order factor in our reports. It does happen, however, that we meet patients with precisely this pattern, and at such times the idea is invaluable.

Second-Order Factor QV: Behavior Control versus Sociopathy

We include this second-order factor because it has been found repeatedly in factor analyses, and because of its importance in clinical and industrial settings, and in contemporary U.S. life. The typical major primaries on this factor include G+ (group conformity), Q3+ (ability to bind anxiety), and N (shrewdness). In our interpretation of this second-order factor we usually also take a close look at the person's scores on O (guilt) and F (fun-loving).

To date, much more is known about the correlates of the two major second-order factors found in the questionnaire realm, namely extraversion and anxiety. Somewhat less is known about sociopathy, and the behavioral correlates of the other three remaining second-order factors are still less well defined.

INTERPRETATION OF THE 16 PF

Our method of interpreting a 16 PF profile is straightforward. First, we look for peculiarities in the faking good, faking bad, and random scales. Next we examine the primaries that load on the major second-order factors, namely extraversion and anxiety. These often provide a capsule summary of the rest of the profile. After this, it is our custom to comment on the most extreme scores in the profile, in order of their deviation from the average.

As we comment on the first-order factors, we gradually begin to form hypotheses about the personality under study. From our experience with the test, we find that client's scores tend to fit certain patterns that we have found to be of importance in the past. We have tried in vain to systematize these patterns, but occasionally a set of score elevations does ring a bell.

Finally, we generally attempt to integrate the 16 PF data with other test data that we have collected on the individual in question. We feel that it is most unwise, at this stage in the development of personality assessment, to base the diagnosis or description of a person on the results of only one test (Karson & O'Dell, 1987b).

Although we have not had great success in codifying the "combinations" of scores that we interpret, Krug (1981) has recently developed a system of pattern analysis based on the second-order factors that may eventually prove useful. He classified four of the five second-order factors mentioned before (extraversion, anxiety, tough poise, and independence) into low (1), medium (2) and high (3) scores, leading to codes such as 1313 (low extraversion and tough poise, high anxiety and independence). These codes were then computed on some seventeen thousand cases who had been given various forms of the 16 PF. From this analysis, characteristics of persons with the 81 possible codes were developed, with respect to such things as occupation and clinical scales. Unfortunately, however, at present there exists only very scanty information about the correlates of these four-point code types. Consequently, we feel that users must await future studies before this system may be used with much practical benefit.

In short, Krug has attempted to introduce to 16 PF interpretation the sort of pattern analysis that has proved so popular with the MMPI. At the moment, his approach must be regarded as experimental. It must also be kept in mind that Cattell himself has stated that he prefers using the first-order factors for 16 PF interpretation (Cattell, Eber, & Tatsuoka, 1970).

Our work with the 16 PF suggests that test misuse with this questionnaire largely involves making simple errors when using the hand-scoring stencils, along with not attending properly to the motivational distortion scores. This results in such mistakes as not making the necessary changes in the sten scores when required, as, for example, when the sten score for either faking good or faking bad is 7 or more. Interpretive failures generally involve being unaware of or unfamiliar with the base rate of a specific sample or occupational group, and using only a scale-by-scale interpretive scheme rather than an integrated consideration of the related factors. One should invariably look at a cluster of related factors when making a descriptive statement. This kind of error is also related to overinterpreting or underinterpreting certain scale scores as well as second-order factors. This sort of mistake frequently stems from not being sufficiently familiar with the primaries that lead to higher-order factors and their interrelationships.

CASE EXAMPLE: MR. ALGER F—A CASE OF BIPOLAR DISORDER[*]

Reason for Referral

This forty-five-year-old, Caucasian male was a self-referral. He is married, with several children. He has worked in an important position in an overseas bank for many years. Testing included a long interview, the 16 PF Forms A and B, the MMPI Form R, the Shipley Institute for Living Scale, and the Bender-Gestalt Test.

General Observations

He began the interview by stating that he had numerous problems that worried him greatly. He described having had occasional homosexual contacts; his wife is apparently aware of this situation. He reported that this problem seemed to be under control until about three years ago.

More importantly, he indicated that he has hardly been sleeping at all, and that his alcohol intake has recently doubled, to about half a fifth a day. He said that when he meets a younger man, he goes overboard and either lends or gives him substantial sums of money. Following this he feels elated for three or four days, and "then it's awful." He indicated that for the past three weeks his "black feelings" were more acute and they appeared to last longer. He described them as being "like something unclean, a sick feeling." He mentioned that after his homosexual encounters he feels that he has been victimized, although he really enjoys the company of younger men. Thereafter, however, what seems to be an archaic superego emerges.

[*]This case example is adapted from *A Guide to the Clinical Use of the 16 PF* by Dr. Jerry W. O'Dell and Dr. Sam Karson. Copyright © 1976 by the Institute for Personality and Ability Testing, Inc., Champaign, Illinois. All rights reserved. Reproduced by permission.

He described going into a depression and reported that he'd had suicidal thoughts; these also had increased in severity in the past few weeks. He also briefly described having what sounded like a hypomanic state about three years ago, lasting about two months. He mentioned that his sister has seen many psychiatrists, and described her as alternating between states of depression and being, as he called it, "hyper."

He portrays his wife of twenty years as calm and strong-willed. His family life seems as routine as can be expected under the circumstances. He holds a professional degree, and did his undergraduate work at one of the nation's finest schools.

At the end of the interview he left the impression of an extremely tense, withdrawn, depressed, worried, and suicidal individual (see Figure 3–1).

16 PF Interpretation

The response set scales indicate that there was a higher than average tendency to exaggerate his symptoms (faking bad = 7), and an even greater response set on his part not to respond to the items as most people do (random = 8). The high faking bad score appeared to be related to a "cry for help," as was the very low motivational distortion score. (He noted during the interview that he was feeling "at the end of his rope.") The high random score may in turn have been related to his inability to concentrate on the task at hand because of the great distress he was experiencing. His high random score also would suggest close scrutiny of scales F, 4, 6, and 8 on the MMPI; all of these measures are interrelated.

His extremely low scores on A (warmth) and H (boldness) suggest a schizoid personality, who predictably tends to be very much a "loner" (Q2 = 10). At the very least, his minimum second-order Extraversion score of 1 shows him to be quite introversive, and he is seen as rather glum and serious (F = 4).

Further, at present he seems quite worried and is experiencing much guilt (O = 8). All of the other anxiety indicators are also strongly in the direction of high anxiety (C−, L+, Q3−, and Q4+), as shown in the second-order anxiety score of 8. It is not a good sign that he possesses below average ego strength (C = 3) and is below average with regard to his ability to bind anxiety (Q3 = 4). Behavior control or compulsivity is below average (G = 2, Q3 = 4), so that alcohol abuse and other forms of acting out come as no surprise.

His H of 1, I of 9, and Q3 of 4 also suggest identity problems, and an inability to integrate an ego ideal toward which he consistently strives. The C− and I+ combination indicates a marked vulnerability to stress in a narcissistic person (M+, G−) who tends to be more swayed by his feelings (I+, M+) than by his intelligence (B+).

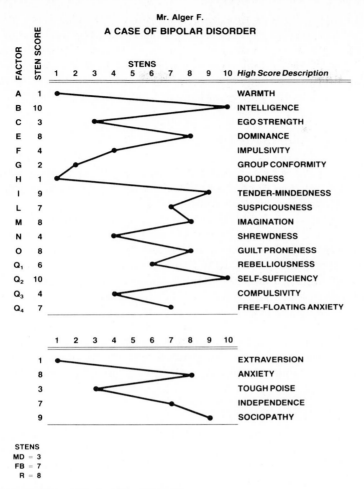

Mr. Alger F.

A CASE OF BIPOLAR DISORDER

FACTOR	STEN SCORE	High Score Description
A	1	WARMTH
B	10	INTELLIGENCE
C	3	EGO STRENGTH
E	8	DOMINANCE
F	4	IMPULSIVITY
G	2	GROUP CONFORMITY
H	1	BOLDNESS
I	9	TENDER-MINDEDNESS
L	7	SUSPICIOUSNESS
M	8	IMAGINATION
N	4	SHREWDNESS
O	8	GUILT PRONENESS
Q_1	6	REBELLIOUSNESS
Q_2	10	SELF-SUFFICIENCY
Q_3	4	COMPULSIVITY
Q_4	7	FREE-FLOATING ANXIETY

1		EXTRAVERSION
8		ANXIETY
3		TOUGH POISE
7		INDEPENDENCE
9		SOCIOPATHY

STENS
MD = 3
FB = 7
R = 8

Figure 3–1 16 PF profile on Mr. Alger F.

There is also a large amount of anger in him (E+, L+), and he does not handle it well. Concurrently, the presence of much depression and some suicidal risk is indicated (F = 4, O = 8), with current feelings of frustration and irritability (Q4 = 7).

Yet, despite all of his problems, he still manages to earn the maximum score on intelligence (B = 10)! Surely this attribute will eventually serve as a valuable asset in psychotherapy.

Still, some form of intensive treatment, including hospitalization, is indicated for this desperate man, because of his great number of serious personality problems. These include a schizoid personality (A = 1, H = 1, Q2 = 10, F = 4), identity problems (H = 1, I = 9, Q3 = 4), serious problems with alcoholism and impulse control (G = 2, Q3 = 4), high anxiety (C−, L+, O+, Q3−, Q4+), and probable depression (F−, O+, and Q4+).

Evaluation on Tests Other Than the 16 PF

On the Shipley he answered all items correctly, attesting to his high intellectual level. The Bender reproductions were sloppy and poorly spaced, with the drawn lines shaky, tremulous, and rather uneven.

He produced a valid MMPI profile of 87542/ with respective T-scores of 92, 85, 78, and 75. Persons with this code have been typically described as feeling strongly alienated as well as showing notable psychic distress, such as anxiety, worry, and difficulties in functioning efficiently. He was also further depicted as shy, socially uncomfortable, fearful, lacking in self-confidence, and feeling inferior. Guilt feelings and feelings of inadequacy regarding sex are often indicated in a profile of this type. Because of the relatively high level of anxiety, a person with this code may well be led to drink excessively in an attempt to relax. Insomnia and suicide attempts are common correlates of his strongly pathological profile code. Such attempts frequently involve self-mutilation or punishment.

Follow-Up

This patient was diagnosed officially as a manic-depressive (bipolar disorder), clearly at the depressive end of the cycle when he was seen for testing. He voluntarily entered inpatient treatment, where lithium therapy was used successfully.

It is interesting to note that, after completion of hospitalization, he began intensive individual psychotherapy and made excellent progress. Within twelve months he was back at work, but he continued with psychotherapy.

KARSON CLINICAL REPORT ON MR. ALGER F

The following is a computerized interpretation of the patient's profile, produced by the *Karson Clinical Report* (reproduced by permission of IPAT). It is interesting to the writers to see just how similar this report is to that produced by the human interpreter. We have omitted the print-out of the score profile, warnings about appropriate professional usage, and so on.

Computerized Report

Certain elements in his profile make one wonder just how withdrawn and schizoid he is. He probably has a history of poor interpersonal relationships and of conflicting family interactions. It is clearly evident that his capacity for abstract verbal skills is exceptionally high. He is so painfully shy, timid, and cautious that he is virtually unable to take any chances. These extreme withdrawal tendencies make life very difficult for him. An extraordinary degree of self-sufficiency would point to good work habits. However, he may be too much of a loner and unable to relate well to others. He is such a low group conformer, with so little regard for the opinions of other people, that he may well have difficulty in adjusting satisfactorily to the demands of life. He's a highly sensitive, tender-minded, sentimental person who is probably more vulnerable to stress than his peers. His below average ego strength suggests the presence of much emotional instability and many neurotic conflicts with limited frustration tolerance and below average capacity for developing an effective network of ego defenses. From a psychodynamic point of view, a major problem would appear to center around his strong feelings of assertiveness and need for control. He may resort to fantasy activity or daydreaming at a time when he ought to be responding to the exigencies of the stimulus situation confronting him. Consequently, attending to routine details is probably not his strong suit. He appears to be especially guilt prone and likely to worry unnecessarily at times.

He is quite serious and sober in his outlook on life with regard to personal obligations. He is typically responsible and dependable. He is seen as someone who tends to be suspicious of other people's motives and who displaces and projects his angry feelings. He is frequently seen as too forthright and direct, and perhaps clumsy in his relations with others. He does not appear to be an obsessive person, and this lack of compulsivity might make it hard for him to function in certain jobs requiring sustained accuracy and attention to detail. His free-floating anxiety is above average and suggests higher than average feelings of tension and frustration.

ASSETS AND LIABILITIES OF THE 16 PF

The measurement of human personality is not a simple matter. Hence, like all personality tests, the 16 PF has both strong and weak points. The reviews of the test in the *Mental Measurements Yearbooks* give a good overview of the virtues and deficiencies of the instrument. Wholeben (1985), in his recent test critique of the 16 PF, presents as balanced an evaluation of the test as one is likely to find in a brief review. Moreover, we are in agreement with his views on the basis of our many years of clinical, industrial, and research work with the 16 PF.

The 16 PF has almost too many good features to summarize in a brief chapter. In many ways its psychometric properties are exemplary. The test has been revised five times over the years. In its most recent standardization, norms were collected on over fifteen thousand people. Reliability of the test appears to be adequate. The amount of validity data on the 16 PF is simply staggering; the publisher states that there are over three thousand research papers, chapters, and books on the test. Anyone looking at the 16 PF *Handbook* (Cattell et al., 1970) will be impressed by the sheer number of coefficients and regression equations provided. Further, the theoretical basis of the 16 PF is probably as sound as that of any personality test in existence. Workable scales to detect response sets are readily available.

In a recent chapter by the present authors (1987b), both the MMPI Form R and the 16 PF Forms A and B were used to study psychiatric medical evacuations and alcoholism in the U.S. Foreign Service. These results demonstrated that the 16 PF and the MMPI constitute a useful test battery with psychiatric patients. These findings, as well as earlier work, make us question Butcher's conclusion (1985, p. 1136) in his review of the 16 PF in the Ninth *Mental Measurements Yearbook,* that the test "is not recommended for routine clinical use." We would agree with him only in the case of psychiatric inpatients. Otherwise, his statement runs counter to our own extensive clinical and research experience with the 16 PF (Karson, 1959, 1960; Karson & Wiedershine, 1961).

From the standpoint of the clinician, the test offers many advantages and practical virtues. First of all, it is fun to use! Moreover, the factors in the 16 PF are fascinating and lend themselves readily to psychodynamic and behavioristic interpretations. Also, the 16 PF is available in five forms; if those are not sufficient, the publisher provides similar tests for younger and older children, and adolescents. The 16 PF was admittedly designed for use with normals and is, consequently, especially well suited to the occupational screening applications that are more and more a major part of clinical and industrial practice. Documentation on the test is extensive, despite its admitted shortcomings. The longest single form of the test is made up of only 187 items. Thus, even if two forms are given at once, the test is much more manageable for the client than a longer test like the MMPI. The test may be administered by relatively untrained personnel, and in group settings. Finally, a vast array of scoring and interpretive services are available to the test user.

There are many somewhat negative features about the test, as one would expect in an instrument that has been in existence for thirty-five years. A common complaint is simply that since the test was developed on normals, it may not be useful with pathological conditions, especially for psychiatric patients. We believe that our work with the test over the years has handily disproved this idea. Many reviewers of the test have complained about what they consider the poor documentation in the *Handbook* and other publications on the test. There is much truth to this; but at the same time it is refreshing to find a test with such a wealth of documentation, deficient as it is in some ways.

The test is certainly not without its psychometric problems. Although reliability appears adequate, there is some evidence that alternate-forms reliability is not as high as it should be. This may be simply because the scales, at ten or thirteen items each, are rather short and thus potentially unreliable. One really cannot win here. If longer scales are to be obtained on an instrument of reasonable length, then it is almost essential that there be item overlap between the scales, as in the MMPI. But this introduces a whole new set of psychometric problems. Validity coefficients calculated between 16 PF scales and outside criteria hit a maximum of about $r = +.30$ to $+.40$. This is approximately the range found with the MMPI, but clearly not outstanding. Such, however, is the state of the art at present, and it is unlikely to change soon.

The 16 PF is commonly criticized because no one really knows just how many features underlie human personality. Cattell feels that there are perhaps sixteen (plus twelve in the psychopathological realm), Eysenck two or three, and so on. Carefully done item factor analyses of the test, including one by the present writers (Karson & O'Dell, 1974a), have in general verified the existence of most of Cattell's sixteen factors, while not finding others. Unfortunately, various other studies seem to verify differing sets of the original sixteen factors. It is our feeling that it may well be a very long time before psychology reaches the point at which there is substantial agreement about the number of dimensions that are needed to measure human personality.

CONCLUSIONS

In summary, the 16 PF is a very successful personality test, whose use is growing every year. It is easy to administer and has a wide variety of scales, many of which we have found to be of great clinical importance. The test has a sound theoretical base, adequate psychometric properties, and decent documentation.

On the basis of over three decades of using the 16 PF in a wide variety of clinical, industrial, and governmental situations, we are confident that the 16 PF has earned a permanent place in the clinician's armamentarium.

REFERENCES

Allport, G. A., & Odbert, H. S. (1936). Trait-names: A psycholexical study. *Psychological Monographs, 47,* Whole No. 211.

Butcher, J. N. (1985). Review of the Sixteen Personality Factor Questionnaire. In J. V. Mitchell (Ed.), *The ninth mental measurements yearbook* (pp. 1391–1394). Lincoln: University of Nebraska—Lincoln.

Cattell, R. B. (1946). *The description and measurement of personality.* Yonkers, NY: World Book Company.

Cattell, R. B. (1957). *Personality and motivation structure and measurement.* Yonkers, NY: World Book Company.

Cattell, R. B. (1973). *Personality and mood by questionnaire.* San Francisco, CA: Jossey-Bass.

Cattell, R. B., Eber, H. W., & Tatsuoka, M. M. (1970). *Handbook for the Sixteen Personality Factor Questionnaire.* Champaign, IL: Institute for Personality and Ability Testing.

IPAT Staff. (1986). *Administrators manual for the 16 PF.* Champaign, IL: Institute for Personality and Ability Testing.

Karson, S. (1959). The Sixteen Personality Factor Test in clinical practice. *Journal of Clinical Psychology, 15,* 174–176.

Karson, S. (1960). Validating clinical judgments with the 16 PF test. *Journal of Clinical Psychology, 16,* 394–397.

Karson, S., & O'Dell, J. W. (1974a). Is the 16 PF factorially valid? *Journal of Personality Assessment, 38,* 104–114.

Karson, S., & O'Dell, J. W. (1974b). The personality makeup of the American air traffic controller. *Aerospace Medicine, 45,* 1001–1007.

Karson, S., & O'Dell, J. W. (1976). *A guide to the clinical use of the 16 PF.* Champaign, IL: Institute for Personality and Ability Testing.

Karson, S., & O'Dell, J. W. (1987a). Computer-based interpretation of the 16 PF: The Karson Clinical Report in contemporary practice. In J. N. Butcher (Ed.), *Computerized psychological assessment.* New York: Basic Books.

Karson, S., & O'Dell, J. W. (1987b). Personality profiles in the U.S. Foreign Service. In J. N. Butcher & C. D. Spielberger (Eds.), *Advances in personality development* (Vol. 6). Hillsdale, NJ: Erlbaum.

Karson, S., & Wiedershine, L. J. (1961). An objective evaluation of dynamically oriented group psychotherapy. *International Journal of Group Psychotherapy, 11,* 166–174.

Krug, S. F. (1978). Further evidence on the 16 distortion scales. *Journal of Personality Assessment, 42,* 513–518.

Krug, S. E. (1981). *Interpreting 16 PF profile patterns.* Champaign, IL: Institute for Personality and Ability Testing.

Lorr, M., Nerviano, V., & Myhill, J. (1985). Factors common to the ISI and 16 PF inventories. *Journal of Clinical Psychology, 41,* 773–777.

O'Dell, J. W. (1971). Method for detecting random answers on personality questionnaires. *Journal of Applied Psychology, 55,* 380–383.

Wholeben, B. (1985). Sixteen Personality Factor Questionnaire. In J. J. Keyser & R. C. Sweetland (Eds.), *Test critiques* (Vol. 4). Kansas City, MO: Test Corporation of America.

4

The California Psychological Inventory

Harrison G. Gough

Why would anyone want to use a test like the California Psychological Inventory (CPI; Gough, 1957), a multivariate device scaled for interpersonal and normative themes in behavior? One answer can come from a perusal of published studies, to examine the uses to which the inventory has been put by different authors. Another answer can come from a consideration of the stated aims of the test, to see if these are relevant to the purposes the potential user has in mind. A third can come from familiarity with the techniques used to construct and validate the scales, to determine whether they correspond to the paradigmatic preferences of the evaluator. As there should be at this stage in the development of instruments for appraising personality, there are many instruments from which to choose, each with its own background, intentions, and methodological characteristics.

Let us begin our look at the CPI with a survey of some of the more interesting studies that have been done to date. One area of concentrated attention has been that of academic achievement, at various levels of the educational ladder. Performance criteria have been studied in high schools

(Alker & Wohl, 1972; Davids, 1966; Linton, 1967; Snider, 1966), colleges (Gough & Lanning, 1986; Griffin & Flaherty, 1964; Stroup & Elft, 1969), medical school (Gough & Hall, 1975), dental school (Gough & Kirk, 1970), optometry school (Kegel-Flom, 1974, 1985), and centers for higher education (Demos & Veijola, 1966).

Related studies have dealt with achievement within certain subgroups, such as high-aptitude students (Hogan & Weiss, 1974; Holland, 1959; Nichols & Holland, 1963; Purkey, 1966, 1970), black students (Pfeifer & Sedlacek, 1974), students of Hispanic background (Gill & Spilka, 1962), the mathematically precocious (Haier & Denham, 1976; Weiss, Haier, & Keating, 1974), and the verbally gifted (Viernstein, McGinn, & Hogan, 1977).

Attention has been given to special aspects of performance, such as graduation versus dropout from high school (Gough, 1966; Irvine, 1979); attrition in college (Hill, 1966); independent versus rule-following achievement patterns (Domino, 1968, 1971; Ross, 1980); interest and attainment in certain fields such as mathematics (Aiken, 1963; Keimowitz & Anspacher, 1960), theology (Query, 1966), and psychology (Gough, 1983); cross-cultural verification of CPI configurations for forecasting academic performance in Greece (Repapi, Gough, Lanning, & Stefanis, 1983) and Italy (Gough, 1964); and cheating on examinations by college students (Hetherington & Feldman, 1964).

Another major topic of study is creativity, including cinematographic creativity (Domino, 1974) and creativity among architects (Hall & MacKinnon, 1969), young scientists (Garwood, 1964; Parloff & Datta, 1965), engineers (McDermid, 1965), mathematicians (Helson, 1971; Helson & Crutchfield, 1970), and research scientists (Weiss, 1981).

Another major theme has been the study of persons in different occupations, for instance managers (Barron & Egan, 1968; Gough, 1984; Rawls & Rawls, 1968), teachers (Gough, Durflinger, & Hill, 1968; Kegel-Flom, 1983; Veldman & Kelly, 1965), police officers (Gettys & Elam, 1985; Hogan, 1971; Hogan & Kurtines, 1975; Leitner & Sedlacek, 1976; Pugh, 1985), engineers (Brown, Grant, & Patton, 1981; Scissons, 1979), accountants (DeCoster & Rhode, 1972), nurses (Dyer, Cope, Monson, & Von Drimmelen, 1972), data processing personnel (Morris & Wise, 1972), and paraprofessional telephone counselors (King, McGowen, Doonan, & Schweibert, 1980).

With respect to personal and social problems, there is a large bibliography—for instance, studies of criminal and delinquent behavior (Laufer, Johnson, & Hogan, 1981; Mizushima & DeVos, 1967), drug abuse (Burger & Collins, 1982; Goldstein, 1974; Kay, Lyons, Newman, Mankin, & Loeb, 1978; Kurtines, Hogan, & Weiss, 1975; McGuire & Megargee, 1974), alcoholism (Kurtines, Ball, & Wood, 1978; Selzer, Vinokur, & Wilson, 1977), the Type A coronary-prone personality (Burke & Weir, 1980; Musante, MacDougall, Dembroski, & Van Horn, 1983; Palladino & Motiff,

1981), pathological gambling (McCormick, Taber, Kruedelbach, & Russo, 1987), stress in the first year of medical school (Boyle & Coombs, 1971), visual impairment (Adrian, Miller, & de L'Aune, 1982), and illness susceptibility (Hong, Wirt, Yellin, & Hopwood, 1979).

Finally, from the many reports on particular topics, the range can be suggested by studies of leadership (Carbonell, 1984; J. C. Hogan, 1978; Megargee, 1969), athletic interests and performance (Johnson, 1972; Schendel, 1965), migration (Mazer & Ahern, 1969), social intelligence (Sipps, Berry, & Lynch, 1987), mate selection (Buss, 1984; Buss & Barnes, 1986), sense of direction (Bryant, 1982), behavioral genetics (Dworkin, Burke, Maher, & Gottesman, 1976; Loehlin, 1987), life-span developmental psychology (Block, 1971; Cartwright, 1977; Helson, Mitchell, & Moane, 1984; Helson & Moane, 1987; Helson & Wink, 1987), anger arousal (Biaggio, 1970), coping ability among women who become victims of rape (Myers, Templer, & Brown, 1984), and adult health as related to adolescent health and personality (Bayer, Whissell-Buechy, & Honzik, 1980).

PURPOSES

The intention of the CPI is to furnish measures of a sufficiently large number of folk notions about personality so that all, or nearly all, kinds of ordinary interpersonal behavior can be forecast and rationalized either from a single scale, or (more often) from a small cluster of scales that will be reasonable from both conceptual and psychometric standpoints. For instance, college-going among high school graduates can be modestly predicted from the CPI scale for Achievement via Conformance (Ac), but a much more satisfactory level of accuracy is attained if the scales for Dominance (Do), Capacity for Status (Cs), and Good Impression (Gi) are added to the equation (Gough, 1968). It might be noted that in this equation the Do, Cs, and Ac scales receive positive weights, whereas the Gi scale is weighted negatively.

Many inventories seek to assess personality traits. A trait is a theorized element of personality showing certain consistencies over time and certain predictive powers across situations. Scales for traits must satisfy a number of psychometric requirements, such as internal homogeneity of items, representative sampling of the trait domain by the items, and minimal covariation with other trait measures. Scales for traits rest on a *definitional* view of measurement.

Although trait words are used to name some (but not all) of the CPI scales, trait measurement is not intended, and indeed no claims are made in this regard. CPI scales have two *instrumental* purposes, namely (1) to forecast what people will say and do in defined, consequential situations, and (2) to identify individuals who will be described and talked about by others in predictable and informative ways.

For instance, the scale for Dominance seeks to forecast the extent to which persons will do things in defined settings that are consensually classified as dominant, and in particular as prosocially dominant, and to identify persons who will be described by others as dominant, strong, assertive, and the like. Examination of the items in the Do scale for unidimensionality or homogeneity, or for their coverage of the implied trait domain of dominance, or for their relationships to other vectors or criteria, may be of interest but will have little to do with the stated purposes of the measure.

Abundant evidence concerning the prediction of acts from scores on the Do scale may be found in the recent papers by Buss and Craik (1980, 1981, 1983) and in the *Administrator's Guide* (Gough, 1987) for the inventory. Persons with high scores on Do tend to speak up early in group meetings, direct and manage others, initiate new activity, and learn people's names quickly. The importance of context for the high-Do person has been demonstrated in a series of studies by Megargee and his associates (Carbonell, 1984; Megargee, 1969; Megargee, Bogart, & Anderson, 1966). Dyads were formed of one person scoring high on Do and another scoring low. Then the dyad, or team, was assigned an experimental task that required one person to direct or take charge, and the other to do the bidding of the leader.

When the instructions emphasized task completion and the performance of the team, the high-dominant member assumed control at about a chance level; but when the instructions emphasized the appraisal of leadership qualities in the experiment, the dominant member took charge in nearly every instance. One exception to this generalization occurred when low-dominant males were paired with high-dominant females. In these dyads, under the leadership instructions, the low-dominant males served as leaders in most of the trials. However, postexperimental debriefing indicated that the high-dominant women had, in fact, maneuvered their male partners into carrying out the conventionally sex-appropriate role.

These laboratory findings coincide with the observation from everyday life that high-dominant persons can be excellent followers, when deference makes sense and is prosocial. For example, vice-presidents of the United States usually have strong leadership drives of their own, but, once elected in this subordinate role, typically become assiduous and steadfast supporters of whatever decisions their president may make. In other words, high scorers on Do will manifest dominant behavior when— and for the most part only when—the sanctioned goals and defined purposes of the setting call for such behavior.

High scorers on Do are very characteristically viewed by others as dominant, confident, assertive, and ambitious, whether or not their behavior is currently dominant or nondominant, and are seldom if ever described as shy, submissive, withdrawn, or timid (Gough, 1987, p. 53).

Another major intention of the CPI is to represent, or map, the social-psychological topography as it actually exists, as opposed to providing a set of scales uncorrelated with each other. Suppose, for example, that in everyday life most people see sociability and social presence as related, even though they can point out the differences between the two concepts and recognize the utility of having both at hand. What does this mean for the CPI Sy (Sociability) and Sp (Social Presence) scales? The answer is obvious, following on the topographical purpose just mentioned. That is, the two scales should be correlated at just the level that the functional concepts correlate in folk usage.

Because all of the CPI scales, save that for Femininity/Masculinity, are scored so that higher values are associated with the conventionally favored end of the continuum, one would anticipate primarily positive coefficients in the interscale matrix. Note that this is a theoretically desired outcome, and not just a weakness or deficiency in the inventory. In fact, after excluding the F/M (Femininity/Masculinity) scale, there were only 7 negative, as against 183 positive, coefficients in the matrix for males, and also 7 negative as against 183 positive in the matrix for females (Gough, 1987, p. 33).

A third theoretical principle embedded in the CPI is that of intensification or saturation of measurement. This concept can be approached by way of measures of intelligence. In early years, most intellectual measures were reported as single scores. Later, for instance in the Wechsler Adult Intelligence Scale (WAIS; Wechsler, 1955), a profile of assessment was given that included subtests for different ways of appraising the talent. Insofar as there is a general or overall g-factor in ability, assessable by a single scale, the Wechsler test offers redundant but nonetheless useful intensification of measurement.

Likewise in the MMPI (Hathaway & McKinley, 1943), which contains a number of scales for different kinds of psychopathological reactions, one could ask, "Why use a profile of subscales to assess the general, overall factor of maladjustment?" Most clinicians would promptly answer, "Because it is helpful in understanding the particularities and nuances of this maladjustment to have separate—even if highly correlated—subscales for syndromes such as hysteria, depression, psychasthenia, and schizophrenia."

This functional/pragmatic point of view can be carried over to the CPI and to its inclusion of subscales for different facets of interpersonal and normative behavior. For instance, in the interpersonal realm, there are seven separate scales, each focusing on a particular way or style in which the general factor of interpersonal poise and self-assurance is expressed. Consider, as an example, the Do and Sp (Dominance and Social Presence) scales from this cluster. For both sexes, the correlation between the two scales is usually about .60. In the factor analysis of the inventory reported in the *Guide* (Gough, 1987), both have strong loadings on the first, or interpersonal, dimension. Why, then, retain both scales on the profile sheet?

The reason is that even though highly similar in factorial properties, each scale picks up interesting and consequential nuances of style. Act frequency (Buss & Craik, 1984) analyses of archival data showed specifics for Do such as "I took charge of the group," "I organized the group to attain its goals," and "I talked a great deal at the meeting." When the same analysis was conducted on the Sp scale, however, these were among the strongest act implications: "I danced at the party," "I took the lead in livening up a dull party," and "I charmed my new acquaintance with clever conversation." These differences in act expectations for the Do and Sp scales are important in arriving at an integrated, coherent picture of the full personality and its modes of functioning.

Finally, the theoretical decision to scale the CPI for folk concepts should be mentioned again. Some inventories are scaled for concepts from a particular theory or point of view, for example the Myers-Briggs Type Indicator (Myers & McCaulley, 1985), based on the theoretical writing of C. G. Jung (1923). Others incorporate scales derived by factor analysis of a large pool of items, for instance the Guilford-Zimmerman Temperament Survey (Guilford & Zimmerman, 1949). Some tests, such as the Minnesota Multiphasic Personality Inventory (MMPI), are scaled for diagnostic concepts possessing a particular relevance for certain settings. The logic underlying all of these instruments is reasonable, and each test will be of value to the user depending on the purposes the user has in mind. The CPI is aimed at the ongoing flow of ordinary, everyday life, and seeks to measure the classificatory and predictive concepts that people everywhere use to comprehend their own behavior and that of others.

STRUCTURE AND CONSTRUCTION OF THE SCALES

The present version of the CPI (Gough, 1987) contains twenty folk concept scales that are included on the profile sheet. Then there are three vector scales for the basic structural themes in the inventory, and a number of special-purpose scales that are available for use at the pleasure of the examiner. The three categories will be described in sequence.

In the first edition of the CPI there were eighteen folk measures (Gough, 1957). The CPI is an "open" system, from which scales may be removed if and when they no longer serve any useful purpose, and to which scales may be added as augmentation appears to be desirable. Over the years, both additions and subtractions have been made.

Thirteen of the twenty folk scales were developed by the method of criterion keying, in which items were selected that correlated significantly ($p \leq .05$) with external criteria, such as nominations by peers for

Do (Dominance), grades in high school for Ac (Achievement via Conformance), and scores on measures of cognitive ability for Ie (Intellectual Efficiency).

The two new scales in 1987 were for Empathy (Hogan, 1969) and Independence. Because the development of the In (Independence) scale has not previously been described, a short account of its construction should be helpful. Independence as a folk concept involves two components: resourcefulness and competence on the one hand, and distance and detachment on the other. In a sample of 236 couples, each member was described by the other on the 300-item Adjective Check List (Gough & Heilbrun, 1983). A cluster of adjectives—some indicative of independence and some contraindicative—was specified, and then scores on this independence cluster were obtained by examining the descriptions of each woman by her male partner, and of each man by his female partner.

These were the adjectives in the two parts of the independence criterion:

> *Indicative items:* cool, independent, individualistic, mature, realistic, self-controlled, strong
>
> *Contraindicative items:* dependent, fearful, frivolous, immature, self-pitying, spineless, submissive, suggestible, unstable, weak

The score for each person on this cluster was obtained by counting the number of positive items checked by the spouse, and subtracting from this total the number of negative items checked. The range of possible scores could thus vary from a low of -10 to a high of $+7$.

Then the scores for each person on the independence criterion were correlated with the 462 CPI items, for the total sample of 472 subjects and for the male and female samples separately. Items were sought that had statistically significant ($p \le .05$) correlations in the total sample, and nonzero correlations in the same direction for each sex separately. Here are some examples of the items found and their scoring for the In scale.

> "I usually expect to succeed in things I do." (true)
>
> "I feel nervous if I have to meet a lot of people." (false)

Thirty items were selected, ten scored for a "true" and twenty for a "false" response. When scored as a scale on a sample of 400 college students, the interitem alpha reliability coefficient was .70. Test–retest coefficients for high school students tested a year apart were .60 for 102 males and .64 for 128 females. Then, in a sample of 198 college students not used to develop the scale, scores on In were correlated with ratings of independence made by assessment staff observers on the basis of a full day of interaction and observation. The consensual staff ratings of independence correlated .42 ($p \leqslant .01$) with the In scale in the total sample, and .47 and .37 within the male and female subsamples of 99 students each. It appears from these data that the In scale has acceptable, albeit modest, reliability, and that it does in fact relate significantly to observers' ratings of independence.

What about the Do scale, which is also in the CPI interpersonal cluster, and which might be considered a possible indicator of independence itself? First, in regard to item overlap, there are only eight items in common to the two scales. That is, 22 of the In items do not appear on the Do scale, and 28 of the 36 Do items do not appear on In. Nonetheless, the two scales are strongly intercorrelated, with coefficients typically of about .73 to .74. In spite of this, when one looks to descriptive implications and expectable acts, differences between Do and In are easy to discern. Two acts correlating significantly with In but not with Do were "I interrupted a conversation" and "I let somebody else pay for cocktails." Two acts associated with high scores on Do, but not with In, were "I had more to say than anyone else" and "I spoke first at the meeting." In the descriptive realm, attributes of distance, coolness, and privacy are more strongly stressed for In, and attributes of affiliation, involvement, and power-seeking for Do.

Four of the twenty folk scales were developed by internal consistency methods, specifically Social Presence, Self-acceptance, Self-control, and Flexibility. In this method, items believed to be related to the concept are first identified and then scored as a preliminary scale on a research sample. Each item, with dummy weights of 1 and 0, is then correlated with the total score. Items from the preliminary set that fail to correlate significantly with the total are dropped, and new items from the full inventory that do correlate significantly may be added. After two or more iterations of this kind, a final set is selected in which internal homogeneity is maximized.

The remaining three scales, for Good Impression, Communality, and Well-being, were developed by mixed strategies, in which both internal consistency and relationships to nontest criteria were considered. The *Guide* (1987) may be consulted for a more complete explanation of the development of these three scales.

For interpreting scores on the folk scales, standard scores on the profile sheet will be helpful. Standard scores are linear transformations of the raw scores, so that for the general population the average will be 50 and the standard deviation 10. Scores in the 40-to-60 range will be more or less undifferentiating. Scores from 60 to 70 and from 30 to 40 carry moderate implications, and scores of 71 or above and 29 or below warrant stronger inferences. The psychological meanings found in past research on each scale may be summarized as follows.

Measures of Interpersonal Style and Orientation

Do (Dominance) (36 Items)   Higher scores indicate a prosocial dominance, self-assurance, task orientation, and enterprise. Lower scores indicate hesitancy about taking the initiative, equivocation, and feelings of vulnerability.

Cs (Capacity for Status) (28 Items)   Higher scores indicate ambition, breadth of interests, versatility, and self-confidence. Lower scores indicate dislike of competitive situations, feelings of unease in social encounters, and apathy.

Sy (Sociability) (32 Items)   Higher scores suggest sociability, gregariousness, and an alert and active social manner. Lower scores suggest caution, self-denial, reticence, and a subdued or unassuming social demeanor.

Sp (Social Presence) (38 Items)   Higher scores are associated with verbal fluency, wittiness, spontaneity, and a tendency to be somewhat self-centered. Lower scores are associated with narrowness of interests, inhibition, a liking for routine, and a readiness to feel guilty.

Sa (Self-acceptance) (28 Items)   Higher scores relate to feelings of personal worth and self-esteem, talkativeness, and effective skills in self-presentation. Lower scores indicate self-doubt, withdrawal, suppressive ego defenses, and ambivalence about self.

In (Independence) (30 Items)   Higher scores are associated with the twin elements of competence and detachment, and are diagnostic of resourcefulness, poise, and feelings of self-sufficiency. Lower scores are associated with the avoidance of conflict, a need for support from others, a tendency to delay or avoid taking the initiative, and feelings of dependency.

Em (Empathy) (38 Items)   Higher scores suggest optimism, perceptiveness about social nuances, likability, and leadership potential. Lower scores suggest difficulty in understanding how others think and feel, conservative ethical values, and discomfort in complex and unpredictable social situations.

Measures of Normative Orientations and Values

Re (Responsibility) (36 Items)   Higher scores are related to rule-awareness and ethical perceptiveness, as opposed to blind or slavish rule-following. Lower scores are related to dissatisfaction, undependability, and self-indulgence.

So (Socialization) (46 Items)   Higher scores suggest conscientious, well-organized, rule-respecting behavior, but (with very high scores) the possibility of overconformity. Lower scores suggest waywardness, undependability, moodiness, and counteractive or rebellious attitudes.

Sc (Self-control) (38 Items)   Higher scores indicate strongly positive feelings about normative constraints, a tendency to suppress or even deny hostile and erotic impulses, and suppressive moral attitudes. Lower scores indicate a sort of undercontrol, with relative freedom of expression of aggressive and erotic feelings, and a pleasure-seeking approach to life.

Gi (Good Impression) (40 Items)   This scale has two functions. For raw scores of about 31 and above, there is an indication of overly favorable self-description, to the point of faking good. For above-average scores but short of this high level, the implications are for a social style overemphasizing prosocial qualities, exaggerated but superficial conformance to convention, and shallow insight. Lower scores indicate individualistic tendencies, easy irritability, and impatience.

Cm (Communality) (38 Items)   This scale also has two functions. For raw scores of 27 or below, one must consider random answering or inattention to the content of the items. For below-average scores above this level, there is a suggestion of unconventionality, changeableness, and complexity of inner life. Higher scores suggest stability, conventionality, and a general satisfaction with things as they are.

Wb (Well-being) (38 Items)   Two functions are served by this scale. For very low raw scores of 20 and below, there is a possibility of undue or unwarranted emphasis on problems, or faking bad. Lower scores short of this point suggest dissatisfaction, worry, and a tendency to complain. Persons with higher scores tend to be insightful, open-minded, and rational in their judgments of self and others.

Measures of Cognitive and Intellectual Functioning

Ac (Achievement via Conformance) (38 Items)   Higher scores suggest ambition, capability, and the capacity to do well in clearly defined and controlled environments. Lower scores suggest distractibility, undependability, and resistance to rules or any kind of strict control.

Ai (Achievement via Independence) (36 Items)   Higher scores are associated with achievement drives that function well in ambiguous, open, or only partially defined settings. High scorers tend to be clear-thinking, intelligent, and independent. Low scorers tend to be rather narrow in interests, easily discouraged from doing their best, and poorly motivated in both educational and occupational matters.

Ie (Intellectual Efficiency) (42 Items)   The intention of the scale is to assess the extent to which intellectual abilities are efficiently used. High scorers tend to be seen as capable, logical, and resourceful. Low scorers tend to be seen as low in self-esteem, below average in ability, and poor in expressing their feelings and ideas.

Measures of Role and Personal Style

Py (Psychological mindedness) (28 Items)   Higher scores indicate insightfulness about people (but not necessarily warmth or sympathy), foresight, critical judgment, and independence. Lower scores indicate conventionality, intellectual shallowness, and uncertainty about one's own ability.

Fx (Flexibility) (28 Items)   Higher scores suggest cleverness, zest, and imagination, but also carelessness and instability in goal-seeking; persons with high scores seek and welcome change, and become impatient in repetitious or routine circumstances. Lower scores suggest conservative attitudes, conventionality, and a certain deliberateness of manner, but also self-discipline, thoroughness, and sense of duty. Persons with low scores seek stability and avoid situations where rapid changes are likely to occur.

F/M (Femininity/Masculinity) (32 Items)   Interpretation of this scale is different for men than for women. For males, higher scores are associated with sensitivity, worry, nervousness, and feelings of ambivalence about self, but also with a certain talent for aesthetic and imaginative thinking. Lower scores are associated with self-confidence, independence, and good ability in dealing with stress and conflict, but also with obstinance and indifference to the feelings of others. For females, higher scores are associated with interpersonal warmth, sympathy for others, and generosity, but also with vulnerability to stress, dependency, and lack of self-confidence. Lower scores are associated with independence, self-reliance, and ego strength, but also with skepticism about the intentions of others, difficulty in accepting any subordinate role, and willfulness.

More extensive discussions of the implications of each scale, as well as suggestions for configural interactions of two or more scales, may be found in the interpretational monographs of McAllister (1986) and Rodgers (1983). For instance, Em and Py have somewhat similar intentions and usually correlate at about .56, but in an occasional profile one will be elevated (60 or more) and the other low (45 or below). Here is what McAllister (1986, p. 60) suggests for persons with a high-Py, low-Em configuration: "They are objectively very accurate in reading people, but they remain aloof and unresponsive on an emotional level." For the configuration of Wb at 35 or below in standard score terms, and F/M at 60 or above, Rodgers (1983, p. 75) remarks: "This combination is often associated with psychophysiologic symptomatology of one sort or another, perhaps especially headaches or gastrointestinal upset or a functional skin condition. It seems to reflect a combination of moderate dependency or affiliative needs in a situation in which these are not being satisfied and are associated with moderate distrust of and alienation from others." Systematic presentation and evaluation of validational data for all the scales except In may be found in Megargee's (1972) *CPI Handbook*.

THE STRUCTURAL SCALES

Factor and smallest-space analyses of the CPI (Bernstein, Garbin, & McClellan, 1983; Karni & Levin, 1972; Levin & Karni, 1970) have repeatedly indicated the presence of two basic themes, one pertaining to interpersonal style and manner of behavior and the other to the incorporation of normative values. On the CPI profile sheet, the seven scales assessing different specifics of interpersonal style are presented first, followed by the seven scales that report different facets of the normative domain. There also appears to be a theme of overall elevation, indicative of the respondent's sense of self-realization and also of the general level of competence as this would be judged by an observer.

Separate measurement of these three structural dimensions should add an attractive feature to the yield from the inventory, particularly if these three scales could be kept orthogonal to each other (uncorrelated) so as to generate a theoretical model. Over the years attempts were made to develop separate scales for the interpersonal and normative dimensions (see Nichols & Schnell, 1963), but the realization/competence axis went unnoticed. For the new edition of the CPI (Gough, 1987), a decision was therefore made to attempt the development of three new scales, one for each of the structural vectors.

The first of these scales, called v.1 (vector 1), assesses the interpersonal factor. Lower scores on v.1 are associated with a more outgoing, involved, interpersonally responsive orientation, and high scores with a more inwardly directed, private, and intrapersonally focused inclination. Some sample items are: "I usually don't like to talk much unless I am with people I know very well" (true), "I'm not the type to be a political leader" (true), "A person needs to 'show off' a little now and then" (false), and "I like to be the center of attention" (false).

The second scale, called v.2, assesses the normative factor. Lower scores on v.2 are associated with rule-questioning, rule-resisting, and even rule-violating dispositions. Higher scores are associated with rule-accepting, rule-observing, and even rule-cathecting tendencies. Several illustrative items are: "I take a rather serious attitude toward ethical and moral issues" (true), "I set a high standard for myself and I feel others should do the same" (true), "I sometimes wanted to run away from home" (false), and "If the pay was right I would like to travel with a circus or carnival" (false).

These two scales, taken conjointly, define four life-styles or ways of living. In the *alpha* quadrant, composed of persons who seek out and enjoy interpersonal engagement and who readily accept normative sanctions, one finds individuals with managerial, leadership, and executive drives. At their best, alphas can be inspirational and charismatic leaders, but at their worst they can be invasive, officious, and meddlesome.

In the *beta* quadrant, composed of persons who are comfortable with normative constraints and whose perspectives are more inward and private, one finds individuals who are thoughtful, reflective, and generous. At their best, betas are virtuous, steadfast, and compassionate. At their worst they are conformist, unresponsive, and judgmental.

The *gamma* quadrant combines a lively involvement in the shared interpersonal world with dubiety concerning the norms under which that world is governed. At their best, gammas are innovative, insightful about the imperfections of the social structure, and adept in defining new and better ways of living. At their worst, gammas are disruptive, counteractive, and asocial in their behavior.

The *delta* quadrant combines an introversive temperament with rule-questioning attitudes. At their best, deltas are complex, creative, and imaginative. At their worst they are fragmented, internally conflicted, and prone to psychopathological reactions.

The four quadrants defined by v.1 and v.2, to repeat, betoken four types of people, each type having its own potentiality and particular kind of fulfillment, and each type having its own pitfalls and dangers to be avoided. A schematic representation of this type theory is given in Figure 4–1.

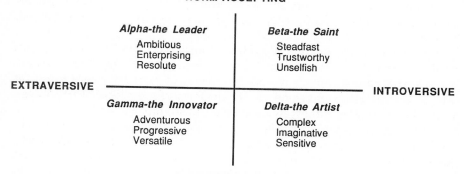

Figure 4–1 The typology formed by the v.1. and v.2 scales of the CPI.

Figure 4–1 presents the v.1 and v.2 axes of extraversive to introversive interpersonal orientation, and norm-questioning to norm-accepting perspectives on social values. The descriptions of the four types are for persons at the highest level of fulfillment and integration.

The v.3 scale was developed to index the level of self-realization and competence. Its psychometric requirements were to be uncorrelated or relatively uncorrelated with v.1 and v.2, but positively correlated with all of the CPI folk scales except for F/M. Its psychological requirements were to reflect feelings of fulfillment or actualization on the one hand, and a confirmable level of competence on the other. A pragmatic concern was to make the scale long enough so that seven levels of attainment could be defined by cutting the distribution of scores at suitable intervals.

The technique of analysis used to develop v.3 was to correlate each CPI item ($N = 462$), using dummy weights of 1 for true and 0 for false with scores on the v.1 and v.2 scales, and with the sum of the standard scores on the Wb, To, and Ie scales. These three scales were chosen as markers for level because of the evidence in the Karni and Levin (1972) analysis that they constituted purer and more independent indicators of level than did the sum of all scales. The desired pattern of correlation for an item to be included in v.3 was zero or close to zero with both v.1 and v.2, and then either high positive or high negative with the criterion formed by Wb + To + Ie. Perfect correspondence to this paradigm was impossible to find, with the result that the v.3 scale did turn out to have a low negative correlation of $-.17$ with v.1 and a low positive correlation of .14 with v.2. In this same cross-validating sample, v.1 and v.2 had a correlation of $-.02$.

Some representative items from the 58-item v.3 scale are "I read at least ten books a year" (true), "I seldom worry about my health" (true), "People today have forgotten how to feel properly ashamed of themselves" (false), and "I would have been more successful if people had given me a fair chance" (false). Persons with high scores on v.3 tend to be described by others as intelligent, resourceful, and insightful. Persons with low scores tend to be described as complaining, narrow in interests, and self-defeating.

In a recent life-span study, Helson and Wink (1987) obtained CPI protocols from 107 adult women who had also been studied twenty-three years earlier while seniors in college. Levels of maturity were rated for the subjects at age twenty-one and at age forty-three, using biographical, social-demographic, interview, and other data, but not any information from the CPI or its scales. Then the v.3 scale (and other measures of self-realization or competence) were correlated with these indices of maturity. Some representative findings for v.3 with criteria at age 43 were correlations of .34 ($p \leq .01$) with occupational status, .24 ($p \leq .05$) with satisfaction concerning pay, $-.34$ ($p \leq .01$) with use of tranquillizers, and $-.24$ ($p \leq .05$) with use of sleeping pills. Helson and Wink concluded that women with high scores on v.3 had a good sense of engagement with others, autonomy, rewarding interpersonal relationships, and a general satisfaction in living. All of these findings seem to be consonant with the stated aims of the v.3 scale as a measure of feelings of self-realization and competence.

We can now turn to the full presentation of the theoretical model of personality generated by the life-style indicators of the v.1 and v.2 quadrants, and the levels of fulfillment indexed by v.3. The three-dimensional representation or cuboid is given in Figure 4–2.

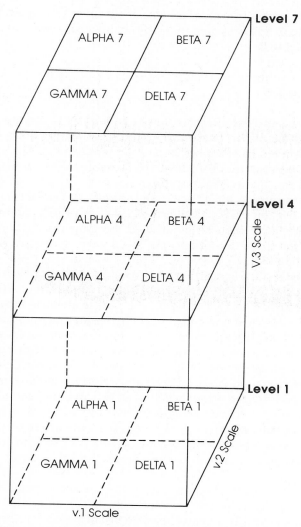

Figure 4–2 The cuboid theoretical model.

For each life-style or type there are seven levels of realization, going from the lowest or unintegrated level at the bottom to the highest or well-realized level at the top. The location of any person can be easily stated by use of the Greek letter for type and Arabic numeral for level. Thus, an alpha-4 would be someone of the alpha type functioning at an average level of competence. A beta-7 would be an excellent example of the beta personality functioning in a superior way. A gamma-1 would be someone of the gamma life-style, in friction with the culture and dissatisfied with current status. A delta-5 would be a person of introversive, rule-questioning dispositions functioning at a relatively good level of integration. In interpreting a CPI protocol, as will be seen in the case analysis at the end of this chapter, classification with respect to type and level is an important first step in formulating a coherent and distinctive personality portrait.

SPECIAL-PURPOSE SCALES

The third category of scales for the inventory is composed of measures intended for use in particular situations, but probably of little interest to examiners in other settings. An example of such a scale is that for Managerial Potential (Mp), developed (Gough, 1984) to assess interest in and talent for managerial pursuits.

Another example is the scale for Anxiety developed by Leventhal (1966, 1968). Dicken's (1963) scales for social desirability and acquiescent response sets should also be mentioned. Scoring instructions and normative data for these and other special purpose scales are given in the *Guide* (Gough, 1987).

A more detailed exposition is needed for the unipolar Femininity and Masculinity (F/M) CPI scales developed by Baucom (1976, 1980) and by Kanner (1976). The F/M scale on the profile sheet is bipolar, in that females tend to score at one end of the continuum and males at the other. The reason for this bipolarity is that in the realm of observational data (ratings and descriptions by observers), the concepts of masculinity and femininity are strongly negatively correlated. Typical coefficients of from − .90 to − .99 are found when adjectival ascriptions of *feminine* and *masculine* are correlated, in either within-sex or combined samples. That is, ordinary observers almost never ascribe both terms to someone being rated; if one of the adjectives is checked, then the other is almost never endorsed. Because all of the folk scales of the CPI seek to represent the actual topography of social usage, bipolarity of scoring for F/M is appropriate.

In the self-report domain, however, an interesting finding has emerged (Bem, 1974; Spence & Helmreich, 1979): subscales for the feminine axis are typically uncorrelated with subscales for the masculine. That is, from a score on a unipolar scale for femininity, nothing can be inferred about the probable score of the same respondent on a unipolar scale for masculinity. A shorthand way of putting these two findings together is to say that in the O-data realm masculinity and femininity are bipolar, whereas in the S-data realm they are unipolar.

Does this mean that unipolar measurement is impossible on the CPI, because of the bipolarity of F/M? The answer is no indeed. One method of deriving unipolar M and F scales is simply to subdivide the F/M scale into its feminine items (those scored for true) and its masculine items (those scored for false, but in this case now scored for true). These two subscales of 15 and 17 items, respectively, are essentially equivalent to the M and F subscales in the work of Bem (1974) and Spence and Helmreich (1979). This method of decomposing the F/M scale was first reported by Kanner (1976) and later applied in a paper by Babl (1979).

Baucom (1976, 1980) has developed separate masculinity and femininity scales for the CPI that are orthogonal in the S-domain, and that can be used to generate quadrants for the androgynous, male-typed, female-typed, and undifferentiated. Baucom has published a number of studies using his two scales, for example on marital satisfaction (Baucom & Aiken, 1984), and on testosterone titers among women (Baucom, Besch, & Callahan, 1985). On the CPI, the furor over unipolar versus bipolar measurement of the M/F theme seems to resolve itself mostly into a matter of the interests of the examiner. If unipolar assessment is wanted, then either the Kanner or the Baucom scale or both can be used. If the folk topography of everyday usage is to be assessed, then the F/M scale in its customary bipolar form should be employed.

ADMINISTRATION

The current form of the CPI contains 462 items in a booklet that can either be administered by an examiner, or self-administered by respondents with good reading skills. The examiner reads aloud the instructions on the cover of the booklet, and then asks the respondents to mark their reactions as true or false on the CPI answer sheet. Testing time is ordinarily about one hour. If more time is needed, the inventory can be given in two sittings, with part of the booklet to be covered in the first and the remainder in the second. Any questions concerning the meaning of items should be answered, but no suggestions should be made as to a desired or appropriate response. The inventory can be given to persons of about age fourteen and older, although apparently valid results have been attained with use of single scales (abstracted from the booklet) with grade school children (Dinitz, Scarpitti, & Reckless, 1962).

Scoring can be done with hand-scoring templates available from the publisher, or answer sheets may be returned to the publisher for computer scoring. There is also a computer-scored narrative that furnishes interpretive comments on each of the folk scales, assigns the respondent to a type/level classification, reports and comments on several special-purpose scales and indices, and ends with a CPI-based formulation of the personality by means of the 100 descriptions in the California Q-set (Block, 1961). This Q-sort description seeks to estimate what an actual observer (counselor, spouse, close friend, etc.) would say about the respondent, not what the respondent would say about self. Because the Q-sort items are assigned estimated numerical values, the CPI-based description can be verified by correlating it with a Q-sort formulation obtained from a real-life observer or panel of observers.

LIMITATIONS OR CONSTRAINTS ON USAGE

No test, including the CPI, can serve every purpose or be the instrument of choice in every setting. For instance, if one's interest is in appraising the kind and degree of psychiatric pathology, then the MMPI would be a better inventory to use than the CPI. If one wishes to assess psychoanalytic themes such as orality and obsessional thinking, then an inventory like the Lazare-Klerman-Armor (1966, 1970) would be a more appropriate test than the CPI. Occupational interests and orientations are better measured by the Strong-Campbell Interest Inventory (Hansen & Campbell, 1985) or the Self-Directed Search (Holland, 1985) than by the CPI.

Another limitation, less obvious than those just stated, relates to the examiner's competence and training. Interpretation of a complex, multivariate device like the CPI requires advanced training in personality theory and psychometrics, as well as supervised practicum experience in which the CPI and other tests are used in intensive case analyses. The American Psychological Association regularly publishes guidelines for the proper professional use of tests like the CPI, and all reputable publishers observe these guidelines in the sale or release of testing materials. Most states also have licensing or certification laws for psychologists, in which personality test usage is a controlled activity. Psychological diagnosis, whether of the normal or of the disturbed personality, is an art for which professional training and experience are essential. Elsewhere, I have discussed the processes of inductive thinking that enter into psychodiagnostic interpretations (Gough, 1971), and the kind of information that the test user must have in order to carry out these activities (Gough, 1965).

CASE EXAMPLE

To illustrate use of the CPI in the study of an individual, we turn now to case B, that of a nineteen-year-old college female taking part in a study of career goals and vocational aspirations. She was in her second year of school, thinking of a major in some combination of biological and social sciences that would allow her to enter a graduate program later in one of the helping professions. Her Scholastic Aptitude Test (SAT) scores were 550 for verbal and 590 for mathematical, and her college grade point average (GPA) to date was about 2.70 (C+ to B−). She felt that her GPA was an underestimate of her true academic ability. She had only a few really close friends but had many acquaintances whose company she enjoyed. In regard to health, she saw herself as above average, with no known problems.

The financial condition of the family was excellent: B's father was a businessman, and her mother also worked on a part-time basis. B did not think the parents and children were very close to each other emotionally. According to B, her mother had rather old-fashioned views and was somewhat stricter with her three children than were other mothers. She described her father as a workaholic and not very open-minded about views different from his own. In general, however, B felt that she received good psychological support from her mother and a strong sense of safety and security from her father. Her parents seemed to share basic values and to get on quite well with each other.

Responsibility was one of the virtues emphasized at home, and B had regular chores that she was assigned. In retrospect, B felt that independence was underemphasized, with her parents too often intervening and telling her *how* to do something, as well as what to do. When B was in high school she began to see a certain boy, but her parents did not approve of him and made things difficult. This experience made B retreat somewhat into herself and hold back on revealing her inner feelings to others.

B wanted to have a career in a field where she could help others, not medicine but something allied to it, and thought she was well suited to such work. She also wanted to get married, planned to have at least one child, and expected to stop working when her child was in grade school.

Recently B had been developing an interest in religious matters and had started to participate in some discussion groups. She liked the people she met on these occasions and was thinking a lot about morality and other religious and philosophical issues.

In the research project, B was interviewed by several staff members and also observed and rated in a variety of experimental situations, such as leaderless group discussions. In the ratings made by these staff observers, B was ranked as below average in dominance but above average in responsibility, sensitivity to others, and personal adjustment.

As shown in Figure 4–3, B's type/level classification on the CPI was delta-7. From the computer narrative for her CPI protocol, these remarks were made concerning her type/level classification:

> The scores on v.1 and v.2 obtained by Case B place her in the Delta quadrant. Delta's cathexes are centered on a private, internal world,

FEMALE NORMS

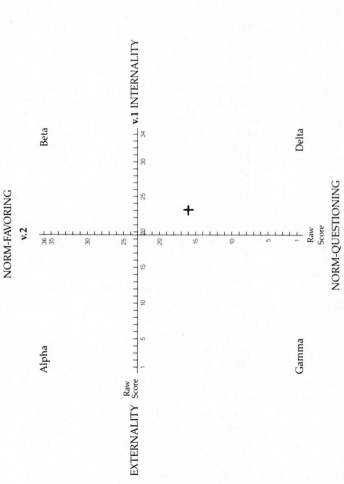

Figure 4–3 Type and level classifications for case B.

and on a personal as opposed to a traditional or sanctioned system of values. Deltas are reflective, idiosyncratic, and detached. At their best, they are ideationally and imaginatively creative, aesthetically perceptive, and visionary. At their worst, they are fragmented, withdrawn, at odds with themselves, and prone to decompensation.

In regard to level, Case B is at the seventh or highest level. One can therefore expect unusual adeptness in dealing with abstract or complex ideas, originality, broad interests, and a strong sense of individuality or detachment.

The full profile of scores is given in Figure 4–4. There are eight scales with standard scores greater than 60: Sociability, Social Presence, Empathy, Good Impression, Well-being, Tolerance, Intellectual Efficiency, and Flexibility. There are only two scales below 50—Dominance and Femininity/Masculinity—and none below 40. Emphasis in interpretation should therefore be placed on her high scores more than on these two lower scores.

Here are the comments on each of the eight high scores from the computer narrative:

Sy (Sociability)—enjoys the company of others; is outgoing and talkative; initiates humor.

Sp (Social Presence)—is above average in poise and self-confidence; has a good sense of humor; is imaginative; has broad interests.

Em (Empathy)—is perceptive about people and about social situations; is versatile; adapts easily to a wide range of demands; is an interesting, observant person.

Gi (Good Impression)—wants very much to be accepted as an upright and helpful person; seeks to control or deny any egoistic or narcissistic tendencies; will be seen by others as moderate, controlled, and calm, but also as somewhat moralistic.

Wb (Well-being)—has a buoyant, upbeat view of her own physical and psychological functioning; is good-natured, contented, and energetic; is optimistic and confident about her ability to cope with the demands of everyday life.

To (Tolerance)—values rationality and logic in dealing with others; tries to be fairminded and tolerant; seen by others as trustworthy, mature, and insightful.

Ie (Intellectual Efficiency)—is an intelligent, resourceful, clear-thinking person; verbally fluent, with a flair for discussion and analysis; feels sure of self, equal to nearly any challenge; has a stable, optimistic view of the future.

Fx (Flexibility)—adapts well to change and new conditions; easily becomes bored and impatient with routine and pedestrian events; is clever and spontaneous, but also somewhat careless and erratic; is seen by others as versatile and capable, but also as changeable and inconstant.

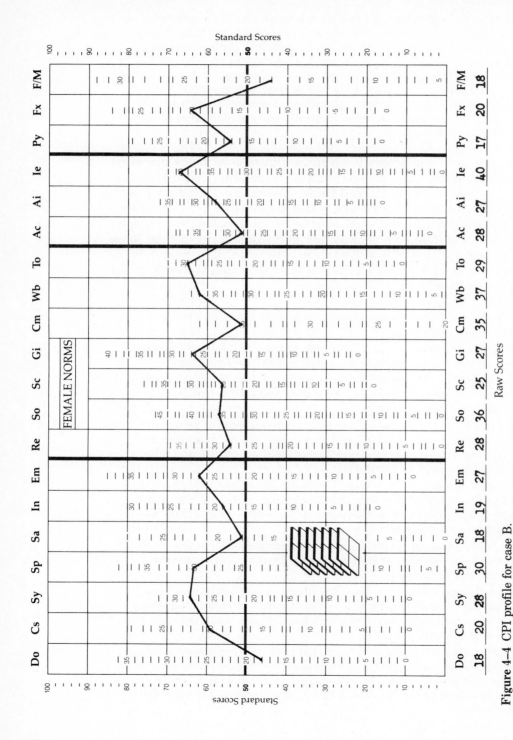

Figure 4–4 CPI profile for case B.

These eight interpretive summaries, along with the type/level guidelines, constitute a starting point for an integrated formulation of B's personality. In this overall formulation, any contradictory indications from the specific scales need to be reconciled with the general, configurated picture that is being drawn, and the recurring strands need to be brought together into a totality.

The interpretational manuals of McAllister (1986) and Rodgers (1983), mentioned earlier, are helpful in moving to this next step. For instance, what can be inferred from the higher score on Sy and the lower score on Do, two scales that usually go together? McAllister (p. 37) noted this sign, and remarked of persons showing it, "They are interested in people, but are likely to be mild mannered, agreeable, cooperative, and acquiescent."

Rodgers (p. 75) described a combination in which To, Ac, Ai, Ie, Py, and Fx were all elevated (above 50 on the profile sheet), and wrote: "The configuration is increasingly significant as one or all of this group increases in elevation. The configuration is commonly associated with good intelligence and strong interest in intellectual matters."

McAllister (p. 59) discussed another configuration that can be discerned on B's profile, one that involves elevated scores on Em, So, and a special combination of scales called the Social Maturity Index. B's scores on the Em (Empathy) scale and the Social Maturity Index were both above 60, and her score on So was 58. This is McAllister's interpretation: "They are likely to be morally mature, and show evidence of good character development, as defined by a respect for but not worship of rules and conventions, as well as an ability to respond intuitively and sympathetically to the needs of others."

In general, then, B's profile shows evidence of a thoughtful, tolerant, and insightful way of dealing with others, firmly internalized moral and ethical standards, good problem-solving abilities, adaptive flexibility, and a feeling of good health and competence.

How would a perceptive observer react to and describe B? In the CPI computer narrative, an attempt is made to estimate what such an observer would say, by way of a sorting of the 100 descriptive items in Block's (1961) California Q-set. When an observer formulates a description of someone by means of the Q-set, each item is sorted into one of nine categories, going from the five items that are most salient, or most true, or most descriptive of the person, down through the middle range, and on to the five items that are least salient, or least true, or least descriptive.

The sorting is *ipsative,* which means that the values assigned to the 100 cards (going from a high of 9 through a middle of 5 to a low of 1) must add to a constant number. In other words, the distribution of ratings is fixed, with the same number of items required to be placed in each category. Thus, for everyone described by means of the Q-set, there will be five most salient descriptions *for that person,* and five that are least true or salient.

From the CPI protocol, an estimation is made of how each of the 100 items would be sorted by an actual observer. For validational purposes, the CPI-based Q-sorting can be correlated with a Q-sorting furnished by an actual observer, such as a counselor or therapist, a spouse, a close friend, a parent, or anyone else who knows the respondent well. Note that the CPI-based Q-sort seeks to estimate what an observer would say, not what the respondent would say about self.

From the computer narrative for B, here are the 10 items identified as most likely to be true, arranged in order of probability (the larger the number, the stronger the inference from the CPI):

1. Appears to have a high degree of intellectual capacity (7.98).
2. Is cheerful (7.93).
3. Behaves in a giving way towards others (7.32).
4. Emphasizes being with others; gregarious (7.09).
5. Behaves in a sympathetic and considerate manner (7.02).
6. Has warmth; has the capacity for close relationships; compassionate (6.78).
7. Responds to humor (6.65).
8. Is protective of those close to her (6.42).
9. Is productive, gets things done (6.32).
10. Values own independence and autonomy (6.30).

The 10 items identified by the computer narrative as least likely to be descriptive of B were:

1. Is guileful and deceitful; manipulative, opportunistic (1.26).
2. Shows condescending behavior in relations with others (2.56).
3. Has hostility towards others (2.58).
4. Feels victimized by life; self-pitying (2.86).
5. Feels a lack of personal meaning in life (3.05).
6. Is basically distrustful of people in general; questions their motivations (3.09).
7. Is fastidious (3.20).
8. Extrapunitive; tends to transfer or project blame (3.36).
9. Is emotionally bland; has flattened affect (3.35).
10. Has a brittle ego-defense system; has a small reserve of integration; would be disorganized and maladaptive when under stress or trauma (3.46).

The Q-sort estimations from the CPI are very favorable, as would be expected from the folk scale profile and the classification at level 7 on v.3.

How do all of these inferences from the CPI correspond to what B's life history interviewer had to say about her? This chapter will close with the character sketch written by the interviewer, from which each reader can judge for himself or herself the relative accuracy of the CPI interpretation.

B is a very capable, responsible, honest, thoughtful, steady, and quiet young woman. She takes her time before she speaks, and pauses between words. She calmly and confidently then goes forward. I see this consistent, controlled motion as the single most prominent characteristic of B.

She has few mood swings, doesn't get overly excited or enthusiastic on the one hand, nor despondent or angry on the other. She would not be offensive to anyone. I'd assume that most people would like her polite, considerate, and kind manner, although few would have an immediate or very strong reaction. It is easy for her to get lost in a crowd: she doesn't stand out. Nonetheless, she can surprise you, for instance in the calm and dispassionate way in which she described the details of her family life, her disappointment in her father, and her changing beliefs and values.

Thus, her quiet manner is not indicative of passivity or submissiveness. She is certainly not showing passivity when she clearly and forcefully (albeit unemotionally) criticized her father. So, although she is not a lively or extraverted person, she does reveal strength of character and intellectual abilities that should continue to develop with age.

I was very much touched by her perceptive and sincere explanation of how her values and opinions are changing, in particular becoming different from those of her parents. She commented on how her father believed that the United States should have more strongly attacked North Vietnam in that war, by bombing and other methods. At one time, she accepted her father's views, but now she is persuaded that they were wrong, and that they failed to recognize the cruelty of the war and the innocence of most of its victims. It has not been easy for her to change her views, but when her psychological growth and life experiences made change necessary she faced these issues candidly. I was very moved and impressed by her report of these matters.

Another observation that fits with the portrait of a calm, steady, rational, and tolerant young woman is her approach to career planning. She wants to become a _____ [one of the helping professions], and has keen anticipations of her future life in this work. At the same time, she recognizes the difficulties in gaining admission to the training program, and that there are fall-back possibilities that would be satisfying to her if she fails to win admission to her first choice. Her approach, in other words, is realistic in regard to being well-prepared as an applicant, and also in being ready with alternative plans should they prove to be necessary.

REFERENCES

Adrian, R. J., Miller, L. R., & de L'Aune, W. R. (1982). Personality assessment of visually impaired persons using the CPI and the MMPI. *Journal of Visual Impairment and Blindness, 76,* 172–178.

Aiken, L. R., Jr. (1963). Personality correlates of attitude toward mathematics. *Journal of Educational Research, 56,* 476–480.

Alker, H. A., & Wohl, J. (1972). Personality and achievement in a suburban and an inner city school. *Journal of Social Issues, 28,* 101–113.

Babl, J. D. (1979). Compensatory masculine responding as a function of sex role. *Journal of Consulting and Clinical Psychology, 47,* 252–257.

Barron, F., & Egan, D. (1968). Leaders and innovators in Irish management. *Journal of Management Studies* (Dublin), *5,* 41–60.

Baucom, D. H. (1976). Independent masculinity and femininity scales on the California Psychological Inventory. *Journal of Consulting and Clinical Psychology, 44,* 876.

Baucom, D. H. (1980). Independent CPI masculinity and femininity scales: Psychological correlates and sex-role typology. *Journal of Personality Assessment, 44,* 262–271.

Baucom, D. H., & Aiken, P. A. (1984). Sex role identity, marital satisfaction, and response to behavioral therapy. *Journal of Consulting and Clinical Psychology, 52,* 438–444.

Baucom, D. H., Besch, P. K., & Callahan, S. (1985). The relationship between testosterone concentration, sex role identity, and personality among females. *Journal of Personality and Social Psychology, 48,* 1218–1226.

Bayer, L. M., Whissell-Buechy, D., & Honzik, M. P. (1980). Adolescent health and personality: Significance for adult health. *Journal of Adolescent Health Care, 1,* 101–107.

Bem, S. L. (1974). The measurement of psychological androgyny. *Journal of Consulting and Clinical Psychology, 42,* 155–162.

Bernstein, I. H., Garbin, C. P., & McClellan, P. G. (1983). A confirmatory factor analysis of the California Psychological Inventory. *Educational and Psychological Measurement, 43,* 687–691.

Biaggio, M. K. (1980). Anger arousal and personal characteristics. *Journal of Personality and Social Psychology, 39,* 352–356.

Block, J. (1961). *The Q-sort method in personality assessment and psychiatric research.* Springfield, IL: Thomas. (Reprinted 1978, Consulting Psychologists Press, Palo Alto, CA.)

Block, J. (1971). *Lives through time.* Berkeley, CA: Bancroft Books.

Boyle, B. P., & Coombs, R. H. (1971). Personality profiles related to emotional stress in the initial year of medical training. *Journal of Medical Education, 46,* 882–888.

Brown, J. S., Grant, C. W., & Patton, M. J. (1981). A CPI comparison of engineers and managers. *Journal of Vocational Behavior, 18,* 255–264.

Bryant, K. J. (1982). Personality correlates of sense of direction and geographical orientation. *Journal of Personality and Social Psychology, 43,* 1318–1324.

Burger, G. K., & Collins, H. A. (1982). Relationships between MMPI and CPI types for male heroin users. *American Journal of Drug and Alcohol Abuse, 9,* 281–287.

Burke, R. J., & Weir, T. (1980). Personality, value, and behavioral correlates of the Type A individual. *Psychological Reports, 46,* 171–181.

Buss, D. M. (1984). Marital assortment for personality dispositions: Assessment with three different data sources. *Behavioral Genetics, 14,* 111–123.

Buss, D. M., & Barnes, M. (1986). Preferences in human mate selection. *Journal of Personality and Social Psychology, 50,* 559–570.

Buss, D. M., & Craik, K. H. (1980). The frequency concept of disposition: Dominance and prototypically dominant acts. *Journal of Personality, 48,* 379–392.

Buss, D. M., & Craik, K. H. (1981). The act frequency analysis of interpersonal dispositions: Aloofness, gregariousness, dominance, and submissiveness. *Journal of Personality, 49,* 175–192.

Buss, D. M., & Craik, K. H. (1983). Act prediction and the conceptual analysis of personality scales: Indices of act density, bipolarity, and extensity. *Journal of Personality and Social Psychology, 45,* 1081–1095.

Buss, D. M., & Craik, K. H. (1984). Acts, dispositions, and personality. In B. A. Maher & W. B. Maher (Eds.), *Progress in experimental personality research* (Vol. 13, pp. 241–301). New York: Academic Press.

Carbonell, J. L. (1984). Sex roles and leadership revisited. *Journal of Applied Psychology, 69,* 44–49.

Cartwright, L. K. (1977). Personality changes in a sample of women physicians. *Journal of Medical Education, 52,* 467–474.

Davids, A. (1966). Psychological characteristics of high school male and female potential scientists in comparison with academic underachievers. *Psychology in the Schools, 3,* 79–87.

DeCoster, D. T., & Rhode, J. G. (1972). Analysis of certified public accounting subgroups and accounting student personality traits using the California Psychological Inventory. *Journal of Vocational Behavior, 2,* 155–162.

Demos, G. D., & Veijola, M. J. (1966). Achievement–personality criteria as selectors of participants and predictors of success in special programs in higher education. *California Journal of Educational Research, 17,* 186–192.

Dicken, C. F. (1963). Good impression, social desirability, and acquiescence as suppressor variables. *Educational and Psychological Measurement, 23,* 699–720.

Dinitz, S., Scarpitti, F. R., & Reckless, W. C. (1962). Delinquency vulnerability: A cross-group and longitudinal analysis. *American Sociological Review, 27,* 515–517.

Domino, G. (1968). Differential prediction of academic achievement in conforming and independent settings. *Journal of Educational Psychology, 59,* 256–260.

Domino, G. (1971). Interactive effects of achievement orientation and teaching style on academic achievement. *Journal of Educational Psychology, 62,* 427–431.

Domino, G. (1974). Assessment of cinematographic creativity. *Journal of Personality and Social Psychology, 30,* 150–154.

Dworkin, R. H., Burke, B. W., Maher, B. A., & Gottesman, I. I. (1976). A longitudinal study of the genetics of personality. *Journal of Personality and Social Psychology, 34,* 510–518.

Dyer, E. D., Cope, M. J., Monson, M. A., & Van Drimmelen, J. B. (1972). Can job performance be predicted from biographical, personality, and administrative climate inventories? *Nursing Research, 21,* 294–304.

Garwood, D. S. (1964). Personality factors related to creativity in young scientists. *Journal of Abnormal and Social Psychology, 68,* 413–419.

Gettys, V. S., & Elam, J. D. (1985). Validation demystified: Personnel selection techniques that work. *The Police Chief, 52*(4), 41–43.

Gill, L. J., & Spilka, B. (1962). Some nonintellectual correlates of academic achievement among Mexican-American secondary school students. *Journal of Educational Psychology, 53*, 144–149.

Goldstein, J. W. (1974). Motivations for psychoactive drug use among students. In B. Kleinmuntz (Ed.), *Readings in the essentials of abnormal psychology* (pp. 371–375). New York: Harper & Row.

Gough, H. G. (1957). *Manual for the California Psychological Inventory*. Palo Alto, CA: Consulting Psychologists Press.

Gough, H. G. (1964). A cross-cultural study of achievement motivation. *Journal of Applied Psychology, 48*, 191–196.

Gough, H. G. (1965). The conceptual analysis of psychological test scores and other diagnostic variables. *Journal of Abnormal Psychology, 70*, 294–302.

Gough, H. G. (1966). Graduation from high school as predicted from the California Psychological Inventory. *Psychology in the Schools, 3*, 208–216.

Gough, H. G. (1968). College attendance among high-aptitude students as predicted from the California Psychological Inventory. *Journal of Counseling Psychology, 15*, 269–278.

Gough, H. G. (1971). Some reflections on the meaning of psychodiagnosis. *American Psychologist, 26*, 160–167.

Gough, H. G. (1983). Personality correlates of time required to complete work for the Ph.D. degree in psychology. In C. D. Spielberger & J. N. Butcher (Eds.), *Advances in personality assessment* (Vol. 3, pp. 105–128). Hillsdale, NJ: Lawrence Erlbaum Associates.

Gough, H. G. (1984). A managerial potential scale for the California Psychological Inventory. *Journal of Applied Psychology, 69*, 233–240.

Gough, H. G. (1987). *Administrator's guide for the California Psychological Inventory*. Palo Alto, CA: Consulting Psychologists Press.

Gough, H. G., Durflinger, G. W., & Hill, R. E., Jr. (1968). Predicting performance in student teaching from the California Psychological Inventory. *Journal of Educational Psychology, 59*, 119–127.

Gough, H. G., & Hall, W. B. (1975). The prediction of academic and clinical performance in medical school. *Research in Higher Education, 3*, 301–314.

Gough, H. G., & Heilbrun, A. B., Jr. (1983). *The Adjective Check List manual— 1983 edition*. Palo Alto, CA: Consulting Psychologists Press.

Gough, H. G., & Kirk, B. A. (1970). Achievement in dental school as related to personality and aptitude variables. *Measurement and Evaluation in Guidance, 2*, 225–233.

Gough, H. G., & Lanning, K. (1986). Predicting grades in college from the California Psychological Inventory. *Educational and Psychological Measurement, 46*, 205–213.

Griffin, M. L., & Flaherty, M. R. (1964). Correlation of CPI traits with academic achievement. *Educational and Psychological Measurement, 24*, 369–372.

Guilford, J. P., & Zimmerman, W. S. (1949). *The Guilford-Zimmerman Temperament Survey: Manual of directions and interpretation*. Beverly Hills, CA: Sheridan Supply Company.

Haier, R. J., & Denham, S. A. (1976). A summary profile of the nonintellectual correlates of mathematical precocity in boys and girls. In D. P. Keating (Ed.), *Intellectual talent: Research and development* (pp. 225–241). Baltimore: Johns Hopkins University Press.

Hall, W. B., & MacKinnon, D. W. (1969). Personality inventory correlates of creativity among architects. *Journal of Applied Psychology, 53*, 322–326.

Hansen, J. C., & Campbell, D. P. (1985). *Manual for the SVIB-SCII* (4th ed.). Stanford, CA: Stanford University Press.

Hathaway, S. R., & McKinley, J. C. (1943). *The Minnesota Multiphasic Personality Inventory*. Minneapolis: University of Minnesota Press.

Helson, R. (1971). Women mathematicians and the creative personality. *Journal of Consulting and Clinical Psychology, 36,* 210–220.

Helson, R., & Crutchfield, R. S. (1970). Mathematicians: The creative researcher and the average Ph.D. *Journal of Consulting and Clinical Psychology, 34,* 250–257.

Helson, R., Mitchell, V., & Moane, G. (1984). Personality and patterns of adherence and nonadherence to the social clock. *Journal of Personality and Social Psychology, 46,* 1079–1095.

Helson, R., & Moane, G. (1987). Personality change in women from college to midlife. *Journal of Personality and Social Psychology, 53,* 176–186.

Helson, R., & Wink, P. (1987). Two conceptions of maturity examined in the findings of a longitudinal study. *Journal of Personality and Social Psychology, 53,* 531–541.

Hetherington, E. M., & Feldman, S. E. (1964). College cheating as a function of subject and situational variables. *Journal of Educational Psychology, 55,* 212–218.

Hill, A. H. (1966). A longitudinal study of attrition among high aptitude college students. *Journal of Educational Research, 60,* 166–173.

Hogan, J. C. (1978). Personological dynamics of leadership. *Journal of Research in Personality, 12,* 390–395.

Hogan, R. (1969). Development of an empathy scale. *Journal of Consulting and Clinical Psychology, 33,* 307–316.

Hogan, R. (1971). Personality characteristics of highly rated policemen. *Personnel Psychology, 24,* 679–686.

Hogan, R., & Kurtines, W. (1975). Personological correlates of police effectiveness. *Journal of Personality, 91,* 289–295.

Hogan, R., & Weiss, D. S. (1974). Personality correlates of superior academic achievement. *Journal of Counseling Psychology, 21,* 144–149.

Holland, J. L. (1959). The prediction of grades from the California Psychological Inventory and the Scholastic Aptitude Test. *Journal of Educational Psychology, 50,* 135–142.

Holland, J. L. (1985). *The SDS professional manual—1985 revision.* Odessa, FL: Psychological Assessment Resources.

Hong, K. M., Wirt, R. D., Yellin, R. D., & Hopwood, J. (1979). Psychological attributes, patterns of life change, and illness susceptibility. *Journal of Nervous and Mental Disease, 167,* 275–281.

Irvine, R. W. (1979). Structure of school, personality, and high school dropouts. *Journal of Negro Education, 48,* 67–72.

Johnson, P. A. (1972). A comparison of personality traits of superior skilled women athletes in basketball, bowling, field hockey, and golf. *Research Quarterly, 43,* 409–415.

Jung, C. G. (1923). *Psychological types.* New York: Harcourt, Brace.

Kanner, A. D. (1976). Femininity and masculinity: Their relationship to creativity in male architects and their independence from each other. *Journal of Consulting and Clinical Psychology, 44,* 802–805.

Karni, E. S., & Levin, J. (1972). The use of smallest space analysis in studying scale structure: An application to the California Psychological Inventory. *Journal of Applied Psychology, 56,* 341–346.

Kay, E. J., Lyons, A., Newman, W., Mankin, D., & Loeb, R. C. (1978). A longitudinal study of the personality correlates of marijuana use. *Journal of Consulting and Clinical Psychology, 46,* 470–477.

Kegel-Flom, P. (1974). Predicting unexpected achievement in optometry school. *American Journal of Optometry and Physiological Optics, 51,* 775–781.

Kegel-Flom, P. (1983). Personality traits in effective clinical teachers. *Research in Higher Education, 19,* 73–82.

Kegel-Flom, P. (1985). Predicting optometry school grades from intellectual and nonintellectual admission variables. *American Journal of Optometry and Physiological Optics, 62,* 901–907.

Keimowitz, R. I., & Anspacher, H. L. (1960). Personality and achievement in mathematics. *Journal of Individual Psychology, 16,* 84–87.

King, G. D., McGowen, R., Doonan, R., & Schweibert, D. (1980). The selection of paraprofessional telephone counselors using the California Psychological Inventory. *American Journal of Community Psychology, 8,* 495–501.

Kurtines, W. M., Ball, L. R., & Wood, G. H. (1978). Personality characteristics of long-term recovered alcoholics: A comparative analysis. *Journal of Consulting and Clinical Psychology, 46,* 971–977.

Kurtines, W., Hogan, R., & Weiss, D. S. (1975). Personality dynamics of heroin use. *Journal of Abnormal Psychology, 84,* 49–51.

Laufer, W. S., Johnson, J. A., & Hogan, R. (1981). Ego control and criminal behavior. *Journal of Personality and Social Psychology, 41,* 179–184.

Lazare, A., Klerman, G. L., & Armor, D. (1966). Oral, obsessive, and hysterical personality patterns: An investigation of psychoanalytic concepts by means of factor analysis. *Archives of General Psychiatry, 14,* 624–630.

Lazare, A., Klerman, G. L., & Armor, D. (1970). Oral, obsessive, and hysterical personality patterns: Replication of factor analysis in an independent sample. *Journal of Psychiatric Research, 7,* 275–290.

Leitner, D. W., & Sedlacek, W. E. (1976). Characteristics of successful campus police officers. *Journal of College Student Personnel, 17,* 304–308.

Leventhal, A. M. (1966). An anxiety scale for the CPI. *Journal of Clinical Psychology, 22,* 459–461.

Leventhal, A. M. (1968). Additional data on the CPI anxiety scale. *Journal of Counseling Psychology, 15,* 479–480.

Levin, J., & Karni, E. S. (1970). Demonstration of cross-cultural invariance of the California Psychological Inventory in America and Israel by the Guttman-Lingoes smallest space analysis. *Journal of Cross-Cultural Psychology, 1,* 253–260.

Linton, T. E. (1967). The CPI as a predictor of academic success. *Alberta Journal of Education, 13,* 59–64.

Loehlin, J. C. (1987). Heredity, environment, and the structure of the California Psychological Inventory. *Multivariate Behavioral Research, 22,* 137–148.

Mazer, M., & Ahern, J. (1969). Personality and social class position in migration from an island. *International Journal of Social Psychiatry, 15,* 203–208.

McAllister, L. W. (1986). *A practical guide to CPI interpretation.* Palo Alto, CA: Consulting Psychologists Press.

McCormick, R. A., Taber, J., Kruedelbach, N., & Russo, A. (1987). Personality profiles of hospitalized pathological gamblers. *Journal of Clinical Psychology, 43,* 521–527.

McDermid, C. D. (1965). Some correlates of creativity in engineering personnel. *Journal of Applied Psychology, 49,* 14–19.

McGuire, J. S., & Megargee, E. I. (1974). Personality correlates of marijuana use among youthful offenders. *Journal of Consulting and Clinical Psychology, 42,* 124–133.

Megargee, E. I. (1969). Influence of sex roles on the manifestation of leadership. *Journal of Applied Psychology, 53,* 377–382.

Megargee, E. I. (1972). *The California Psychological Inventory handbook.* San Francisco: Jossey-Bass.

Megargee, E. I., Bogart, P., & Anderson, B. J. (1966). Prediction of leadership in a simulated industrial task. *Journal of Applied Psychology, 50,* 292–295.

Mizushima, K., & DeVos, G. (1967). An application of the California Psychological

Inventory in a study of Japanese delinquency. *Journal of Social Psychology, 71,* 45–51.

Morris, J. L., & Wise, J. J. (1972). Personality characteristics of data processing personnel. *Australian Psychologist, 7,* 173–179.

Musante, L., MacDougall, J. M., Dembroski, T. M., & Van Horn, A. E. (1983). Component analysis of Type A coronary-prone behavior pattern in male and female college students. *Journal of Personality and Social Psychology, 45,* 1104–1117.

Myers, I. B., & McCaulley, M. H. (1985). *Manual: A guide to the development and use of the Myers-Briggs type indicator.* Palo Alto, CA: Consulting Psychologists Press.

Myers, M. B., Templer, D. L., & Brown, R. (1984). Coping ability of women who become victims of rape. *Journal of Consulting and Clinical Psychology, 52,* 73–78.

Nichols, R. C., & Holland, J. L. (1963). Predicting first year college performance of high aptitude students. *Psychological Monographs, 77,* 7, Whole No. 570.

Nichols, R. C., & Schnell, R. R. (1963). Factor scales for the California Psychological Inventory. *Journal of Consulting Psychology, 27,* 228–235.

Palladino, J. J., & Motiff, J. P. (1981). Discriminant function analysis of Type A/B subjects on the California Psychological Inventory. *Journal of Social and Clinical Psychology, 1,* 155–161.

Parloff, M., & Datta, L. E. (1965). Personality characteristics of the potentially creative scientist. In M. Parloff & L. E. Datta (Eds.), *Science and psychoanalysis* (Vol. 3, pp. 91–106). New York: Grune & Stratton.

Pfeifer, C. M., Jr., & Sedlacek, W. E. (1974). Predicting black student grades with non-intellectual measures. *Journal of Negro Education, 43,* 67–76.

Pugh, G. (1985). The California Psychological Inventory and police selection. *Police Science and Administration, 13,* 172–176.

Purkey, W. W. (1966). Measured and professed personality characteristics of gifted high school students and analysis of their congruence. *Journal of Educational Research, 60,* 99–103.

Purkey, W. W. (1970). *Self-concept and school achievement.* Englewood Cliffs, NJ: Prentice-Hall.

Query, W. T. (1966). CPI factors and success of seminary students. *Psychological Reports, 18,* 665–666.

Rawls, D. J., & Rawls, J. R. (1968). Personality characteristics and personal history data of successful and less successful executives. *Psychological Reports, 36,* 911–918.

Repapi, M., Gough, H. G., Lanning, K., & Stefanis, C. (1983). Predicting academic achievement of Greek secondary school students from family background and California Psychological Inventory scores. *Contemporary Educational Psychology, 8,* 181–188.

Rodgers, D. A. (1983). Configural interpretation of the CPI. In J. T. Webb, K. M. McNamara, & D. A. Rodgers (Eds.), *Configural interpretations of the MMPI and CPI* (rev. ed., pp. 55–76). Columbus: Ohio Psychology Publishing Company.

Ross, H. G. (1980). Matching achievement style and instructional environments. *Contemporary Educational Psychology, 5,* 216–226.

Schendel, J. (1965). Psychological differences between athletes and nonparticipants in athletics at three educational levels. *Research Quarterly, 36,* 52–67.

Scissons, E. H. (1979). Profiles of ability: Characteristics of Canadian engineers. *Engineering Education, 69,* 822–836.

Selzer, M. L., Vinokur, A., & Wilson, T. D. (1977). A psychological comparison of drunken drivers and alcoholics. *Journal of Studies on Alcohol, 38,* 1294–1312.

Sipps, G. J., Berry, W., & Lynch, E. M. (1987). WAIS-R and social intelligence: A test of established assumptions that uses the CPI. *Journal of Clinical Psychology, 43,* 499–504.

Snider, J. G. (1966). The Canadian high school achievement syndrome as indicated by the California Psychological Inventory. *Ontario Journal of Educational Research, 9,* 43–47.

Spence, J. T., & Helmreich, R. L. (1979). *Masculinity and femininity: Their psychological dimensions, correlates, and antecedents.* Austin: University of Texas Press.

Stroup, A. L., & Elft, J. H. (1969). The CPI as a predictor of college academic success. *Alberta Journal of Educational Research, 15,* 191–194.

Veldman, D. J., & Kelly, F. J. (1965). Personality correlates of a composite criterion of teaching effectiveness. *Alberta Journal of Educational Research, 11,* 102–107.

Viernstein, M. C., McGinn, P. V., & Hogan, R. (1977). The personality correlates of differential verbal and mathematical ability in talented adolescents. *Journal of Youth and Adolescence, 6,* 169–178.

Wechsler, D. (1955). *Manual for the Wechsler Adult Intelligence Scale.* New York: Psychological Corporation.

Weiss, D. S. (1981). A multigroup study of personality patterns in creativity. *Perceptual and Motor Skills, 52,* 735–746.

Weiss, D. S., Haier, R. J., & Keating, D. P. (1974). Personality characteristics of mathematically precocious boys. In J. C. Stanley, R. J. Haier, D. P. Keating, & L. H. Fox (Eds.), *Mathematical talent: Discovery, description, and development* (pp. 126–139). Baltimore: Johns Hopkins University Press.

5

The Children's Apperception Test (CAT)

Leopold Bellak, M.D.
Helen Siegel, M.A.

The term *apperception* was probably first used by Leibnitz but was given its current meaning by the Austrian philosopher Johan Friedrich Herbart (1777–1841), who employed *apperception* to "denote assim-

The CAT, by L. Bellak and S. S. Bellak, is published by CPS Inc., P.O. Box 83, Larchmont, New York 10538. The test and related material is also published in French by the Centre de Psychologie Appliquée, Paris, France; in Italian by the Organizzazioni Speciali, Florence, Italy; in English for the British Empire by the Australian Council for Educational Research, Hawthorn, Victoria, Australia; in German by Verlag für Psychologie, Göttingen, Germany; in Spanish by Editoriale Paídos, Buenos Aires, Argentina; and in Portugese by Mestre Jou, São Paulo, Brazil. An adaptation for India has been devised by Uma Chowdhury, with the help of B. S. Guha and L. Bellak, published by Manasayan, New Delhi, India. The test has also been published in Japan.

The original CAT, consisting of 10 plates depicting animals in various situations, was published in 1949. It was followed in 1952 by the Children's Apperception Test, Supplement (CAT-S), and in 1965 by the Children's Apperception Test, Human (CAT-H), consisting of an exact substitution of human figures for the original animal ones. Most of the remarks in this chapter refer to all three versions of the test. A few of them refer to the original CAT—for convenience's sake, sometimes designated as CAT-A. A discussion of the CAT-H and the CAT-S is also included in this chapter.

ilation of new presentations by old ones of a similar kind" (Johnston, 1972, p. 282).

In that age of polymath, Leibnitz not only spoke of drive *(Trieb)* and repression *(Verdraengung),* but also, fascinated by the theory of harmony in music, he devised an elaborate calculus for quantifying the strength and weakness of presentations *(Vorstellungen)* or images. Once generated, he said, these presentations become indestructible parts of the soul.

It does not take too much license to say that Herbart had already spoken of apperceptions as meaningful perceptions (in distinction to the atomistic notions of sensations and perceptions, as propounded by Wundt, Weber, Fechner, and Mach) and that new perceptions are being influenced by the apperceptive mass of previous experience.

It was another Viennese philosopher, Christian von Ehrenfels (1859–1932) who wrote a book about *Gestalt Qualitäten* (configurational qualities), also in relation to music for a start. He became the inspiration for Wertheimer, Koehler, and Koffka.

Freud almost certainly knew of Herbart, and learned about his concepts via Bretano and his disciples in Vienna, but unfortunately neither Herbart nor Freud had yet heard of operational definitions and controlled experimentation. To the everlasting loss of general psychology as well as that of psychoanalysis, Gestalt psychology never became integrated into psychoanalysis.

I (L.B.) am making this large and complex detour not only to provide an appropriate historical background, but also to make a slightly sarcastic aside. Many of Freud's propositions had been made, in part, by his predecessors. Hume, in fact, stated *"Nihil est in intellectu quid non antea fuerit in sensibus:* There is nothing in the mind which was not previously a sensory experience"—as good a brief statement of the perceptual theory of personality as one could ask for.

I do not want to minimize Freud's contributions: he established continuity between childhood perceptions and adult ones, although the latter often manifest themselves in neurotically distorted ways (in a new Gestalt); he established continuity between daytime thinking and the Gestalten in dreams. With the help of Herbart, Gestalt psychology, and Freud, we are able to use apperceptive techniques to understand these connections. Freud's unparalleled contribution was the introduction of *causality,* in the form of that continuity, thereby making psychology a science and permitting us to make lawful inferences.

What is galling is that despite the foundation of psychoanalysis and apperceptive techniques in what had originally been mainstream psychology, it was looked at askance by academic psychology for decades. Only later did the academicians do some *Nach entdecken*—some latter-day rediscovering of its basic principles: academic psychologists "discovered," a couple of decades ago, that perception and emotion coexist. Under the ill-defined and controversial term *cognitive psychology,* the basic tenets of apperception and much of psychoanalysis have become respectable.

I was personally fortunate enough to have had my early schooling in Vienna, with a training analysis with Ernst Kris just a couple of blocks up the hill from Freud, while also taking some courses at the Vienna Psychoanalytic Institute and the Vienna Medical School, just about half-way between Kris's couch and Freud's office at 19 Bergasse.

Thus, when I came to Harvard in 1940 (with Gordon Allport as the enlightened department chairman) and to the Harvard Psychological Clinic under R. W. White and Henry A. Murray, and there found the early versions of the TAT (half its present size, and with different pictures), I took to it like the proverbial duck to water.

Sometime in 1948, Kris and I met again in New York and had time to discuss Harvard, American psychology, and eventually the TAT as well. We arrived at the idea that, judging from the role of animals in fairy tales and the like, animal pictures might have a special appeal for children.

I then asked a friend of mine, Violet Lamont, who was an excellent professional artist, to draw some pictures of animals in a variety of social situations, which I specified, toward the idea of illuminating crucial relationships. We started with a large number of pictures. Sonya Bellak and I, together with a number of graduate students, then took these pictures to nurseries, kindergartens, and elementary schools and started the slow process of weeding out the unproductive ones and substituting new pictures, until we finally arrived at ten plates that seemed to produce consistently good stories and to illuminate basic aspects of these children's personalities, with some construct validity derived from teachers' reports. Currently, there is a bibliography of about sixty items relevant for the use of the Children's Apperception Test (Bellak, 1980/1949).

The proposition that animal pictures might have a better "pull" than human pictures aroused a great deal of interest in American psychology. A number of Ph.D. theses and other research projects explored this hypothesis, with highly variable results (Bellak, 1965a, 1965b, 1986). Mostly this seemed due to attempts to take shortcuts or to the use of inferior equivalent pictures for the human situations. After I provided a careful set of human figures matched to the animal series, several research endeavors established the equivalence of the human and animal series (Bellak, 1986, p. 251; Bellak & Hurvich, 1966). Despite these data, the fact remains that some children prefer the animal pictures, whereas others show a preference for the human forms. On the whole, judging by sales of the CAT, the profession still seems to prefer the animal pictures. Subsequently, a supplement to the CAT was also designed (Bellak, 1980/1952), which will be discussed later.

I am now exploring the usefulness of an additional five pictures, to be used in conjunction with the basic ten. I have come to feel that it might be particularly useful to add pictures that are likely to "pull" themes reflecting issues of current concern to society, such as sexual or aggressive abuse, drug use, exposure to disasters, and the experience of divorce.

THE NATURE AND PURPOSE OF THE CAT

The CAT consists of ten pictures depicting animals in various social situations. It is designed for maximum usefulness with children of both sexes, primarily between the ages of three and ten. After the establishment of appropriate rapport with the child, the cards are presented as outlined in the section of this chapter on administration. The responses are recorded verbatim and later analyzed as discussed in the section on interpretation.

The CAT is a projective method or, as we prefer to call it, an *apperceptive* method—a method of investigating personality *by studying the dynamic meaningfulness of the individual differences in perception of standard stimuli.*

The test is a direct descendant of Henry Murray's Thematic Apperception Test (TAT), but it does not compete with the TAT or substitute for it. Unsurpassed as I believe the TAT is for adult personality investigation, it is nevertheless relatively unsuited for young children, to the same degree that the CAT is unsuited to adults. Ideally, I should like to see the CAT used for children from three to ten, and the TAT used for adolescents and adults.

The CAT was designed to facilitate our understanding of a child's relationship to the most important figures in his life, and to illuminate his drives, conflicts, and anxieties, as well as, more generally, the dynamics and structure of his personality. To this end, the pictures were designed to elicit response to feeding problems specifically, and oral problems generally; to investigate problems of sibling rivalry; to illuminate the attitude toward parental figures and the way in which these figures are apperceived; and to learn about the child's relationship to the parents as a couple. The last of these is technically spoken of as the *oedipal complex,* with its culmination in the primal scene: the child's fantasies about seeing the parents in bed together. In relation to this, we wish to elicit the child's fantasies about aggression and about acceptance by the adult world, as well as his or her fears of being lonely at night with possible relation to masturbation, toilet behavior, and the parents' response to these. We wish to learn about the child's structure and his or her dynamic method of reacting to and handling the problems of growth.

We believe that the CAT may be clinically useful in determining what dynamic and structural factors might be related to a child's behavior and problems in a group, in school or kindergarten, or at home. The CAT may be profitable in the hands of psychoanalysts, psychiatrists, psychologists, social workers, and teachers, as well as psychologically trained pediatricians. It may be used directly in therapy as a play technique. After the original responses have been given, one may wish to go over them with the child in the form of play and make appropriate interpretations.

Furthermore, the CAT should lend itself to much needed longitudinal research studies on child development: if the CAT were administered to children at half-year intervals from the third year on, we might learn much about the developmental rate of a number of psychological problems thus far studied only in psychoanalytic investigation or other cross-sectional studies, which are necessarily reconstructions and inferences needing further confirmation and/or elaborations. In research studies and clinical use alike, it should be helpful that the CAT is relatively culture-free. Since we deal with animal pictures, it is used equally well with white, black, and other groups of children, except, of course, those groups who might not be familiar with some of the inanimate objects, such as bicycles, and so forth.

Lack of familiarity with the animals depicted does not seem to constitute a problem, since the children simply substitute animals with which they are familiar.

ADMINISTRATION

In the administration of the CAT, account must be taken of the general problems of testing children. Good rapport must be established with the child. This will, in general, be considerably more difficult with the younger child, as well as with the more disturbed one. Whenever possible, the CAT should be presented as a game, not as a test. In cases of children who are obviously aware that it is a test—whether from previous experience with such procedures or from a higher level of sophistication—it will be advisable to acknowledge this fact fully, but to explain carefully that it is not a challenging kind of test in which the child must face approval, disapproval, competition, or disciplinary action.

It will probably be found that much encouragement and prompting are necessary; interruptions are permitted. One must be certain, however, not to be suggestive in one's prompting. After all the stories have been related, one may go over each of them, asking the child for elaboration on specific points, such as why someone was given a particular name, the proper names of places, the characters' ages, and even the outcome of a story. If a child's attention span does not permit this procedure, it would be well to attempt it as soon after administration as possible.

Cain (1961) suggests a supplementary "dream technique," for use on cards 5, 6, and 9, especially, where the characters are often seen as being asleep. In these instances, the examiner's final question is, "What did X dream?" Dreams that children report have been found to contain more unconscious material than the original theme, and to be based more on fantasy.

All side remarks and activities in relation to the story being told should be noted. Blatt, Enger, and Mirmow (1961) advise attending to physical activity, gestures, facial expressions, or posturing accompanying the responses; they view this "elaboration of the response" as equivalent to the adult's verbal productions.

A difficult situation may arise if the child wants the examiner to tell a story; this is primarily a request to be given something rather than to have to give, and is best dealt with in that light. Although it may help to explain that we want to hear what the particular child can make of the picture, it may also be necessary to promise (and to adhere to the promise) to tell a story later or to leave off testing until one can establish a relationship with the child by a giving of one kind or another.

It is helpful to keep all the pictures out of sight except the one being dealt with, since younger children have a tendency to play with all the pictures at once, choosing them at random for storytelling. These pictures have been numbered and arranged in a particular sequence for particular reasons, and should therefore be administered in the order indicated.

If, however, a child is particularly restless and one has some indication as to what problems the current disturbance reflect, one may restrict the test to only those few cards that are likely to illuminate those specific problems. Thus, a child who apparently has sibling rivalry problems might be given cards 1 and 4 in particular.

As discussed elsewhere (Bellak, Hurvich, & Gediman, 1973; Bellak & Goldsmith, 1984), the ego can be studied systematically in the form of twelve functions: (1) reality testing, (2) judgment, (3) sense of reality, (4) regulation and control of drives, (5) object relations, (6) thought processes, (7) ARISE (adaptive regression in the service of the ego), (8) defense functions, (9) stimulus barrier, (10) autonomous functions, (11) synthetic functions, and (12) mastery-competence. These functions can be assessed and conveniently scored on a graph reproduced in the manual for the CAT (Bellak, 1980/1949) and in the Short Form for Recording and Analyzing the CAT (Bellak, 1980/1955). It is useful to keep the twelve ego functions in mind while observing test behavior and to record them as manifestly observable ego functions. These should then be compared to ego function ratings based on the evaluation of the stories.

TEN VARIABLES FOR SYSTEMATIC ANALYSIS OF THE STORIES

The Main Theme

We are interested in what a child makes of our pictures, and then we want to know *why* the child responds with this particular story (or interpretation). Rather than judge by one story, we will be on safer ground if we can find a common denominator or trend in a number of stories. For example, if the main hero of several stories is hungry and resorts to stealing in order to satisfy himself, it is not unreasonable to conclude that this child is preoccupied with thoughts of not getting enough—either food literally or gratification generally—and, in his fantasy, wishes to take it away from others. *Interpretation, then, is concerned with finding common denominators in behavioral patterns*. In this sense we can speak of the *theme* of a story or of several stories. A theme may, of course, be more or less complex. We find that, particularly with our younger subjects, three and four years old, themes are usually very simple. On the other hand, a story may have more than one theme, and themes may sometimes be interrelated in complex ways.

The Main Hero

A basic assumption behind our reasoning so far is, of course, that the stories that our subjects tell are, in essence, about themselves. Since there can be a number of people in a story, it becomes necessary to state that we speak of the figure with which our subject mainly identifies himself as the *hero*. We will have to specify, for this purpose, some objective criteria for differentiating the hero from other figures: the hero is the figure about whom the story is primarily woven, who resembles the subject most in age and sex, and from whose standpoint the events are seen. These statements hold true most of the time, but not always. A subject may, for example, identify with a hero of a different sex; it is important to note such identifications. Sometimes an identification figure secondary in importance in a story may represent the subject's more deeply repressed unconscious attitudes. In general, the interests, wishes, deficiencies, gifts, and abilities with which the hero is invested are those that the subject possesses, wants to possess, or fears that he or she might possess. Some figures will represent split-off self-representations, and others will reflect object representations. The whole gamut of object relations can be observed. It will be important to observe the *adequacy* of the hero—that is, his or her ability to deal with whatever circumstances may exist in a way considered adequate by the society to which he or she belongs. The adequacy of the hero serves as the best single measure of the child's ego strength. An exception, of course, is any story that is a blatant example of wish fulfillment. With careful scrutiny, the real inadequacy should become apparent.

Main Needs and Drives of the Hero

The story behavior of the hero may have one of a variety of relationships to the storyteller. The needs expressed may correspond directly to the needs of the child. These needs may be, at least in part, expressed behaviorally in real life, or they may be the embodiment of the direct opposite of real-life expression and constitute the fantasy complement. In other words, very aggressive stories may sometimes be told by a very aggressive child or, conversely, by a meek, passive-aggressive one who has fantasies of aggression. To a certain extent, the needs of the hero may not reflect the needs of the storyteller so much as they do the drive quality that he perceives in other figures. In other words, he may be describing the aggression feared from various objects, or referring to idealized expectations, such as brilliance or fortitude, ascribed to significant figures in his life and only in part internalized in himself. In short, the behavioral needs of the hero expressed in the story must be examined and understood in the light of all the varieties and vicissitudes of drive modification, and must be subsumed under the broader concepts of projection or apperceptive distortion.

It is the difficult task of the interpreter to determine to what extent the manifest needs of the hero correspond to various constituents of the storyteller's personality and, in addition, what the relationship of these constituents is to the narrator's manifest behavior. It is here that comparison with the actual clinical history is most useful and entirely appropriate under clinical circumstances (as distinct from a research setting). If a child is reported to be particularly shy, passive, and withdrawn, but his CAT stories overflow with aggression, then the compensatory nature of the fantasy material is obvious.

Figures, objects, or circumstances introduced must be considered. Thus, a child who introduces weapons of one sort or another in a number of stories (even without using them in context) or who has food as an integral part of his stories (even without eating it) may be tentatively judged on such evidence as having a need for aggression or for oral gratification, respectively. Since the introduction of a figure or circumstance not pictorially represented is extremely significant, this should be duly noted, possibly by adding an exclamation mark to the analysis sheet. External circumstances such as injustice, severity, indifference, deprivation, and deception (included with the figures and objects introduced) help to indicate the nature of the world in which the child believes himself or herself to be living.

Figures, objects, or circumstances may be omitted. If so, we must consider the possibility of dynamic significance. The simplest meaning is usually an expression of the wish that the figure or object were not there. This may express plain hostility, or mean that the figure or object is severely conflict-arousing, possibly because of its positive value.

The Conception of the Environment

This concept is, of course, a complex mixture of unconscious self-perception and apperceptive distortion of stimuli by memory images of the past. The more consistent a picture of the environment appearing in the CAT stories, the more reason we have to consider it an important constituent of our subject's personality and a useful clue to his or her reactions in everyday life. Usually two or three descriptive terms will suffice, such as succorant, hostile, exploiting or exploitable, friendly, dangerous, and the like.

Identification is important: With whom does the child identify in the family? It is also important to observe the role that each parent takes with regard to his or her adequacy and appropriateness as an identification figure—for instance, whether a male child after the age of five identifies with the father or with an older brother or uncle, rather than with his mother or a younger sister. Although the process of identification will not be completed until the end of puberty, the early history may be of great importance.

Figures Seen as . . .

We are interested in the way children view the figures around them and how they react to them. We know something about the quality of object relationships—symbiotic, anaclitic, oral dependent, and so on—at different stages of development and in different personalities. In a broader schema, however, we may descriptively speak of supportive, competitive, and other relationships.

Significant Conflicts

When we study the significant conflicts, we want to know not only the nature of the conflicts, but also the *defenses that the child uses against anxiety engendered by these conflicts.* Here we have an excellent opportunity to study early character formation as coping mechanisms, and we may be able to derive ideas concerning prognosis.

There are those conflicts that all children experience as they grow from one phase to the next. Thus, beginning at age three, we ought not to be alarmed to find evidence of the oedipal struggle and defenses against the fantasied relationships. Some conflicts are part of normal growing up, whereas others may have pathological significance.

Nature of Anxieties

The importance of determining a child's main anxieties hardly needs emphasizing. Those related to physical harm, punishment, and the fear of lacking or losing love (disapproval) and of being deserted (loneliness, lack of support) are probably the most important. It will be valuable to note the context in which the child's defenses against the fears that beset him or her occur. We will also want to know the form that the defense takes: whether it be flight, passivity, aggression, orality, acquisitiveness, renunciation, regression, and so on.

Main Defenses against Conflicts and Fears

CAT stories should not be studied exclusively for drive content but should also be examined for the defenses against these drives. Not infrequently, such a study of defenses will actually offer more information, in that the drives themselves may appear less clearly than do the defenses against these drives. On the other hand, the defensive structure may be more closely related to the child's manifest behavior. By means of studying drives and defenses, the CAT often permits an appraisal of the character structure of the subject.

Aside from a search for the main defense mechanism, it is also valuable to study the molar aspects of the stories. For instance, some subjects will choose obsessive defenses against a picture of disturbing content. They may produce four or five themes, each very short and descriptive, manifestly different but dynamically similar. Sometimes a succession of themes for one and the same picture shows the subject's attempts to deal with a disturbing conflict; successive stories may become more and more innocuous, showing an increase in defensive operation.

The concept of defense has to be understood in an increasingly broader sense, as a form of *coping*—that is, of the person's general ability and mode of meeting external and internal stimuli and tasks. With the advances in ego psychology and a focus on the problems of adaptation, a study of these functions is likely to play an increasing role in the exploration of projective methods. We want to know not only the nature of the defensive maneuvers but also the success with which they are employed, or, rather, the sacrifice such maneuvers demand from the functioning personality.

The concept of perceptual vigilance may be thought of in connection with projective methods. Various studies have suggested that stress not only increases the defensive projective function of the ego, but also improves its cognitive acuity at the same time.

In the study of children's stories, it must be remembered that we view the nature of pathogenicity of defenses and other structural concepts in terms of *age-appropriateness*. What may be quite normal at one age may be pathological at another. In the absence of reliable norms for what precisely is age-appropriate, not only in the projective literature but in any literature at all, some very rough, fallible guidelines have to be adhered to.

Adequacy of Superego as Manifested by "Punishment" for "Crime"

The relationship of the chosen punishment to the nature of the offense gives us an insight into the severity of the superego: a psychopath's hero who murders may receive no punishment other than a slight suggestion that he may have learned a lesson for later life, whereas a neurotic may produce stories in which the hero is accidentally or intentionally killed or mangled, or dies of an illness, following the slightest infraction or expression of aggression. On the other hand, a nonintegrated superego, sometimes too severe and sometimes too lenient, is also frequently met in neurotics. A formulation of the circumstances under which a person's superego can be expected to be too severe, and under what other conditions it is likely to be too lenient, is, of course, related to the difficult problem of acting out. In addition, however, it is a generally valuable piece of information.

Integration of the Ego

This is, of course, an important variable to assess, for in its many aspects it reveals the general level of functioning. To what extent is the child able to compromise between drives and the demands of reality on the one hand, and the dictates of the superego on the other? The adequacy of the hero in dealing with the problems with which the storyteller confronts him is an important aspect of this variable.

We are also interested in formal characteristics: Is the child able to tell appropriate stories, which constitute a certain degree of cognizance of the stimuli? Or does she leave the stimulus entirely and tell a story with no manifest relation to the picture because she is not functioning well enough to do so and is therefore too preoccupied with her own problems to perceive reality? Does the child find comfort and salvation from anxiety stimulated by the test by giving very stereotyped responses, or is he healthy enough and intelligent enough to be creative and to give more or less original stories? Having produced a plot, can the child attain a solution of the conflicts in the story and within himself that is adequate, complete, and realistic; or do his thought processes become unstructured or even bizarre under the impact of the problem? Does the child show the ability to go from a past background of the story to a future resolution? This will depend on the age of the child as well as on his or her unique personality.

These observations, together with the dynamic diagnosis that the content variables supply—thus facilitating possible classifications of the subject into a nosological category—is one of the main contributions of the CAT. From a formal standpoint, it is useful to consider the child's telling stories for the pictures as a task that he will perform. We may judge his or her adequacy and ego strength and other variables from the standpoint of his or her ability and way of meeting this task. Of course, the adequacy of the ego and its various functions must be considered in relation to the specific age of the child. Consideration should be given to a variety of ego functions, such as drive control (related to the story sequence and outcome), frustration tolerance (related to adequacy of the hero), anxiety tolerance, perceptual and motor adequacy, and others.

TYPICAL THEMES AND RESPONSES TO CAT PICTURES

The CAT pictures as stimuli have been selected because they are likely to illuminate certain dynamic aspects of the child's personality. That fact alone means that stories told to the pictures will have a certain communality, something akin to what Rorschach described as "popular responses." To the extent to which a child gives that sort of response, it is an indication of intact reality testing, in that the subject shares in the common perception of our world. From the child's variations on the general theme, we infer specific dynamics and structural features: someone who totally ignores the stimulus in the story or grossly distorts the commonly perceived response is almost certainly grossly disturbed. If someone introduces figures not in the picture, or grossly omits figures that do exist, we must, of course, infer specific dynamic reasons for this inclusion or omission—a need for the figure introduced (food, parents, weapon) or a fear of the subject or object omitted (denial of aggression, fear of a parent). In short, the typical themes represent a *baseline* that helps us to evaluate the specific features of each storyteller's productions.

When one approaches the interpretation of an apperceptive method such as the CAT, it is best to keep some basic principles firmly in mind. The subject is asked to *apperceive* a situation—that is, to interpret it meaningfully. The subject's interpretation of the stimulus in following our instruction to tell a story exceeds the minimal "objective" stimulus value. He does so, by necessity, in his own way, which must be a function of continually present psychological forces which, at that moment, manifest themselves in relation to the given stimulus material.

If one accepts the idea of a motivational continuity of the personality structure, one may use the following analogy for a testing procedure as well as psychotherapeutic free association: if a river is sampled at various relatively close intervals, the chemical analysis of the content will be highly similar. Any pailful will be representative of the total content. This procedure is commonly followed in public health assays.

Now, if a new tributary joins the river—as compared to a new situational factor in psychological sampling—it may, of course, add factors about which the assayer must know in order to account for changes in content. A primarily genetic theory of personality, like psychoanalysis, maintains that the main contents of the river will remain the primary matrix, which, after a certain point, tributaries can only modify to a greater or lesser degree.

To leave the dangers of further analogies, we believe (and ample experimental literature supports this belief) that interpretations of stimuli in our test material give us a valid sample of the subject's psychic continuum known as *personality*. Still in its formative stages, it is, of course, more changeable in childhood. We can learn about the motivational forces from the fact that any individual response is meaningful for that person; we can furthermore increase our insight by comparing one individual's responses to those of others. To that extent, we are really studying individual differences and making inferences about a given subject by this comparison.

The appendix to this chapter shows the CAT pictures (Figures 5–1 through 5–10) and the typical themes seen as responses to the various plates.

CASE EXAMPLE 1

The following CAT responses are those of a five-year, eight-month-old boy. I had very little background information about the child, and my interpretation of his CAT stories is presented as something of a challenge in the presence of relatively few data. I did gather that the boy lives with his mother and sees his father on weekends. The parents were divorced when he was one year of age. He was brought to a clinic for diagnostic appraisal and evaluation because he was hyperactive and oppositional in school, and was asked to leave his summer camp because he was considered to be too agitated and nervous. The mother is described as overanxious, and the boy has been known to say that he hates her.

Story 1 (Figure 5–1)

Once upon a time there was a mother bird. . . . I mean a sister bird . . . and a brother bird. They were having a chicken soup for breakfast . . . I mean . . . I mean . . . for dinner. Then they went and suddenly this big monster came and they hide under the table and then after that they wound up under the table and flew away and then when they flew back he was gone.

Clinical Notes   I don't know why the child substitutes a "sister bird" for a "mother bird" except that we know he doesn't like his mother, and this might be a defensive denial. Then he introduces a big monster, and we can only assume that that is the way he sees the large chicken in the picture, which started out as the mother bird. It is very suggestive that he refers to mother as the monster and then arrives at a rather magical solution—they hide under the table and the monster flies away. They fly away also, and by the time they return the monster is gone. This appears to be a clear wish to have mother disappear. If it should turn out that this boy does indeed have a sister, less defensiveness would be involved. As it happens, I later learned that the boy is an only child, thus making it a clear case of defensive creation.

Story 2 (Figure 5–2)

Yeah. First these two little monsters fell off the mountain and then the other bear pulled them up by the rope. Then suddenly somebody cut the rope and then they were falling down and there was a parachute and they fell on the parachute.

Clinical Notes   In this story he refers to two of the bears as little "monsters," possibly seeing himself that way—perhaps a self-representation of his aggressive drive (a phenomenon not uncommon, for instance, in children with attention deficit disorder (ADD) (Bellak, 1979). A disaster ensues, however, as in the first story, because somebody cuts the rope and the bears "were falling down." Again, there is a *deus ex machina* introduced in that the bears fall onto a parachute, a not quite realistic view of the use of a parachute. At any rate, the heroes are magically saved. Whether the severance of the rope refers to his parents' divorce, or in some way reflects his tenuous version of object relations, is only something to speculate about at this point. Operationally more reliable is the fact that he appears primed to expect disaster, and then needs to resort to magical resolutions, which is not age-appropriate.

Story 3 (Figure 5–3)

Whew! This reminds me of something. Once upon a time there was a lion and a mouse and they were friends. They lived in the jungle. And then the hunters got the lion and the mouse was chewing the net and then they lived happily ever after.

Clinical Notes   In this third story a lion and a mouse are friends, and then a disaster befalls the lion: the hunters get him, apparently by catching him in a net. Then the mouse chews the net, and the lion escapes, and they live happily ever after. What we see again in this story is a theme the storyteller has used in his first two stories: a disaster befalling people, followed by some magic but clever rescue operation. Whether this deserves the connotation of denial in order to effect a happy resolution is something to be kept in mind: denial is the defense mechanism of choice for affective disorders, so this child might be at risk for a depression or hypomanic behavior.

Story 4 (Figure 5–4)

Mrs. Dog and whatever that is riding a bike—kangaroo—then suddenly ran into a lion. Then they had to turn away and went back. The end!

Clinical Notes   In this story the heroes run into a lion and they have to turn away, apparently because the lion is now considered dangerous. From the context, it seems that the lion may represent father, who is sometimes seen as dangerous, and mother in turn is seen as the refuge.

Story 5 (Figure 5–5)

Once upon a time there was a little teddy bear asleep in his crib and then they—he—was scared. And then they hide his head under the crib and then the big monster came and then he was scared and then another big monster came and scared the other monster away.

Clinical Notes   Here again, we have a little one who feels threatened and frightened and has to hide from a big monster. Then another big monster comes and scares the first monster away, suggesting that indeed the boy views both parents as monsters. Again, we find a repetition of the theme of magical solution.

Story 6 (Figure 5–6)

Once upon a time there was little bears and they lived in a hole. And then it was winter and they hibernate until it wasn't snowing again. And then the lion jumped over the cave and then they were eating honey. And then they came around and went to sleep again. The end.

Clinical Notes   In this story little bears "hibernate." To use this word at age five years, eight months, suggests considerable intelligence. Then the story becomes quite disrupted in its sequence: the lion jumps over the cave, followed by the bears eating honey and going to sleep again. It appears that aggression, in the form of the lion, clearly disrupts the little boy's thought processes, and he finds comfort in oral gratification.

Story 7 (Figure 5–7)

[Puts finger to his mouth.] Once upon a time there was a little monkey and the tiger hated the monkey and he was running after him. And he climbed up the tree and the tiger tried to climb up the tree after him. But he couldn't and the hunter shot him. The end.

Clinical Notes   The aroused aggression now leads the child to put his finger into his mouth when he looks at card 7. In this story we have a tiger who hates a little monkey and who tries to climb a tree to catch the monkey. But he is not able to do so because a hunter, introduced as another *deus ex machina,* intervenes and shoots the tiger. It appears plausible—but not certain—that the tiger is a representation of mother, and the boy is expressing death wishes toward her.

Story 8 (Figure 5–8)

Once upon a time there was a mother and a kid and a father. And then somebody came over for his birthday. And then they drank some coffee and they had some cake and at the end of the day he opened his presents and then that's the end.

Clinical Notes   In this story the child has created an intact family— a mother, a father, and a child—in a happy oral scene, probably in a defensive attempt to deal with the aggression aroused in the previous stories. In view of the parent's divorce, this is probably a wishful story.

Story 9 (Figure 5–9)

Looks like something I said about the bear. Once upon a time there was the kid and he opened the door and then the little bunny ran away and then . . . and then . . . and then . . . he came back and then he had a party and that's the end.

Clinical Notes   In this story there is a little bunny that runs away when the child opens the door, but then the bunny comes back and they have a party. I believe the child is revealing a wish to run away from home, but realizes that that probably wouldn't work, and so falls back on a kind of wishful, magical (happy, oral) solution.

Story 10 (Figure 5–10)

There was two little puppies and they went to the bathroom to play hide and seek. And then they went and the other puppy found the other puppy in hide and seek. And then they live happily ever after.

Clinical Notes   The storyteller ignores the fact that one dog is larger than the other. Instead, they are transformed into two puppies who play together in the bathroom, perhaps revealing a wish for a sibling or a friend. In this story, we have an outspoken denial of one of the popular responses to this picture, namely that the big dog is either spanking or grooming the little dog. This time we must assume that, indeed, denial already plays a more than customary role in this child's dynamics, even allowing for age. This may represent part of his unsuccessful attempt to deal with his hostility toward mother. Depression is likely to play an important role as the behavioral expression of his anger. The question arises as to whether his hyperactivity is not the result of a great deal of hostility toward the maternal figure, which he attempts to deal with by being hyperactive, while at the same time feeling a great deal of anger. The hyperactivity is one way of channeling his feelings of aggression; but when the latter become excessive, depression is likely to play a role.

Overall Summary

In distinction to the analysis of the next case, the foregoing is an example of a rather cursory, unsystematic, clinical inspection, as one might engage in when the CAT is simply used as a supplement to an interview.

In all, what I culled from this initial assessment of this boy's CAT is that this hyperactive and oppositional child is scared of disasters and monsters, scared for his life. He is often adaptive enough to try to arrive at a reasonable and happy ending (stories 1, 2, and 3); but with card 6 it becomes more difficult for him to deny his fears and his anger. The feelings now become disruptive, and he needs magical solutions. We see a wishful solution in card 8 and an outspoken denial in card 10, a defense that, in excess, could put this child at risk for an affective disorder.

In terms of therapy, it will be necessary to work through the child's rage at his mother. There is some indication in these stories that the boy suffers from attention deficit disorder (ADD) since in story 2 he speaks of a little monster, possibly as a self-representation. Because of their problems with impulse control, children with ADD often view themselves as wild animals or monsters (Bellak, 1979).

The mother's overanxiousness and the trauma of the parents' divorce might be sufficient to account for the pathology revealed in the CAT stories. Only additional testing and further history will permit a reliable differential diagnosis.

Supplementary Information and Interpretation

Subsequent to my "blind" reading of the boy's CAT, as presented here, the psychologist who evaluated him added the following background material.

With regard to the family background, the father was hyperactive as a child and was medicated with Ritalin. He was reported to have had aggressive outbursts all through his life. As an adult, he is an alcoholic and is described as depressed a great deal of the time. When he drinks, he becomes vicious, throws things, and is very aggressive. He is unemployed.

The boy's mother had parents who were both alcoholics, although they appear to be recovered at the present time. Recalling her childhood, the mother remembers a father who had frequent aggressive outbursts, who drank a great deal of the time; and she recalls both parents as being absent from the home a majority of the time. The mother is the oldest of three children, was oppositional and defiant as a child, and was forced to spend several years in a predelinquent home for girls, in part for refusing to attend school. She is overanxious, possibly borderline, and is not employed. She has gone back and forth to many different modes of therapy, and was diagnosed as borderline at New York Hospital. At the same institution, the boy was diagnosed as having conduct disorder, socialized aggression, with the possibility of later developing a sociopathic personality.

After looking over my clinical notes, the psychologist who has taken the boy into treatment, added the following observations:

From his acquaintance with the child, he feels strongly that the magical thinking he reveals is pathological for a five-year, eight-month-old, and views it as preoedipal regression, especially in view of the fact that the CAT revealed several instances of magical thinking.

He feels that the boy's "happily ever after" endings represent some denial and reversal of affect or undoing of conflicts presented by the pictures.

With regard to my clinical notes on card 4, specifically the change of animal, he believes this may represent unstable object relations, lack of self-object differentiation, and the like.

He feels that the disruption in sequence, which I noted in the story to card 6, is an indicator of ego fragmentation, perhaps an indicator of ADD or a borderline condition, or both.

I noted that story 8 was a wishful story. He feels it is primarily a reconciliation fantasy in a child who has two parents who have been divorced since he was about a year old, and are both still not remarried.

At the end of my diagnostic statements, I noted that I felt the boy might be liable for a depression or hypomanic behavior. He concurs strongly with my observation, nothing that, as per family history, the father is depressed as an adult and the mother described as generally hypomanic or overanxious or borderline. In terms of ADD, he thinks that the mother does not suffer from this condition, but that the father might. He feels that the fragmentation in narrative sequence noted in story 6 suggests the possibility of the boy suffering from ADD or a borderline condition (evidenced by the change of objects in story 1—mother changed to a sister—and the change of animal in story 4).

He was impressed with how many of the boy's stories showed defensive withdrawal (1, 4, 5, 6, 9), which supports the possibility of either depression or a borderline condition; he adds that depression was noted on the Rorschach in several responses to objects underneath the ground or underwater. Some of the boy's responses on the Rorschach approximated confabulation, supporting the borderline, magical thinking revealed in my reading of his CAT.

With regard to my noting that the boy's CAT reveals a child who is scared of disasters and monsters, scared for his life, he agrees that the child apparently views his parents as being suddenly helpless in the care of him (rope suddenly cut in story 2). In story 7, the boy has the tiger suddenly hating the monkey: he feels this brings out the issue of the child's hateful remarks about the mother reflecting his identification with the aggressor in feeling that the mother hates him. He notes that although the mother consciously states that she loves the boy and is proud of him, at the same time she conveys a hatred of him and the feeling that he is an uncaring monster, noting that he kicks and hits other children, does not listen to the teacher, runs away frequently, has lied and stolen, is very demanding of toys and will yell and scream unendingly if he does not get his way.

In sum, it would appear that the psychologist's observations, based on his more extensive knowledge of the boy and his family, seem quite consistent with what I was able to glean from a cursory reading of the CAT.

CASE EXAMPLE 2

Kenneth was eight years, five months old at the time of testing, with an IQ of 89 on the Stanford-Binet. Entered in a parochial school before he was five years old, he proved to be so severe a behavior problem that the sisters refused to keep him. Things were no better in the public school, where he proved to be an academic problem as well in his inability to learn to read.

Kenneth is tall for his age, thin, and undernourished. He wears glasses. The mother appears to be a heavy, ignorant, placid woman who does not want her placidity disturbed. She apparently rejects Kenneth, preferring the younger child, a girl about four years old. The father, high-strung and unstable, expects his son to be perfect and believes that perfection in children is attained by beating them. He also openly shows his preference for the younger girl.

The boy's behavior at school is markedly aggressive: he has assaulted several children quite severely, has stolen from girls' pocketbooks, has removed articles from the teacher's desk, and is constantly noisy and restless.

Kenneth does not come home for lunch as do the other children, because his mother finds it too much trouble to fix lunch for him.

Kenneth loses bladder control by night or day and soils himself occasionally at school.

Story 1 (Figure 5–1)

She's going to eat the food up [pointing to the big one], then the little one's won't have any. Then they're going to start crying. Then she's going to make some more . . . [prompted]. The mother will give him some food when it's cooked [pointing to chick without bib]. [Prompted] . . . They all had their food already—all the others.

Clinical Notes   For this first story, note the description of descriptive, interpretive, and diagnostic levels as an example of diagnostic inferences from the primary data to a diagnostic level.

Descriptive Theme	Interpretive Theme	Diagnostic Level
The mother will eat all the food, depriving the little ones.	If there is food, the mother eats it all up.	Mother seen as depriving children of basic needs (food, love).
They will cry.	And children cry.	Subject feels unhappy.
She will relent and make more and give bibless chick the food.	Mother relents and cooks more for one.	Mother seen as responding to crying.
All the others already had some.	The others having already received theirs.	Subject feels especially deprived in relation to others (sister? mother?). Subject clearly identifies with deprived child in stimulus (check minus bib).

This first story already suggests an atmosphere of deprivation and unhappiness, with the subject feeling especially neglected.

Story 2 (Figure 5–2)

The daddy bear is trying to pull the rope away from the momma and the baby bear. The father bear wants to win, and the little ones wants to win. The father pulls and pulls and can't get it away. So the baby is losing. [Prompted] . . . The baby will fall down. [Prompted] . . . The mamma will fall down too.

Clinical Notes   There are some inconsistencies in this story. Even though the father cannot get his way, in the next sentence the subject states that the baby is losing, conveying his basic feeling of helplessness.

Story 3 (Figure 5–3)

[Sits up straight, big smug grin] The lion is waiting for the rat to come out of the hole so he can eat him up—eat him up for his dinner. He's resting. The rat is coming out. The lion don't know the rat is coming out. [Prompted] . . . The lion will chase the rat, and the rat will run into the hole, and then the lion will run into the wall and get a bump on his head [big smile].

Clinical Notes   This story continues the struggle between father and the boy. This time the boy wishfully outwits the father. It must be considered significant that he identifies himself with the rat, rather than the little mouse that is usually seen. The rat constitutes a more aggressive and more dangerous, and at the same time a socially much less acceptable, dirty self-image.

The theme of devouring is worth noting but may not be given too much pathological significance here, since the stimulus tends to suggest this theme. However, we will see that the theme recurs in later stories in a much more clearly pathological form.

Story 4 (Figure 5–4)

[Big smile at examiner] He's going to crash right into the momma with his bike. The momma will get hurt. Then he's going to run over her. The balloon will bust and he'll run over the milk and stuff and they'll spill all over the place. . . . Then she'll get up and run into the tree 'cause her hat's over her head and she can't see and she'll get a bump on her head again.

Clinical Notes   Judging by the smile at the examiner, subject feels happy at releasing aggression, of which he apparently can't get enough. The way he destroys food suggests that the food itself is a frequent source of irritation, probably also identified with the mother. There is obviously a tremendous need for aggression against the mother, some of it possibly sexually fused (crashing into her).

Story 5 (Figure 5–5)

The mamma bear is under the covers so she's afraid there might be a ghost around the house. The baby sticks its head out and screams. Then the rats come out under the bed and pushed the bed up near the window. The ghost puts its hand in and grabs the mamma bear and puts the momma in the garbage pail, with her head first, and then the ghost takes the baby bears and takes them home and eats them. Then the ghost goes to bed—he's too full.

Clinical Notes   This must be considered a rather bizarre story, even for an eight-and-a-half-year-old boy. We seem to deal with multiple iden-tification in this story, in that the rat in story 3 suggests that the rats in the present story who are so hostile to the mother also represent the subject. Probably the ghost is also an identification figure, further dis-guised for defensive displacement from consciousness.

The tremendous amount of hostility again becomes apparent in his refinement of detail, specifying "with her head first." Probably if the ghost is our hero, the baby bears are here identified with the baby sister; but the possibility of another shift of identification, wherein the aggressor also becomes the victim, cannot be excluded. This story suggests an ex-treme of nocturnal anxiety, among other things, by a projection of the child's own aggressive impulses. Again, incorporation plays a clear pathological role. This theme is illustrative of Bertram Lewin's (1950) oral triad: the wish to devour, to be devoured, and to sleep. This suggests that the subject is likely to develop a severe affective disorder of a manic-depressive nature. Hand in hand with the bizarreness of the story, one would be inclined to predict that this boy might well go on to an adult psychosis, which may at first appear to be of a manic-depressive variety and later become a schizophrenic disorder with affective features (schizoaffective disorder].

Story 6 (Figure 5–6)

> The baby bear is asleep in a cave and the lion's going to come in and eat him up. The lion came in and took the baby bear far away in the forest and ate him up and left the bones there. Then the lion came and took the other baby bear and took him to the forest and ate him up and left the bones there too. There's one there, asleep and fat. The father woke up and saw the two babies gone and he saw the bones walking around and he jumped on the bones and they died 'cause they were poison bones. Just the father and mother jumped. The bones came near the baby and he died and the bones died too. [*Note:* Questioning caused resentment, but examiner is certain that "they died" referred to father and mother.]

Clinical Notes   This must also be considered a rather bizarre story even for the subject's age level, in that it is a very unusual response to this or any other CAT picture and is so little suggested in its details by the stimulus. In a continuation of the theme of oral incorporation, the father figure is seen again as orally aggressive, although the latter part of the story shows some defensive switching, with the father in a somewhat protective role; at the same time, the father is a victim, as are the mother and the baby sister. Earlier in the story our hero himself also has to die. In other words, we deal with an abundance and diffusion of hostility and aggression, as well as intraaggression.

The walking bones are probably the most bizarre feature of the story, since the idea of poison occurs often enough in children without clear-cut or serious pathological implications, connoting fears of orally incorporating harmful objects related both to the mother's milk and to fantasies of oral impregnation.

Story 7 (Figure 5–7)

> A lion is chasing a monkey and the monkey is climbing up the tree and the lion breaks down the tree. The monkey jumps to the next tree and the lion grabs him by the tail and eats him up and only the bones are left. Then the tiger goes to one of the houses and eats the people

and takes the clothes and said [voice pitched high and dramatic], "I'm the greatest king in the whole jungle." The end.

Clinical Notes   Here we see a further perseveration of the theme of eating up people (or animals) with a reference to remaining bones. Again, this is mainly directed against the father figure (king) and all father figures (greatest king) in the whole jungle—a wild and primitive place in which this boy seems really to be living. The references to bones, particularly as in story 6 (poisoned bones of malevolent power) is the kind of literal organic concept seen in the Rorschach and also in Figure Drawing responses, and consistent with psychosis.

Story 8 (Figure 5–8)

They're having a party. The mother bear's grandma says, "You go get the lunch." He don't want to. The momma tells secrets to the father about the baby and he don't like it. He got breakfast, dinner, and lunch and went out to get candles for the birthday cake. It was his birthday, and he got matches too and lighted the candles and blew them out. Then he cut the cake for the grandma, mother, and father. Then he ate and went to bed and the grandma went home and to bed.

Clinical Notes   This story appears extremely innocuous after the previous ones. The introduction of matches to light the candles suggests the possibility of a urethral complex, since fire, as well as water, has this diagnostic significance in TAT and CAT stories.

Story 9 (Figure 5–9)

The momma bear came out of bed and made supper for the baby. The baby's looking and the momma's dead, and the ghost came in and killed the baby. The papa came in and saw it and he took a bottle out. The ghost saw it and shot the father. Then the cops came and saw it and sent the ghost to the electric chair.

Clinical Notes   This story is one of extreme aggression directed against the mother, younger sibling, and father, as well as tremendous intraaggression. In all, this is an extremely disturbed story. It does not consider the stimulus at all, and diffuse, uncontrolled hostility abounds throughout.

Story 10 (Figure 5–10)

The little doggie don't want to get hit. He's crying 'cause he don't want to get in the tub. The mother sits down and hits and hits and he barks and barks. He starts to run away into the tub. He turns the water on and takes a bath and she'll pet him and give him dessert, breakfast, and supper, and pet him and put him to bed.

Clinical Notes   In this story the hostile and fearful relationship between mother and child clearly emerges, with mother seen as coercive and punishing. Remarkable is his running into the tub as an attempt at compliance with the "aggressor." Food obviously plays a tremendous role in gratification. Although it is only reasonable to point out that children generally go to bed after having eaten, the frequent association of the two in this subject's stories suggests that it is also part of the oral triad.

Postscript to Case 2

Kenneth was never known to me personally.* I made my interpretations and predictions solely on the basis of his CAT stories and information about his background as printed *in toto* in this section.

Some years later, it occurred to me to try to check on the dire prognosis I had made, based on my interpretation of the boy's CAT material. I contacted the psychologist, whom I had not seen in many years. It is through her strenuous efforts to trace this boy's subsequent career that the following tragic history can be made available.

Kenneth moved from his home town. After a few years, a social worker from the new domicile requested information on him because, at about age thirteen, he assaulted his sister sexually; threatened to kill her if she told anyone; and, when discovered in the act by his mother at one time, almost strangled the mother. The father, who had previously told the school's social worker to mind her own business, that he knew how to handle the boy, then told the social worker she should take care of him—"He is all yours."

Kenneth was then sent to a state school. He ran away several times. At some time later, according to a relative, he seemed to adjust better for several years, worked, got married, and had a daughter. After about three years of marriage, he met another young woman, who became pregnant by him. Meeting her in a park near her childhood home, he strangled her to death. He was executed at age twenty-eight, just about twenty years after taking the test reported here.

The CAT report that Kenneth was an exceedingly disturbed boy was hardly overstated. Extreme aggression and hostility are noted throughout. The report failed to predict overt mayhem, although that fact was obvious from the behavioral report. What the CAT supplies is the bizarreness of the aggression and the general severe pathology. It has been impossible to obtain institutional records to ascertain whether a psychosis

---

*Kenneth's CAT stories and the background information on the child were furnished to me by a psychologist who had taken a course in the CAT with me.

was diagnosed at any point. The crime for which Kenneth was executed certainly sounds like a direct repetition of his earlier tendencies to choke someone to death, and most likely was the result of sudden loss of control rather than premeditation. This makes the sentence a puzzling one. It is unlikely that any amount of therapy at that late date would really have made him a safe person to have around, but at the same time it is very unlikely that he could have been a person of sound mind who was aware of the consequences of his act while engaged in it. It is probably a reflection of the nature of our criminal justice system that this man was executed rather than hospitalized.

This whole story underlines points I have made elsewhere (Bellak & Barten, 1969): that it is necessary not only to screen children psychologically at school entrance, but also to have the legal right to *insist* on treatment, to remove a child from a pathological home, and/or to provide treatment of the parents, if necessary without their voluntary consent.

THE CHILDREN'S APPERCEPTION TEST—HUMAN FIGURES (CAT-H)

In this version of the CAT (Bellak, 1980/1965), human figures in exactly the same situations as in the CAT are substituted for the animals. A fourteen-page manual reviews the literature concerning the use of animal versus human figures in projective techniques and discusses the process of transposing the animal figures to human form. A copy of Haworth's Schedule of CAT Responses (1963) is included in the manual, as is a bibliography of pertinent literature.

SUPPLEMENT TO THE CHILDREN'S APPERCEPTION TEST (CAT-S)

The CAT Supplement (CAT-S) (Bellak & Bellak, 1980/1952) was designed to supply pictures that might illuminate situations *not necessarily pertaining to universal problems,* but occurring often enough to make it desirable to learn more about them, as they exist in many children. Ten pictures have been designed (see Bellak & Bellak, 1952), any one of which may be presented to children in addition to the regular protocol CAT. For instance, CAT-S picture 5, depicting a kangaroo on crutches, might be given to a child with a temporary or permanent disability or with a history of disability, and might permit one to learn about the psychological effects of this somatic problem on the child. Or a child with any kind of psychosomatic disorder or hypochondriasis might project this onto the stimulus. Picture 10, depicting a pregnant cat, might permit us to learn what fantasies a boy or girl may have about the mother's pregnancy.

The plates are constructed like pieces of a jigsaw puzzle, with different, irregularly shaped outlines. Children who do not relate stories readily can manipulate these forms in play techniques. An eleven-page manual discusses the play technique and includes a bibliography of relevant literature.

CASE EXAMPLE 3

Clinical Notes on a Sexually Abused Four-Year-Old Girl

The following are three CAT stories to the regular plates by a four-year-old girl who, by history, is believed to have been sexually abused by her father in the form of his fondling her vagina, putting his penis near her vagina, and taking her into the men's bathroom and touching her vagina with his mouth and fingers.

Story 1 (Figure 5–1)

And the bird said, "Go in your room." So the bird said, "Don't you dare go in my room!" [She pushes the card back and rocks in her chair.] And she did. That's it. The end.

Clinical Notes   As a tentative notion, one might suspect that the "Don't you dare go in my room," accompanied by the child rocking in her chair and then bringing the story to a very prompt and abrupt end, is also consistent with the experience of sexual abuse. It is, however, not clear who originally said, "Don't you dare go in my room," unless it is a variation of "Don't you dare go in her room," if said by mother.

Story 8 (Figure 5–8)

Hm. The monkey can't. And the baby said "Cut it out!" "Cut out the cert." *What is cert?* Cert . . . the baby monkey . . . right . . . hide from the big monkey. The big monkey is going to touch his pee pee. *What happens?* Put it upside down. [She turns the card upside down.] And then they lived happily ever after.

Clinical Notes   We don't know what this word *cert* means. It may well just be one of those family idiosyncratic words that are frequent coins of exchange just within one family. But there is nothing equivocal about the big monkey touching his "pee pee," very clearly referring to some sexual touching, even though it is not clear from the story who is touching whose "pee pee." We do not know if the father monkey is touching himself, or if the sexual fondling involves his touching the baby monkey. We could probably elicit this information by further inquiry.

Story 9 (Figure 5–9)

And then the rabbit went in the crib and he was sleeping and snoring and there was the bed. And then he had a bad dream. *About what?* Like I don't know. Like what my Daddy did. Went in the room. I need to go to the bathroom again. [She runs over to her mother who takes her to the bathroom. When she comes back she continues the story.] He took me in a boat and I stopped it. *What are you talking about?* My Daddy. *What did you stop?* Nothing. Touching my pee pee. And then they went on a boat in a cruise and that's the end. [She hands the card over to the examiner.]

Clinical Notes   Here we see a reference to a bad dream in relation to something that Daddy did, again strongly suggestive of sexual abuse. This aspect of the story was apparently stimulating to the child, enough so that she actually had to go to the bathroom, a crossing from sexual to urethral arousal, which is not infrequent. We don't know exactly what his taking her in a boat means, but whatever was involved, she stopped him. When the examiner asks what she stopped in relation to the father, the child replies, "Nothing. Touching my pee pee." Chances are that this is in reference to the father having made some vaginal contact with the child.

CONCLUSIONS

The CAT has proved itself by a number of criteria to be a useful technique for psychological assessment of children. Judging by sales figures, it has been used increasingly since its original conception and development. It is one of the few survivors among a large number of projective devices developed after World War II that have since disappeared from the scene. It is now published in many different languages in a variety of countries, from New Delhi, India, to Buenos Aires, Argentina.

Suspicious or critical as the academic community was of all the projective techniques, cognitive psychology has made the CAT and other types of apperceptive assessment both methodologically and theoretically more acceptable to academic psychologists. The CAT also has spurred a fair amount of research into various areas of child development. It still lends itself to further research, not only into its own validity and reliability, but also as a method for studying different areas of child development, for example, the Freudian concepts of libidinal development and the development of defenses, and the nature of object relationships and of thought processes. It could also be used longitudinally for the assessment of therapeutic change over time, using, for instance, Chassan's (1979) technique of intensive design for single-case statistics.

The CAT provides *primary data* that lend themselves to use from whatever vantage point one wishes to take. This includes studying the CAT from the standpoint of the currently intense interest in neuropsychological assessment. It can also be studied from the vantage point of the equally fashionable concern with object relations, and specifically with the development and diagnosis of the very topical concern with borderline personality, or from the vantage point of self psychology.

For the clinician, the CAT is an easy tool to use. One doesn't even have to master administration, as one does to use the WAIS. When the CAT is used as an informal supplement to a clinical interview, using only a few of the pictures may suffice, as opposed to making use of the entire set of ten plates.

Children like the CAT. They do not find it traumatic—it engages them, especially the animal pictures. I suspect, in fact, that many psychologists simply enjoy using the CAT for its emotional appeal as well as its varied usefulness.

REFERENCES

Bellak, L., & Bellak, S. S. (1980/1949). *The Children's Apperception Test (CAT)* (7th and rev. ed.). Larchmont, NY: C.P.S., Inc.

Bellak, L., & Bellak, S. S. (1980/1949). *A manual for the Children's Apperception Test—Animal Figures* (7th and rev. ed.). Larchmont, NY: C.P.S., Inc.

Bellak, L., & Bellak, S. S. (1980/1952). *The supplement to the Children's Apperception Test (CAT-S)* (rev. ed.). Larchmont, NY: C.P.S., Inc.

Bellak, L., & Bellak, S. S. (1980/1952). *A manual for the supplement to the Children's Apperception Test (CAT-S)* (rev. ed.). Larchmont, NY: C.P.S., Inc.

Bellak, L. (1980/1955). *Short form for recording and analyzing Thematic Apperception Test and Children's Apperception Test* (rev. ed.). Larchmont, NY: C.P.S., Inc.

Bellak, L. (1980/1965). *The Children's Apperception Test—Human Figures (CAT-H)* (rev. ed.). Larchmont, NY: C.P.S., Inc.

Bellak, L. (1980/1965). *A manual for the Children's Apperception Test—Human Figures (CAT-H)* (rev. ed.). Larchmont, NY: C.P.S., Inc.

Bellak, L. (Ed.). (1979). *Psychiatric aspects of minimal brain dysfunction in adults.* New York: Grune & Stratton.

Bellak, L. (1986). *The TAT, CAT, and SAT in clinical use* (4th ed.). New York: Grune & Stratton.

Bellak, L., & Barten, H. (1969). *Progress in community mental health* (Vol. 1). New York: Grune & Stratton.

Bellak, L., & Goldsmith, L. (1984). *The broad scope of ego function assessment.* New York: John Wiley & Sons.

Bellak, L., & Hurvich, M. (1966). A human modification of the Children's Apperception Test. *Journal of Projective Techniques, 30,* 228–242.

Bellak, L., Hurvich, M., & Gediman, H. (1973). *Ego functions in schizophrenics, neurotics, and normals.* New York: John Wiley & Sons.

Blatt, S., Engel, M., & Mirmow, E. (1961). When inquiry fails. *Journal of Projective Techniques, 25,* 32–37.

Cain, A. (1961). A supplementary dream technique with the Children's Apperception Test. *Journal of Clinical Psychology, 17,* 181–184.

Chassan, J. B. (1979). *Research design in clinical psychology and psychiatry.* New York: John Wiley & Sons.

Haworth, M. (1963). A schedule for the analysis of CAT responses. *Journal of Projective Techniques, 27,* 181–184.

Johnston, W. M. (1972). *The Austrian mind: An intellectual and social history, 1848–1938.* Berkeley: University of California Press.

Lewin, B. (1950). *Psychoanalysis of elation.* New York: W. W. Norton.

Appendix:
The CAT Pictures

Figure 5–1 Chicks are seated around a table on which is a large bowl of food. Off to one side is a large chicken, dimly outlined. Responses revolve around eating, specifically being or not being sufficiently fed by either parent. Themes of sibling rivalry enter in around who gets more, who is well-behaved and not, etc. Food may be seen as a reward or, inversely, its withholding seen as punishment; general problems of orality are dealt with: satisfaction or frustration, feeding problems per se.

From *The Children's Apperception Test (CAT)*. Copyright by Leopold Bellak, M.D., 1949. Seventh and revised edition, 1980. Reprinted by permission of C.P.S., Inc., Box 83, Larchmont, NY 10538.

Figure 5–2 One bear is pulling a rope on one side while another bear and a baby bear pull on the other side. It is interesting to observe whether the child identifies the figure with whom he cooperates (if at all) as the father or the mother. It may be seen as a serious fight with an accompanying fear of aggression or fulfillment of the child's own aggression or autonomy. More benignly, this picture may be seen as a game (tug-of-war, for example). Sometimes the rope itself may be a source of concern, i.e., breakage of the rope as a toy and fear of subsequent punishment; or again, purely as a symbol concerning masturbation with the rope-breaking representing castration fears.

From *The Children's Apperception Test (CAT)*. Copyright by Leopold Bellak, M.D., 1949. Seventh and revised edition, 1980. Reprinted by permission of C.P.S., Inc., Box 83, Larchmont, NY 10538.

Figure 5–3 A lion with a pipe and cane is sitting in a chair. In the lower right corner a little mouse appears in a hole. This is usually seen as a father figure equipped with such symbols as pipe and cane. The latter may be seen either as an instrument of aggression or may be used to turn this paternal figure into an old, helpless one of whom one need not be afraid. This is usually a defensive process. If the lion is seen as a strong paternal figure, it will be important to note whether he is a benign or a dangerous power.

The mouse is seen by the great majority of children, and is often taken as the identification figure. In such a case—by tricks and circumstance—the mouse may be turned into the more powerful one. On the other hand, the mouse may be totally in the power of the lion. Some children identify themselves with the lion while others switch identification one or more times, giving evidence of confusion about role, conflict between compliance and autonomy, etc.

From *The Children's Apperception Test (CAT)*. Copyright by Leopold Bellak, M.D., 1949. Seventh and revised edition, 1980. Reprinted by permission of C.P.S., Inc., Box 83, Larchmont, NY 10538.

Figure 5–4 A kangaroo with a bonnet on her head is carrying a basket containing a milk bottle. In her pouch is a baby kangaroo with a balloon. There is a larger kangaroo child on a bicycle behind her. This usually elicits themes of sibling rivalry, or some concern with the origin of babies. In both cases, the relation to the mother is often an important feature. Sometimes a child who is an older sibling will identify himself with the pouch baby, thus indicating a wish to regress in order to be nearer to the mother. On the other hand, a child who is in reality the younger one, may identify himself with the older one, thus signifying his wish for independence and mastery. The basket may give rise to themes of feeding. A theme of flight from danger may also occasionally be introduced. Our experience thus far suggests that this picture can be related to unconscious fear in the area of father–mother relationship, sex, pregnancy, etc.

From *The Children's Apperception Test (CAT)*. Copyright by Leopold Bellak, M.D., 1949. Seventh and revised edition, 1980. Reprinted by permission of C.P.S., Inc., Box 83, Larchmont, NY 10538.

Figure 5–5 A darkened room with a large bed in the background. In the fore-ground is a crib in which there are two baby bears. Productions concerning the primal scene in all variations are common here; the child is concerned with what goes on between the parents in bed. These stories reflect a good deal of conjecture, observation, confusion, and emotional involvement on the part of the children. The two children in the crib lend themselves to themes of mutual manipulation and exploration between children.

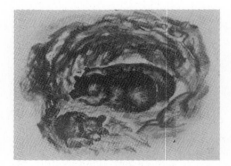

Figure 5–6 A darkened cave with two dimly outlined bear figures in the back-ground and a baby bear lying in the foreground. This again is a picture primarily eliciting stories concerning the primal scene. It is used in addition to Figure 5–5 since practical experience has shown that Figure 5–6 will enlarge frequently and greatly upon whatever was held back in response to the previous picture. Plain jealousy in this triangle situation will at times be reflected. Problems of masturbation at bedtime may appear in response to either Figure 5–5 or 5–6.

Figure 5–7 A tiger with bared fangs and claws is leaping at a monkey which is also leaping through the air. Fears of aggression and manners of dealing with them are exposed here. The degree of anxiety in the child often becomes apparent. It may be so great as to lead to rejection of the picture, or the defenses may be good enough (or unrealistic enough) to turn it into an innocuous story. The monkey may even outsmart the tiger. The tails of the animals lend themselves easily to the projection of fears or wishes of castration.

From *The Children's Apperception Test (CAT)*. Copyright by Leopold Bellak, M.D., 1949. Seventh and revised edition, 1980. Reprinted by permission of C.P.S., Inc., Box 83, Larchmont, NY 10538.

Figure 5–8 Two adult monkeys are sitting on a sofa drinking from tea cups. One adult monkey in the foreground is sitting on a hassock talking to a baby monkey. Here one often sees the role in which the child places himself within the family constellation. His interpretation of the dominant (foreground) monkey as either a father or mother figure becomes significant in relation to his perception of it as a benign monkey or as an admonishing, inhibiting one. The tea cups will, on occasion, give rise to themes of orality again.

From *The Children's Apperception Test (CAT)*. Copyright by Leopold Bellak, M.D., 1949. Seventh and revised edition, 1980. Reprinted by permission of C.P.S., Inc., Box 83, Larchmont, NY 10538.

Figure 5–9 A darkened room is seen through an open door from a lighted room. In the darkened one there is a child's bed in which a rabbit is sitting up looking through the door. Themes of fear of darkness, being alone, desertion by parents, significant curiosity as to what goes on in the next room, are all common responses to this picture.

Figure 5–10 A baby dog is lying across the knees of an adult dog; both figures with a minimum of expressive features. The figures are set in the foreground of a bathroom. This leads to stories of "crime and punishment," revealing something about the child's moral conceptions. There are frequent stories about toilet training as well as masturbation. Regressive trends will be more clearly revealed in this picture than in some others.

6

Sentence Completion Tests

Michael I. Lah

Unlike the other chapters in this book, which focus on individual psychological tests, this chapter focuses on a group of tests called *sentence completion* tests. This name describes a very broad category of tests, which have in common their format, but otherwise vary considerably in their area of psychological functioning of interest, specific focus, purpose, scoring methods, and so forth. Most often, however, discussions of sentence completion tests concern those tests used to assess personality or adjustment. It is this specific subgroup of sentence completion tests on which this chapter will focus.

Sentence completion tests often are less familiar to students than some of the more famous psychological tests, but in fact they are among the most frequently used psychological tests. In a nationwide survey of psychologists (Sundberg, 1961), sentence completion tests as a group ranked fourteenth in frequency of use. In two more recent national surveys of psychologists (Lubin, Larsen, & Matarazzo, 1984; Lubin, Wallis, & Paine, 1971), sentence completion tests ranked 8.5 and 7.5, respectively, in frequency of use. And, in a survey of directors of clinical psychology training programs concerning psychodiagnostic training, sentence completion tests were one of only four objective or projective personality tests recommended by more than 50 percent of the directors as tests with which trainees should be familiar (Piotrowski & Keller, 1984). The goal of this chapter, then, is to introduce readers to this widely used and versatile group of measures.

The chapter begins with a review of some of the history of the development of sentence completion tests. Because of the wide variety of such tests, this review will provide some background on the method and may give the reader a sense of the variety of tests developed and the purposes for which they have been used. Next, some general issues concerning sentence completion tests will be briefly discussed. Four of the better-known sentence completion tests of historical and practical importance will then be described. Finally, the chapter will focus on the most widely used and most researched sentence completion test, Rotter's Incomplete Sentences Blank (1950a, 1950b, 1950c).

THE DEVELOPMENT OF SENTENCE COMPLETION TESTS

Historical Roots

The history of sentence completion tests begins in the late 1890s. Though mostly remembered for his seminal work on the study of human learning and memory, Herman Ebbinghaus also is certified as being the first person to develop a sentence completion test (Ebbinghaus, 1897). This test was developed to assess the intellectual capacity and reasoning ability of school children in Breslau, Germany. This was also the first published account of the development of an "intelligence test" (Wertheimer, 1979). Ebbinghaus's test later was the inspiration for Alfred Binet and Theodore Simon (1905) to incorporate a version of it as one of the tests in their first intelligence scale used to diagnose intellectual deficits in children. Similar tests were continued in the 1908 and 1911 revisions of their scale. Later, when Lewis Terman (1916) revised and expanded the Binet-Simon scale for use in the United States, he retained a variation of the Binet-Simon completion test. To this day, a sentence completion test (the Minkus Completion) continues as one of the tests in the Stanford-Binet Intelligence Scale (Terman & Merrill, 1973). Around the same time as Terman's work on the Stanford-Binet, Marion Trabue (1916) published one of the first uses of a completion test in the United States for the assessment of language skills. From these early roots, use of the completion format spread throughout the fields of psychological and educational assessment. Today, in addition to personality test variants, a wide variety of sentence completion tests, both published and unpublished, continue to be used to assess achievement and intelligence, as well as reading, writing, and language skills.

A second historical root of sentence completion tests was Carl Jung's (1916) use of the "word association" technique to study personality. Although it had been used by Galton, Wundt, and others before him, it was Jung's use of the technique to study personality ("complexes" of emotional disturbance) that contributed greatly to the popularity of the method. Around the same time as Jung's work, in the United States, Grace Kent and Aaron Rosanoff (cited in Rotter, 1951; Watson, 1978) published their Free Association Test, which added to the popularity of the method for the study of various aspects of personality. However, some of the limitations of using a single stimulus word and of subjects being limited to one-word responses prompted later workers to build upon the technique and to use parts of sentences as stimuli, as we shall see.

Although Frederick Wells (1954) notes devising and briefly using a series of "phrase-completions" around 1910, Arthur Payne is widely regarded as the first person to use the sentence completion format systematically in assessing personality. Payne (cited in Rohde, 1946, 1948, 1957) used the technique in the late 1920s to measure personal traits as an aid in vocational guidance counseling of college students and adults. He also used his measure to assess and study personality (e.g., Payne, 1930). A second important early sentence completion test was the one developed by Alexander Tendler (1930) as a measure of "emotional insight," a test to aid in the examination and diagnosis of emotional responsiveness. Noting the problems with test formats used to assess intellectual functions and the limitations of the word association technique, Tendler developed twenty stems, all beginning with "I" (or "My") that would tap a variety of emotional states with a wide range of subjects. Examples are: "I love," "I hate," "I get angry when," "My hero is," "I feel ashamed when," and "I wish for." Tendler also presented some of the first criteria for constructing what now would be called *projective tests,* and presented some of the first general criteria for the intra- and interperson analysis of the responses to this type of test.

Other early researchers used sentence completion tests in exploring a variety of problems and groups of people. Norman Cameron (1938a, 1938b) used sentence completions to study the thought processes of schizophrenic and senile patients. Cameron's use of the method influenced some later psychologists in their use of sentence completion. In a comprehensive study of 50 college males at Harvard University (Murray, 1938), Wheeler developed a test called the Similes Test, a variety of sentence completion, as one of the many test methods used to study this group. Noting the use of the free association (word association) test popularized by Carl Jung and Kent and Rosanoff, Irving Lorge and Edward Thorndike (1941) decided to explore the possible advantages of the similar use of a completion test using 240 stems to explore the presence of 70 different traits in a group of public works employees. Finally, Nevitt Sanford and colleagues (Sanford, Adkins, Miller, & Cobb, 1943) used a sentence completion test as one of the personality tests in their intensive study of 48 children at the Harvard Psychological Clinic. Sanford and co-workers used 30 items, which were scored for the presence of needs, motives, and action patterns in accordance with Henry Murray's (1938) personality theory.

Modern Developments

The modern era of the development of sentence completion tests for the assessment of personality starts with Amanda Rohde's revision and expansion of Payne's questionnaire, cited earlier. Rohde began her work in the late 1930s and, with Gertrude Hildreth, published the first version of their test in 1940. Rohde's test is important because it was designed for general personality assessment, was more carefully constructed than previous tests, had some validation studies done on the measure, and served as a source for later tests developed by other psychologists (cf. Rohde, 1957; Stein, 1949). (A more detailed description of Rohde's test is provided later.)

A second major force that accelerated the pace at which sentence completion tests were developed and employed was the great demand, created by World War II, for psychological assessment instruments for diagnosis, treatment, and personnel selection. Max Hutt (1945) was one of the first to discuss the use of projective methods at U.S. Army medical installations. He differentiated between "structured," "partially structured," and "unstructured" personality tests and cited Cameron's methods, noted earlier, as an example of a partially structured method. Joel Shor (1946) developed his Self-Idea Completion Test along the lines of the word association test, but he wanted to encourage freedom of response and to tap various feelings, attitudes, and areas of interest. His test had 50 sentence stems that related to general life situations as well as ones related to everyday army life, and he varied them from ambiguous (e.g., "If only," "Today, I") to more direct (e.g., "My greatest fear," "Army food," "My most important decision was"). He found the measure useful for understanding personality dynamics for diagnostic and prognostic purposes. Early versions of Shor's test and Tendler's earlier test served as the sources for the development of a sentence completion test called the Personality Projection Sheet, which became a part of the standard psychological test battery used for diagnosis, treatment planning, and disposition at Mason General Hospital in New York, at that time the Army's largest neuropsychiatric hospital (Holzberg, 1945; Holzberg, Teicher, & Taylor, 1947). This measure avoided some of the problems that had been found in scoring and interpreting the Thematic Apperception Test (TAT), and was found to reflect patients' anxiety, guilt feelings, degree of insight, specific complaints, areas of preoccupation, and attitudes toward a variety of people and institutions, and to differentiate neurotic and psychotic patients. The various versions of sentence completion tests used by Shor, Hutt, Holzberg, and others in Army hospitals was one source (along with Cameron's earlier work) for the development of the Incomplete Sentence Test for use in the Army Air Forces convalescent hospitals (Rotter & Willerman, 1947; Wischner, Rotter, & Gillman, 1947). This measure was designed to be a screening instrument and featured an objective system for scoring responses. This test was later revised for civilian use by Rotter and, now known as the Incomplete Sentences Blank (ISB), remains the most frequently used sentence completion test. (A more detailed discussion of the ISB is presented later.)

A final force in the development of sentence completion tests during World War II was the need for the assessment and selection of men for special duty with the Office of Strategic Services. A 100-item completion test was constructed for use by the Assessment Board of the Office of Strategic Services (OSS). Stein (1949) noted that Amanda Rohde had sent a copy of her Sentence Completion Test to Henry Murray before the OSS Assessment Board program began with Murray as its director. Stein notes the similarity of several of the items between the two tests, thus suggesting that Rohde's test probably served as a basis of the initial version of the test used in the OSS program. The test, one of several tests used in assessing candidates to be selected for overseas duty, was administered at one sitting, but in two parts of 50 items each (Murray & MacKinnon, 1946). This test initially was not found useful for easily determining adjustment in several specific areas of interest, but on an in-depth analysis of some cases the measure was found to be very useful in revealing more underlying trends, drives, childhood experiences, interpersonal identifications and conflicts, attitudes toward anxieties and health, and so forth (Symonds, 1947). Morris Stein (1947) noted that use of the Sentence Completion Test in the OSS program was so valuable that he then adapted it for use in the Veterans Administration hospitals. He selected items to contribute information to ten important areas, such as family, the past, drives, inner states, goals, reactions to others, and so forth. The OSS test later was also adapted for civilian use (Hiler, 1959; Kelly & Fiske, 1950) and became known as the Michigan Sentence Completion Test.

Since the end of World War II, the development of sentence completion tests has continued. Today there are a wide variety of completion tests, which have been developed to assess various aspects of personality. In his review of sentence completion research, Goldberg (1965) cites research in the literature on eleven "standard format" sentence completion tests and fifteen "custom-made" tests. Many of these tests (particularly the custom tests) were developed with special purposes in mind, such as the assessment of specific attitudes (e.g., attitudes toward the elderly, blacks, parents and peers, mental hospitals) or exploration of differences between groups (e.g., differences between races, sexes, nationalities). In a later survey of members of the Society of Projective Techniques and Personality Assessment, Goldberg (1968) found mention of the use of 33 different sentence completion tests, 17 published and 16 locally developed. Many sentence completion tests have been developed to assess specific aspects of personality, such as guilt (Mosher, 1961); self-concept, need achievement, and learning attitudes in students (Irwin, 1967); level of ego development (Loevinger & Wessler, 1970); ego strength in chronic psychiatric patients (Stotsky & Weinberg, 1956); and so forth. The most common use of sentence completion tests, however, continues to be for clinical assessment of overall personality characteristics and level of adjustment.

Some Issues in the Development of Sentence Completion Tests

One issue of debate concerning sentence completion tests for personality assessment has been how to categorize them. The answer to this question has implications for how the measures are constructed, used, scored, and so forth. Typically, sentence completion tests have been categorized as projective tests, although there has been some disagreement about this practice. As mentioned before, the tests were developed out of a desire to strike a balance between the limitations of more highly structured assessment methods and the difficulties of scoring and interpreting the highly unstructured projective instruments. It is this in-between nature that has created much of the debate. Some research on sentence completion tests has shown, for example, that subjects can respond to look "good" or "bad" depending on their "mental set" (Meltzoff, 1951). Other research has shown a relationship between measures of social desirability and defensiveness, and willingness to be revealing on sentence completion tests (Crowne & Marlowe, 1964). On the basis of such evidence, some reviewers have concluded that the tests are not projective measures but, in fact, are more like structured interviews or various checklists that merely elicit reports of conscious feelings and attitudes. However, no tests are immune to such influences. Clearly, the Rorschach or the TAT offers a subject much more freedom in how to respond to the stimuli presented, and it is less evident what type of response would be a "good" one. It is also clear, however, that a sentence completion test offers a subject much more freedom of expression than, for example, simply marking yes or no to items on a computer-scored objective test. And, although sentence completion tests do give subjects more structure than some other projective tests and do elicit more consciously revealed information, there is still some disguise of purpose, and how one's responses will be evaluated or interpreted is unclear. Further, as Rohde (1946) has pointed out, even when subjects are defensive, evasive, cryptic, or not telling the truth, their responses can be as revealing as those of a fully open and honest person. Nevertheless, the tests continue to be described most often as "partially structured" or "semistructured" projective tests. The reader is referred to Goldberg (1965) or Watson (1978) for a more detailed review of this issue, and to Campbell (1957) and Lindzey (1959) for their discussions on categorizing various tests.

Because sentence completion tests have been viewed and designed primarily as projective tests, a second major issue has been how to maximize the projective potential of the method while maintaining the method's advantages of ease of administration and interpretation. Test developers have debated how to promote freedom of expression (and projection of aspects of the testee's personality) without eliciting defensiveness or more mundane conscious responses to the sentence stems. Over the years, sentence completion tests have varied on one or more of four main variables. One of the variables has been the amount of structure in the sentence stems. For example, the stem "I" has much less structure than "If I think the job is too hard for me, I." The assumption is that less specific or structured items allow the subject to project more semiconscious and unconscious aspects of personality into the completions. Another variable is whether the stem refers to the testee, to someone else, or to no one (e.g., "I love," versus "He loves," versus "Love is"). Most often the question has been whether first-person stems elicit more personally relevant information or cause greater threat and defensiveness. A third variable has been the stem "pull" or emotional tone, that is, whether the stem has a negative tone ("My greatest fear"), a positive tone ("I like"), or a neutral tone ("A mother"). One argument here is that negative and positive stems elicit responses of the same tone from everyone and that it is the neutral stems that better promote projection. A final variable is the instructional set. Various sentence completion tests have instructed subjects to "work as quickly as you can," "put down the first thing that comes to your mind," "express your real feelings," and other variations. The main argument is that first thoughts or quick responses will be less affected by conscious controls to withhold negative material. But others have found such instructions to promote *less* meaningful responses. There has been research to examine each of these variables and their effects on subjects' responses, although the results have often been contradictory. There is probably most agreement on the issue that sentence stems that are very structured or specific in trying to tap certain content do get more specific responses from testees and are also often more easily scored or categorized. To date, however, there are no definitive answers to these questions, and test constructors have based their decisions on clinical experience and judgment as much as on research findings. Reviews of this literature (e.g., Goldberg, 1965; Watson, 1978) provide more extensive discussions of these issues.

SOME REPRESENTATIVE SENTENCE COMPLETION TESTS

In this section, four of the better-known sentence completion tests will be described in more detail. Each of these tests is designed to be administered individually or in groups for the purpose of general personality assessment. In addition to providing a further introduction to these specific measures, the differences between these four tests (and between them and the Rotter ISB, to be discussed later) will demonstrate some of the varying approaches in sentence completion test construction, mentioned earlier.

The Rohde Sentence Completion Test

Amanda Rohde (1946) noted the need for psychologists, counselors, and other professionals to know the needs, inner conflicts, fantasies, attitudes, aspirations, and adjustment difficulties of the individuals requiring their services. She further noted the difficulties with direct questioning of persons and the advantages of projective methods, which "reveal latent needs, sentiments, feelings, and attitudes which subjects would be unwilling or unable to recognize or to express in direct communication" (p. 170). Therefore, in the late 1930s Rohde developed an instrument "which would have the advantages of the projective techniques, but simplicity of procedure and interpretation to give practical value for psychological diagnosis in schools and other institutions" (p. 170). Starting with the 50 items from Arthur Payne's measure, Rohde and Gertrude Hildreth retained 35 of the items in their original form, modified four, and added 25 new ones, to create a measure with 64 items. The criteria for the items were to present a range of stimuli to elicit information concerning all aspects of the person, to control the responses as little as possible to give the subject freedom of expression, to keep the items comprehensible to persons of a mental age of ten and above, and to keep the measure's length reasonable. Further, the items were arranged in order to lead the subject from "everyday life" to more inaccessible fears, ambitions, inhibitions, conflicts, and so forth (Rohde, 1957).

The 64 items of the Rohde *Sentence Completion Test* are presented in a four-page booklet. The instructions state: "Kindly complete these sentences as rapidly as possible. Try to express your real feelings and opinions" (Rohde, 1957, p. 59). The items are fairly unstructured and (going from initial items to some later ones) include:

"My school work,"

"The future,"

"I want to know,"

"Much of the time,"

"Working,"

"My stomach,"

"Suicide,"

"Death,"

"Love in my life,"

"I am sorry,"

"At home,"

"I feel hurt,"

"My head,"

"No one,"

"I am ashamed."

At the end of the test there are several blank lines for the subject to write any comments he or she may have. Rohde developed a standard scoring system based on Murray's (1938) theory of personality. The content of item responses is scored on the basis of intensity (low, medium, or high) and is analyzed and categorized in terms of reflecting the subject's needs, need integrates, inner states, general traits, and press (environmental forces). She noted that although life situations and various transient emotional states are reflected in responses, the more basic attitudes, sentiments, and "cathections" that are revealed are relatively enduring.

The initial validation of the measure was conducted with ninth-grade students in schools in New York City and New Jersey. The information obtained from the measure compared favorably with teacher ratings of pupils, records, and clinical interviews. Later work was done with some adult populations, and Rohde (1957) presents several examples of test protocols and interpretations for groups of normal, neurotic, and schizophrenic adults.

The Rohde test is important historically and as an example of a sentence completion test with a theoretically based standard system for the clinical analysis and interpretation of subjects' responses. The limitations of the scoring system are that one must be familiar with Murray's personality theory and that the procedure is time-consuming and probably more useful for specific research applications than for general clinical use.

The Sacks Sentence Completion Test

The *Sacks Sentence Completion Test* (SSCT) was developed by Joseph Sacks and others at a Veterans Administration Mental Hygiene Service in New York. Citing it as a variation of the word association technique, they constructed their measure "to obtain significant clinical material in four representative areas of adjustment" (Sacks & Levy, 1950, p. 370). Each of the four areas had several more specific subareas, which were assessed by having four items for each subarea. The four areas (with their subareas) are: *family* (mother, father, family unit); *sex* (women, heterosexual relations); *interpersonal relations* (friends and acquaintances, colleagues at work or school, superiors at work or school, people supervised); and *self-concept* (fears, guilt feelings, goals, attitudes toward one's own abilities, own past, own future). An item pool was created by having twenty psychologists submit items to assess each of the subareas; other items were added from sentence completion tests in the literature. The 280 items amassed were then rated by twenty psychologists as to which were best for assessing each of the fifteen subareas. Those items most often rated as the best were selected for the final version of the measure.

The instructions for the Sacks Sentence Completion Test read: "Below are sixty partly completed sentences. Read each one and finish it by writing the first thing that comes to your mind. Work as quickly as you can. If you cannot complete an item, circle the number and return to it later" (p. 377). The 60 items of the SSCT all have first-person stems. It is not stated by Sacks and Levy, but the choice of all first-person stems is probably based on Sacks's earlier research finding (1949) that first-person stems were more valuable in eliciting relevant information from subjects. Examples of sets of items for a few subareas are:

[father] "If my father would only," "I feel that my father seldom," "I wish my father," "I feel that my father is";

[heterosexual relations] "When I see a man and a woman together," "If I had sex relations," "My feeling about married life," "My sex life";

[colleagues at work] "I like working with people who," "Those I work with are," "At work I get along best with," "People who work with me usually";

[guilt feelings] "The worst thing I ever did," "My greatest mistake was," "I would do anything to forget the time I," "When I was younger."

(Note that on the test form the four items for each subarea are not grouped together as they are here.)

Sacks devised a rating sheet to summarize the responses for the four items in each of the fifteen subareas. It was felt that it is "more desirable to simply point out areas of disturbance and to determine these through a constellation of response" (Sacks & Levy, 1950, p. 374). Each subarea could then be rated on a three-point scale to indicate "no significant disturbance," "mildly disturbed," or "severely disturbed" (appears to require therapeutic aid in handling emotional conflicts in the area). At the end of the sheet is a general summary to list principal areas of conflict and interrelationships among attitudes, and to describe personality structure on several dimensions. Although they do provide examples of the range of responses for each subarea, Sacks and Levy note that these ratings and judgments depend on the clinician's background and acumen.

To assess the validity of the measure, Sacks and Levy had three psychologists rate the degree of disturbance of 100 patients in each of the fifteen subareas. Then, the psychiatrists who had been treating these patients, and had considerable clinical knowledge of them, independently made the same ratings on the 15 subareas. The psychologists agreed on 92 percent of 1,500 ratings, and thus had good reliability. The ratings of the psychologists and those of the psychiatrists compared favorably and supported the SSCT's validity—results, note Sacks and Levy, comparable to validity assessments of the Rorschach and the TAT. The SSCT is a good example of a sentence completion test designed to assess specific content of interest and would be useful for that purpose. The rating sheet is a useful way of grouping the subarea items together and facilitating the analysis of the content of subject responses, although this is not the only way these data could be scored or analyzed.

The Forer Structured Sentence Completion Test

Bertram Forer (1950) stated that he attempted to construct a sentence completion test that could be interpreted in a systematic way and that would reveal valuable diagnostic information for the purpose of therapeutic planning. As its name suggests, the Forer test is one of the more structured sentence completion tests. Forer noted as follows the problem of scoring and classifying responses when one must take into consideration different levels of personality, conflicts, ambivalence, defenses, inconsistency of response, and so forth:

> When the incomplete sentence is minimally structured, the substrate is difficult to determine. The interpreter lacks sufficient information regarding the stimulus situation to determine what the response means. The less the interpreter knows of the stimulus situation, the less able he is to determine the role of the response in the total personality and less able to predict behavior. (p. 17)

Therefore, Forer's test is fairly highly structured; he feels this contributes to objectivity; to better interperson comparisons; and to more systematic, better, and more easily drawn interpretations and diagnostic inferences. Further, Forer feels that highly structured items allow wide coverage of the "attitude-value" system and more easily force the client to express attitudes and reveal interpersonal behavior determined in advance by the examiner to be important.

The Forer *Structured Sentence Completion Test* consists of 100 items. There are separate forms for males and females, which are identical except for relevant pronouns. The instructions for the test read, "Complete the following sentences as rapidly as you can. Write down the first thing you think of" (Forer, 1950, p. 18). The items for the measure were selected with first-person singular, third-person singular, and third-person plural pronouns to get at (respectively) degrees of personal reference, projections of the self by describing another, and perceptions of external "codes" or situations. Although a few items are relatively unstructured (e.g., "Men," "Love is"), most of the items are fairly structured compared to those on other sentence completion tests. Some examples are:

"If I can't get what I want, I";
"When I feel that others don't like me, I";
"If I think the job is too hard for me, I";
"I used to dream about";
"When my father came home, I";
"When she was completely on her own";
"After he made love to her, she";
"When he found he had failed the examination, he";
"Her conscience bothered her most when";
"When they told him to get out, he";
"He felt inferior when";
"People in authority are";
"Most men act as though."

Forer devised an elaborate check sheet to use in categorizing the test responses. The sheet consists of major content categories (e.g., Interpersonal Figures, Dominant Drives, Causes of Own, Reactions to) with more specific areas within each (e.g., for Interpersonal Figures: mother, father, females, males, people, authority). Across the top of each major section of the sheet are other aspects or qualities to be used to cross-categorize the responses. Thus, a response about males might be judged as "accepting," one about females judged as reflecting "dependence," and one about authority as indicating "fear" or "compliance." Each major category has its own set of qualities to use in evaluating responses. After rating all of the subject's responses, one then uses the check sheet to interpret them on the basis of predominant reaction, aberrant responses, and so forth. Forer notes that responses can be analyzed on the basis of structure (language, grammar, etc.), content, and substrates (underlying needs, drives, traits, dynamics, etc.). Forer does not present any normative or validity data for his test. The Forer is another sentence completion test that is focused on tapping specific content areas of interest, and would be useful for that purpose. The check sheet developed by Forer is an example of another way to categorize responses systematically and facilitate interpretation of them.

The Miale-Holsopple Sentence Completion

The test developed by James Holsopple and Florence Miale (Holsopple & Miale, 1954) probably represents the best example of a sentence completion test developed and used with the primary goal of maximizing the potential of the measure as a projective instrument. These authors note that word association methods have been lacking and that the free associations to the varying stimuli of unstructured interviews provide inadequate background from which the examiner can draw inferences. However, the "sentence completion, lying midrange between these two techniques, offers an almost ideal compromise. Furthermore, by giving a subject an opportunity to reveal himself without committing himself, the sentence completion may be constructed to meet the primary requirements of the projective method" (p. 3). Thus, such a measure permits the individual to "behave in a way which is altogether characteristic of him and consistent with the structure of his whole personality" (p. 3). They further note that sentence completion does not have the drawback of requiring the extensive technical training and clinical experience needed to use other projective methods, such as the Rorschach. Holsopple and Miale feel that other sentence completion tests approach the individual too directly, thereby causing the person to feel attacked and exposed, and eliciting conscious attitudes which mask the material from which inferences about unconscious trends could be drawn. This concern is reflected in the design of their test.

The Miale-Holsopple *Sentence Completion* consists of 73 incomplete sentences. The items were drawn from many sources, including previously published sentence completion tests and their own experience with earlier versions of their measure completed by over seventeen hundred individuals from a variety of patient and nonpatient populations. The stems were selected to permit the expression of feelings or thoughts with the minimum of threat. Thus, first-person references and even third-person references were avoided. Further, stems were selected on their ability to elicit a wide variety of responses and to allow subjects maximum flexibility in interpreting the meaning of the sentence. The instructions for the test read: "Complete each sentence in whatever way you wish. If you have trouble thinking of a completion to any sentence, put a circle around the number, and return to the sentence when you have finished the rest" (Holsopple & Miale, 1954, p. 175). Some examples of items include:

"A large crowd,"

"He drew back from the touch of,"

"No one can repair the damage caused by,"

"A person is most helpless when,"

"Few things are less attractive than,"

"Spiders are,"

"People refrain from murder only because,"

"The finger pointed,"

"A naked man,"

"A woman's body,"

"Behind one's back,"

"She couldn't bear to touch,"

"The main difference between a wild and a tame animal is,"

"Worse than being lonely is."

The different "feel" of these items compared to those of the tests described earlier is clear.

Holsopple and Miale see the task of dealing with the data from the sentence completions as a "procedure of interpretation, and . . . not a procedure of scoring" (p. 6). They discuss some of the ways that responses vary (e.g., positive or negative, active or passive subject role, time frame, length) and give examples of characteristic responses for each item. But they believe that attempting to handle the data in a more objective way is premature, and prefer to interpret the responses "sentence by sentence until an acceptable global description is achieved" (p. 6). The data of interest in this process are semiconscious and unconscious desires, conflicts, motives, and aspects of personality organization that are revealed in the subject's completions. Holsopple and Miale go on to provide item-by-item and summary interpretations for thirteen cases. No normative or validity data are provided, and, in fact, the authors question the applicability of reliability and validity to projective tests. The Miale-Holsopple is an interesting and provocative example of one variation of the sentence completion method and its interpretive potential.

THE ROTTER INCOMPLETE SENTENCES BLANK

Julian Rotter's (the "o" is pronounced as in "wrote") *Incomplete Sentences Blank* (ISB) is the most widely used and most researched sentence completion test in current use. As was mentioned at the beginning of the chapter, Sundberg (1961) conducted a national survey of psychologists to determine the psychological tests most frequently used by them and their organizations. In that survey, all sentence completion tests as a group ranked fourteenth in frequency of use. The ISB was the only specific sentence completion test to be listed individually, and it ranked sixty-first. Ten years later, in the survey conducted by Lubin, Wallis, and Paine (1971), the ISB ranked as the tenth most frequently used individual test of the 149 tests in the survey. In the most recent study, by Lubin, Larsen, and Matarazzo (1984), they found the ISB to rank twelfth in frequency of use. Finally, on checking the number of citations listed for various sentence completion tests in *Tests in Print* (Buros, 1974; Mitchell, 1983), one finds 156 citations listed for the ISB, compared to 12 for Forer's test and 11 for Rohde's, the two next most frequently cited sentence completion tests. Because of the popularity and importance of the measure as reflected by these statistics, the ISB will be discussed in greater detail.

Development

As briefly mentioned earlier, the ISB was originally developed for use in the Army Air Forces convalescent hospitals during World War II. At that time a serious need was felt for a screening test that could be given to large groups of individuals to evaluate adjustment and fitness for return to duty. Rotter and Willerman (1947) found that self-rating scales and more structured personality tests did not allow sufficient freedom of response and had not proved to be sufficiently discriminative. On the other hand, projective tests like the Rorschach and the TAT had problems of scoring and interpretation, and projective tests that could be more easily scored had proved inadequate when investigated experimentally. Rotter and Willerman then developed the Incomplete Sentences Test, adapted in part from the various versions of similar tests used by Hutt (1945), Holzberg (1945), Shor (1946), and others at Army hospitals. Wischner, Rotter, and Gillman (1947) also note the influence of Cameron's earlier work (Cameron, 1938a, 1938b).

Rotter and Willerman noted that with earlier sentence completion tests the methods of scoring subject responses had been subjective and relied on a high degree of clinical skill on the part of the interpreter. For this reason, and because their test was intended to serve as a screening measure, one of the primary goals of their work was to develop a scoring method that would provide consistent results and could be reliable with relatively untrained scorers. Starting with 50 items, they reevaluated them and eliminated ones that elicited stereotyped responses or only a narrow range of response. They settled on 40 items (see Table 6–1 for a listing of 10 of the 40 sentence stems). They also changed the instructions, avoiding any reference to responding quickly or with one's first thought. Their scoring procedures involved rating each response on a seven-point scale from $+3$ to -3 for adjusted and maladjusted responses, respectively. They developed a scoring manual with examples of responses for each item, and on examination found good interscorer reliability. (A more detailed description of the scoring procedures is given later.)

A second goal of the development of the ISB (explicated more clearly by Rotter & Rafferty, 1950) was to create an instrument to obtain fairly specific diagnostic information that would be useful for treatment purposes. Included in this goal was the hope that the measure would save the clinician time and give her or him some information helpful in better

Table 6–1 Responses of a Twenty-one-year-old University Student Outpatient to the Rotter Incomplete Sentences Blank

1. *I like* . . . [Blank]
2. *The happiest time* . . . s for me are hanging out with friends and being with my family.
3. *I want to know* . . . why I have been faced with so much adversity this year.
4. *Back home* . . . I am able to relax and enjoy being with my family.
5. *I regret* . . . letting my personal life interfere with my academics.
6. *At bedtime* . . . I am so tired and can't wait to fall asleep.
7. *Boys* . . . are often easier to talk to and deal with.
8. *The best* . . . feeling is knowing that you have accomplished something.
9. *What annoys me* . . . the most is when people gossip and talk behind my back.
10. *People* . . . can be cruel sometimes.
11. _____ . . . is someone who understands and cares and protects.
12. _____ . . . pretty worn out lately.
13. _____ . . . is that the mistakes I'm making academically will hurt my future plans to go to medical school.
14. _____ . . . I worked very hard and learned a lot about myself and other people.
15. _____ . . . deal with any more problems.
16. _____ . . . are a challenge for me and they excite me.
17. _____ . . . I was a happy child.
18. _____ . . . have been pretty good, until lately.
19. _____ . . . often call me uptight which makes me more uptight.
20. _____ . . . from feeling like I put out a lot of energy for others and don't get it back.
21. _____ . . . an organic chemistry test even though I studied really hard.
22. _____ . . . has always been something I love to do.
23. _____ . . . thinks too much sometimes.
24. _____ . . . holds promise and yet I feel as though I need to crack down more now in preparation for it.
25. _____ . . . a vacation and a friend who will give me time.
26. _____ . . . to me is finding someone you can love forever.
27. _____ . . . in a comfortable or interesting conversation.
28. _____ . . . I wish I wasn't so sensitive about things.
29. _____ . . . [Blank]
30. _____ . . . having to deal with gossip and other such problems.
31. _____ . . . has opened my eyes to new and different ideas.
32. _____ . . . [Blank]

Table 6–1 *Continued*

33. _____ . . . with my goal is that I have been disappointing myself lately.
34. _____ . . . I could remember things quickly and retain them.
35. _____ . . . and I are a lot alike and he is so understanding and strong.
36. _____ . . . [Blank]
37. _____ . . . [Blank]
38. _____ . . . is such a release.
39. _____ . . . that I won't get into medical school.
40. _____ . . . are really bitchy.

structuring initial interviews with the patient. They note that "it was not an objective to construct a measure that would describe the 'whole personality' nor necessarily to expose the 'deep layers' of personality or the 'fundamental structure' " (p. 6). Nonetheless, the sentence stems of the ISB are among the least structured, and the material obtained by them can be interpreted much the same as that obtained from other projective measures.

Validity

Murstein (1965) has stated that sentence completion tests are "probably the most valid of all the projective techniques reported in the literature" (p. 777). Of all the sentence completion tests, the ISB has the most consistent evidence supporting its validity for use in diagnosis and the assessment of adjustment (Goldberg, 1965; Watson, 1978). Rotter's and Willerman's (1947) original validity data were based on comparing the overall adjustment scores obtained from the objective scoring system with independent judgments of psychologists regarding patients' psychological fitness for return to duty. A second test was of psychologist ratings of degree of disturbance (no, mild, moderate, or severe) based on the overall ISB protocol as compared to the admission diagnosis given by independent judges. Both studies supported the measure's validity as used. In the original validation of the ISB for use with college students, Rotter, Rafferty, and Schachtitz (1949) compared the overall adjustment score with teacher and psychologist ratings of "adjusted" and "maladjusted" (in need of therapy) students and found good support for the adjustment score. Churchill and Crandall (1955) conducted one of the first independent tests of the measure's validity using college students and married adult women as subjects. They compared the students' ISB scores with requests for help at the campus counseling center. The married women's scores were compared to ratings of adjustment made by clinical psychologists after interviews. The validity of the measure was substantiated in both of these comparisons. In a different area, Getter and Weiss (1968) found the ISB total adjustment score to be a good predictor of frequency of visits to a university health service for somatic complaints. Finally, noting the length of time since its original publication and concomitant changes in U.S. society, Lah (in press) recently conducted two validity studies of the ISB. One compared the ISB scores of a nonselect group of university students with the scores of a sample drawn from students who had visited the university's student mental health service; a significant difference in the predicted direction was found. The second study compared ISB total scores with adjustment scores from a sociometric measure (where students who knew one another fairly well rated members of their respective groups on various dimensions of adjustment) and obtained significant results reaffirming the measure's validity.

Use and Administration

The ISB is widely used in clinical, research, and industrial settings. The measure's versatility allows it to be used in several different ways depending on one's purpose. First, using the objective scoring system to arrive at an overall adjustment score, one can use the measure as a screening device to determine, for example, of new incoming college students which ones may be in need of counseling, of visitors to a health service which ones may have psychological factors associated with their medical complaints, or of clients on a mental health clinic waiting list which ones are most urgently in need of help. A second use is as a clinical instrument to obtain specific information about a patient. For example, the ISB is often used as part of the intake paperwork completed at many clinics or hospitals, where its purpose is to give the clinician a sense of the person and his or her concerns before meeting for the first time. The ISB can be used alone or as part of a battery of psychological tests to gather specific information about the subject's thoughts, feelings, and attitudes, or, in its capacity as a projective test, to be interpreted to obtain better insight into the person. The measure also can be used to assess pre- to posttreatment change, using either the objective scoring system (especially in group comparisons) or clinical interpretations of subjects' responses.

A third major use of the ISB is in research. One of the strengths of the ISB is its scoring system, which yields a numerical score indicating an overall level of adjustment. Thus, in any research where level of adjustment is an important variable, the ISB is an excellent instrument for several reasons:

1. Because it provides a single overall numerical score, statistical analyses are facilitated.

2. The measure is more sensitive in providing a distribution of scores within a more "normal" range, in contrast to many measures of adjustment (e.g., the MMPI) which are more useful in distinguishing levels of more severe pathology.

3. Because the scoring procedures consider positive ("adjusted") responses as well as negative ("maladjusted") ones, the ISB can be used to select "well-adjusted" groups for some research purposes, whereas with most measures of adjustment, "adjustment" is indicated (inferred) by the absence of indicators of maladjustment.

Another research use of the ISB is that because it provides free responses to the sentence stems, this material can be examined and analyzed in a variety of ways for special purposes. For example, special scoring systems for the ISB have been developed to assess expectancies (Lewinsohn & Nichols, 1964); anxiety (Neuringer & Orwick, 1968), dependency (Fitzgerald, 1958); and anxiety, dependency, and hostility (Renner, Maher, & Campbell, 1962).

Administration of the ISB is very easy. The measure can be administered individually or in groups and needs few or no instructions, as the measure is fairly self-explanatory. The ISB is available in three forms: Adult, College, and High School (Rotter, 1950a, 1950b, 1950c). These three forms are identical except for the wording of a few stems, which are changed to make them appropriate for the different populations of interest (e.g., the stem "In school" on the Adult form reads "In high school" and "In the lower grades" on the College and High School forms, respectively). The 40 items of the ISB are printed on the front and back of a single 8½-by-11-inch page. The instructions for the ISB read: "Complete these sentences to express *your real feelings*. Try to do every one. Be sure to make a complete sentence" (Rotter & Rafferty, 1950, p. 7; emphasis in original). Occasionally individuals will ask what they should put down or if they must complete every item. It usually suffices simply to state that there are no right or wrong answers, that they should simply respond however they feel, and that they should try to complete as many of the items as they can. Generally subjects complete the ISB in 20 to 25 minutes, with the range of completion times varying from 10 to 40 minutes.

Scoring

In the objective scoring system, subjects' responses are scored for the presence or absence and the degree of conflict. Completions are scored on a seven-point scale from 0 (most positive) to 6 (most conflict), with 3 being scored as a neutral response, which does not clearly fall into either the positive or the conflict category. Positive responses are those that express a healthy or hopeful frame of mind, such as positive attitudes, optimism, warm acceptance, and good-natured humor. Conflict responses are those that express an unhealthy or maladjusted frame of mind, such as hostility, pessimism, mention of specific problems or symptoms, and negative attitudes. Neutral responses are those that are simple descriptions, common sayings or catch phrases, or simply lacking in personal reference. For example, in response to the stem "People," completions such as "are wonderful and fun to be with," "are different," and "don't like me and I don't like them" clearly reflect different frames of mind. Although the differences are not always so clear, the vast majority of responses can be scored fairly easily. Items that are not completed or are only partially completed and do not provide a sufficiently complete thought are not scored. Rotter and Rafferty (1950) provide a set of general criteria for scoring responses and discuss scoring difficulties such as statements with qualifications, unusually lengthy responses, partial completions, and so forth. The bulk of the scoring manual consists of numerous examples provided for each scoring level for each item; scoring examples for females and males are provided in separate sections. The reader is referred to the scoring manual for a more detailed presentation of the general criteria and specific scoring examples.

After all the items have been scored, the individual item scores are added together to obtain a total score, which provides an overall index of adjustment. If any items were left blank or not scored, the total score is prorated so that it is comparable to those protocols with a full 40 responses. In theory, scores could range from 0 to 240, but in practice total scores usually fall in the range of 85 to 200. Rotter and Rafferty (1950) provide norms for 85 female and 214 male college students. Lah and Rotter (1981) examined student mean scores for the years 1965, 1970, and 1977 and found that they were significantly higher than the 1950 norms. They provided the means for their 150 female and 150 male subjects. Most recently, Lah (in press) found evidence that student ISB scores may be declining and suggests that new norms are needed. Norms for adults or high school students are not available. In determining whether subjects were adjusted or maladjusted, Rotter and Rafferty found a score of 135 to be most efficient. Lah (in press) also provided updated and expanded information on scores one can use to dichotomize groups of subjects as "adjusted" or "maladjusted," depending on the group and one's purpose.

Although numerous scoring examples are provided for each item, scoring the completions does require some judgment on the part of the scorer, and the scoring procedures are probably best described as "semi-objective." Still, the reliability of the scoring procedures has consistently been found to be excellent. Rotter and Rafferty (1950) report interscorer reliabilities between .90 and .96. Lah and Rotter (1981) report interscorer reliabilities between .88 and .93, and reliabilities ranging from .90 to .95 for different scorers rescoring protocols after many years. These reliabilities are typical of those reported in the literature. I have found it relatively easy to obtain high correlations between scorers, although it is sometimes more difficult to prevent high or low scorer bias. For example, if scorer X obtained scores for five protocols of 98, 107, 120, 134, and 147, and scorer Y obtained scores of 104, 112, 126, 141, and 153, the correlation of their sets of scores would be very high (probably over .90), but there is a difference in the average of their scores of 6.0 points. When tested statistically, this difference would probably be significant. It is this type of difference that is more often problematic in assessing scoring reliabilities. To prevent this, scorers must try to follow closely the scoring examples in the manual.

Another potential problem that can contribute to high or low bias occurs if, when one is having difficulty scoring items (e.g., having difficulty deciding whether an item should be scored 4 or 5), one consistently chooses the higher (or the lower) score. Rather, on any later items on which one gets stuck, one should alternate, choosing the higher score once, on the next occasion the lower score, and so on. Finally, scoring several protocols at one sitting is helpful in getting scorers "in tune" with the general criteria and scoring examples. Because of this potential for high or low scorer bias, in research applications where interscorer reliabilities must be checked, performing paired (correlated) t-tests between scorers' mean scores is required in addition to calculating correlation coefficients.

Clinical Interpretation

For the purposes of psychodiagnostic assessment or when seeing someone in a counseling or therapeutic situation, the numerical score obtained from the scoring procedures described here will not be that useful. Rather, one would be interested in the content of the person's responses and the more qualitative inferences one could draw from the responses to obtain an overall picture of the person and his or her personality. For such clinical assessment, Rotter and Rafferty (1950) do not recommend any specific method of interpretation. They state that a clinician's use of the material obtained from the ISB will depend on her or his experience, level of training, and theoretical orientation. They state that the content of the completions can be interpreted from several viewpoints—for example, from a commonsense level or at a symbolic psychoanalytic level, in accordance with Murray's (1938) need-press personality theory or Rotter's social learning theory (Rotter, 1973, 1982), and so forth. Rotter and Rafferty note that the kind of material obtained by the ISB is similar to that obtained by the TAT and, therefore, can be interpreted by any of the methods used for TAT analysis. The scoring manual contains six illustrative cases with interpretations that are consistent with Rotter's (1946) method of TAT analysis (see also Bellak, 1986, who summarizes several TAT interpretation methods and describes his own method). Presented next is an eclectic approach for clinical interpretation of the ISB, which includes some of the more common elements mentioned by interpreters of sentence completions and TAT stories.

Generally, interpreters of sentence completions analyze the material at three different levels. The first level of analysis evaluates the *content* of the responses, that is, what the subject actually stated. Here one simply catalogues the thoughts expressed by the subject and the feelings and attitudes expressed about the specific topic or persons referred to in the completions of the sentence stems. Rotter groups responses according to the categories of *familial* (parents, siblings, spouse); *social* and *sexual* (people in general, opposite sex, social activities); and *general* (educational, vocational, religious, economic) attitudes, as well as for character traits. The procedures, described earlier, of Forer and Sacks for categorizing the content of responses are examples of other methods to facilitate analyzing the content of completions.

The second level of analysis consists of evaluating what are often called the *formal* aspects of the test protocol. This includes looking at the use of language in responses (spelling errors, grammar, word choice, repeated use of words, intensity of descriptors, odd language or neologisms); the length of responses; vagueness or specificity of responses, following of instructions (whether complete sentences were written, or whether completions were given that suggest the subject changed or misunderstood the stems); the handwriting; and the presence of erasures, crossed-out words, or omissions. For example, one obtains different information from the following observations: a subject's responses seem open and revealing except for several stems relating to people, which receive neutral, mundane responses; the subject has a college degree, but the use of language is awkward and contains spelling and grammatical errors; the responses tend to be of short or moderate length except for a few items on which the subject squeezes in several lines of writing; the person's completions are written in neat, tiny, precise, printed letters with no completion extending beyond the space allowed; the subject completes all the items except "Back home" and "My father."

The third level of analysis consists of drawing *inferences* from (making interpretations of) the material obtained from the foregoing analyses. This process involves taking the data from the content and formal analyses and integrating it, looking for relationships between these data and for relationships between the different item responses, in order to arrive at a description of the person and his or her major thoughts and concerns. Some of the factors considered in this process include: the frequency with which something is mentioned (the more often something is mentioned, or is conspicuously omitted, the more important it may be); how common or rare the responses are; patterns of language or word use in association with specific content; the emotions mentioned and the mood of the subject; the relationships between item responses; characteristic behaviors (traits) that are evident; and so forth. Often these final interpretations are subsumed under the categories of *content* and *structural* interpretations. Content interpretations are those that relate to the content of the subject's thoughts; what is on the person's mind; what goals, feelings, attitudes, worries, and so forth are expressed. Structural interpretations have to do with the characteristic patterns of behavior or traits of the individual that distinguish his or her personality, such as hostility, passivity, dependence, introversion, achievement orientation, and so forth.

The sequence of steps one would follow in interpreting a subject's ISB protocol on these three levels would go as follows. First, one would read through the entire protocol to get an overall impression of the person. Next, one would go back over each item and note the specific content mentioned and any relevant formal aspects of the response. Third, one would go over the response and one's previous notes again to begin to draw together these data, and to look for patterns and consistencies (or inconsistencies) in responses. Finally, one would review any patterns and inferences drawn in the previous step and go back to the original responses to check to see how each response fits or does not fit these inferences. This final step may involve going back and forth between the completions and one's interpretations several times. The goal is to arrive at an overall description of the person and his or her concerns. Certainly, these conclusions should be viewed as hypotheses about the individual and must be confirmed and reconciled with other sources of information (e.g., other test data, patient records, interviews, etc.).

Case Study

The following case presents an example of the clinical interpretation of an ISB protocol. The case concerns a twenty-one-year-old female student at a large state university who was a self-referral to the campus mental health service. As part of the usual intake procedures, she completed the *Incomplete Sentences Blank—College Form* along with other paperwork. A complete record of the subject's responses was presented in Table 6–1. When her responses were scored using the objective scoring procedures, her total score was 163, significantly higher than the norms for college students and comparable to the average score of other clinic samples reported in the literature. As mentioned earlier, however, in a therapeutic situation the information obtained from the interpretation of the subject's responses usually is more useful than the numerical adjustment score. The inferences that follow are presented as one interpretative example and certainly are neither exhaustive nor definitive.*

Some overall impressions one gets on first reading this person's responses are of a lot of stress and pressure in reaction to problems experienced with people and academic goals. Regarding some of the formal aspects of her protocol, the individual ("Maryam") appears fairly open and honest in her responses. Her completions are clearly stated and articulate, with no errors or oddities of language use. The responses are of moderate length; the two fairly lengthy responses, which required her to squeeze her completions into the space, refer to her future goals (13 and 24). She made a slight change in item 2 to make the stem plural, but otherwise completed all the items as presented except for five omitted completions (about which more later). The responses were well organized, were legibly written on the blank, and contained only a couple of minor erasures.

Regarding the content of Maryam's thoughts and feelings, her home and family are very positive sources of good times (2, 4); happy memories (17); relaxation (4); and caring, protection, and understanding (11 and 35, regarding her parents). Other people also are sources of positive experiences for her (2; 27, regarding when she feels best), but she also is experiencing considerable conflict with people (9, 10, 19, 20, 30). Gossip and talking behind one's back seem to be a particular source of this conflict. Although her feelings toward males (7, 35) and about being married (26) are positive, female peers are viewed negatively (40) and may be the source of much of the gossip, interpersonal conflict, and lack of support she experiences in response to her efforts (20; 25, regarding her needs). However, she also blames herself in part for some of this conflict (28). In addition to the interpersonal conflict, Maryam is experiencing considerable conflict regarding her work. She works hard (14, regarding high school; 21, regarding failures) and enjoys that (8), has fairly clear goals (13, 39), and sees the future as promising (24). However, she places a lot of importance on these goals and is very concerned about her ability to meet them (13 and 39, regarding her fears). Further, she blames herself for this difficulty (5; 13; 33, regarding problems; 34, regarding her wishes). Finally, it is interesting that the five items she did not complete (1, 29, 32, 36, 37) required her to reflect on herself globally and on her likes, pains, and secret thoughts. One wonders about her ability to tune in to her own needs and feelings and/or her comfort in doing so, and her willingness to acknowledge her needs to herself or others.

*Note that because of copyright restrictions, only 10 of the ISB item stems could be reproduced in Table 6–1. Despite this limitation, the reader should still be able to get a sense of how the subject's responses are analyzed in the following discussion. At times the general nature of an item stem is indicated to help the reader understand the context of the subject's response.

The effects of Maryam's academic and interpersonal problems are several. She feels confused about all these problems (3) and feels she can not deal with any more (15). She is stressed, sometimes thinking too much (23); her nerves are not good (18); she needs a release (38, regarding dance); to take a vacation (25, regarding her needs); or to retreat home where she can relax and be cared for, protected, and understood (4, 11, 35). At the same time, however, she has been letting herself down (33) and feels the need to crack down on herself even more (24). Not surprisingly, she is worn out (12) and exhausted (6). In addition to the stress and pressure, one senses her anger and disappointment with herself and others, and would expect some depression.

If one integrates all these responses, Maryam appears as an open, honest, hard-working young woman who bases much of her self-esteem on her academic accomplishments and on others' caring for her. The strongest and most consistent impression one gets is the importance of future academic goals and how hard she drives herself to achieve them. In fact, there is a self-critical and unforgiving quality in her pursuit, and her academic goals seem to take precedence over her personal life (5). Maryam's hard-working approach is also applied in relationships with people, where she works hard to give a lot to others. One would suspect that she is often disappointed by others, as she currently is, because she would work harder at being a good friend than others might and because she is quite sensitive to others' responses to her (19, 28). Such situations would leave her hurt and disappointed, doubting and criticizing herself, and depressed. Maryam would work hard to satisfy others and make things work (and to avoid conflict and negative emotions), even at the expense of her own needs. For someone who works so hard to achieve goals (and control her life), not achieving her goals, and the concomitant negative emotions, would be very distressing and would prompt her only to strive that much harder to make things work. Her extreme striving to achieve goals and a sense of accomplishment indicates an overcompensation for lack of self-worth or self-esteem.

In considering the source(s) of these characteristics, we have her father, whom she resembles (35), as a model for this approach to life. Other hypotheses are possible about her father's style and its effects on Maryam. Was he also so busy striving to achieve that Maryam experienced insufficient time with or attention from him, and adopted his style out of identification with him or as a way to earn/attract his attention? Was he most responsive to or reinforcing of her active attempts to achieve? Was an emphasis on work and achievement an explicit ethic taught her? One also might wonder if Maryam's family was so warm and caring that she did not develop sufficient ability to be self-caring and self-nurturing and was left unprepared for some of the realities of the outside world (9, 10, 20). Many other hypotheses are possible as well.

In therapy, one would expect Maryam to be open, genuine, cooperative, and hard-working. She would welcome an accepting, supportive, understanding response to her distress. Yet, she would also want a goal-oriented approach to working on her problems. She would want to feel better quickly so that she could get back to her work.

These interpretations fit closely with Maryam's personality and her reason for seeking help. She sought help because she was depressed, crying often, and "losing control of her problems." In addition to other problems in previous months and a physical illness in previous weeks, a recent incident with a boyfriend had caused some talk and rumors among friends. She was very hurt by her boyfriend's subsequent response to her and by the gossip among friends. As all these problems accumulated, Maryam's attempts to get help and support from her two closest female friends left her frustrated, as she felt they were too involved in their own lives to give her much time or attention, something that was even more upsetting because she felt she had given them so much of herself in the past. Maryam was a friendly, hard-working young woman who typically put others' needs ahead of her own and had difficulty acknowledging and expressing her feelings. Most of her disappointment and anger was directed at herself. She stopped coming for help after two visits, when she felt she could "handle things now" and was feeling better.

Assets and Liabilities

The assets of the Incomplete Sentences Blank (and of many other sentence completion tests) are several:

1. The method allows the subject freedom of response and thus can provide more information about the subject than can many objective tests.

2. The measure is easily administered individually or in groups, and administration requires no special training.

3. Administration time is fairly short compared to that for most psychological tests.

4. There is some disguise of purpose in that it is not readily apparent exactly how responses to the stems are scored.

5. The ISB can be scored by a semiobjective scoring procedure that provides a numerical index of overall level of adjustment. In addition, the measure can be interpreted as are other projective methods.

6. Because of the multiple ways the responses may be scored or analyzed, the ISB can be used in many applications for both clinical and research purposes.

7. Sentence completion tests, and the ISB in particular, have the best research evidence in support of their validity as projective methods.

8. The sentence completion method, in general, is a versatile method allowing the development of items or measures for many special assessment needs.

The liabilities of the ISB (and of most other sentence completion tests) are associated with some of its assets:

1. Because the measure allows free responses, scoring is more time-consuming (about fifteen minutes per protocol) compared to objective tests (although the measures are easier to score than are other projectives).
2. Because the measure does provide more structure than other projective methods, subjects can more easily control their responses to withhold information they do not want to reveal. Very uncooperative subjects can provide little useful information.
3. The measure is not as useful with subjects with lower levels of literacy or intelligence.

CONCLUSION

In this chapter an introduction to sentence completion tests has been provided. The method has a long history in psychology, dating back to the development of the very first psychological tests. A wide variety of measures are in current use for a wide range of purposes. In terms of psychological assessment, the most common sentence completion tests are those used for personality assessment. Of these latter measures, standard tests used for the assessment of overall personality and adjustment are among the most frequently used psychological tests, in particular Rotter's Incomplete Sentences Blank. These measures have many advantages and fill a unique place in the psychological assessment armamentarium, providing some different information than can be obtained from objective tests, but without the disadvantages of time consumption and scoring difficulty of clinical interviews or more traditional projective methods. The reader is encouraged to explore this useful and versatile assessment method by referring to some of the works in the literature cited throughout the chapter.

REFERENCES

Bellak, L. (1986). *The Thematic Apperception Test, the Children's Apperception Test and the Senior Apperception Technique in clinical use.* New York: Grune & Stratton.

Binet, A., & Simon, T. (1905). Méthodes nouvelles pour le diagnostic du niveau intellectuel des anormaux. [A new method for the diagnosis of levels of intellectual abnormality.] *L'Année Psychologique, 11*, 191–244.

Buros, O. K. (Ed.). (1974). *Tests in print: II. An index to tests, test reviews, and the literature on specific tests.* Highland Park, NJ: Gryphon Press.

Cameron, N. (1938a). Reasoning, repression and communication in schizophrenia. *Psychological Monographs, 50*(1, Whole No. 221).

Cameron, N. (1938b). A study of thinking in senile deterioration and schizophrenic disorganization. *American Journal of Psychology, 51*, 650–664.

Campbell, D. T. (1957). A typology of tests, projective and otherwise. *Journal of Consulting Psychology, 21*, 207–210.

Churchill, R., & Crandall, V. J. (1955). The reliability and validity of the Rotter Incomplete Sentences Tests. *Journal of Consulting Psychology, 19*, 345–350.

Crowne, D. P., & Marlowe, D. (1964). *The approval motive: Studies in evaluative dependence.* New York: John Wiley & Sons.

Ebbinghaus, H. (1897). Über eine neue methode zur prüfung geistiger fähigkeiten und ihre anwendung bei schulkindern. [On a new method for the testing of intellectual capacity and its application by school children.] *Zeitschrift fur Psychologie und Physiologie der Sinnesorgane, 13*, 401–457.

Fitzgerald, B. J. (1958). Some relationships among projective test, interview, and sociometric measures of dependent behavior. *Journal of Abnormal and Social Psychology, 56*, 199–203.

Forer, B. R. (1950). A structured sentence completion test. *Journal of Projective Techniques, 14*, 15–30.

Getter, H., & Weiss, S. D. (1968). The Rotter Incomplete Sentences Blank adjustment score as an indicator of somatic complaint frequency. *Journal of Projective Techniques, 32*, 266.

Goldberg, P. A. (1965). A review of sentence completion methods in personality assessment. *Journal of Projective Techniques and Personality Assessment, 29*, 12–45.

Goldberg, P. A. (1968). The current status of sentence completion methods. *Journal of Projective Techniques and Personality Assessment, 32*, 215–221.

Hiler, E. W. (1959). The sentence completion test as a predictor of continuation in psychotherapy. *Journal of Consulting Psychology, 23*, 544–549.

Holsopple, J. Q., & Miale, F. R. (1954). *Sentence completion: A projective method for the study of personality.* Springfield, IL: Thomas.

Holzberg, J. (1945). Some uses of projective techniques in military clinical psychology. *Bulletin of the Menninger Clinic, 9*, 89–93.

Holzberg, J., Teicher, A., & Taylor, J. L. (1947). Contributions of clinical psychology to military neuropsychiatry in an Army psychiatric hospital. *Journal of Clinical Psychology, 3*, 84–95.

Hutt, M. L. (1945). The use of projective methods of personality measurement in Army medical installations. *Journal of Clinical Psychology, 1*, 134–140.

Irwin, F. S. (1967). Sentence-completion responses and scholastic success or failure. *Journal of Counseling Psychology, 14*, 269–271.

Jung, C. G. (1916). The association method. *American Journal of Psychology, 21*, 219–269.

Kelly, E. L., & Fiske, D. W. (1950). The prediction of success in VA training programs in clinical psychology. *American Psychologist, 5*, 395–406.

Lah, M. I. (In press). New validity, normative, and scoring data for the Rotter Incomplete Sentences Blank. *Journal of Personality Assessment.*

Lah, M. I., & Rotter, J. B. (1981). Changing college student norms on the Rotter Incomplete Sentences Blank. *Journal of Consulting and Clinical Psychology, 49,* 985.

Lewinsohn, P. M., & Nichols, R. C. (1964). The evaluation of change in psychiatric patients during and after hospitalization. *Journal of Clinical Psychology, 20,* 272–279.

Lindzey, G. (1959). On the classification of projective techniques. *Psychological Bulletin, 56,* 158–168.

Loevinger, J., & Wessler, R. (1970). *Measuring ego development: I. Construction and use of a sentence completion test.* San Francisco: Jossey-Bass.

Lorge, I., & Thorndike, E. L. (1941). The value of the responses in a completion test as indications of personal traits. *Journal of Applied Psychology, 25,* 191–199.

Lubin, B., Larsen, R. M., & Matarazzo, J. D. (1984). Patterns of psychological test usage in the United States: 1935–1982. *American Psychologist, 39,* 451–454.

Lubin, B., Wallis, R. R., & Paine, C. (1971). Patterns of psychological test usage in the United States: 1935–1969. *Professional Psychology, 2,* 70–74.

Meltzoff, J. (1951). The effect of mental set and item structure upon response to a projective test. *Journal of Abnormal and Social Psychology, 46,* 177–189.

Mitchell, J. V., Jr. (Ed.). (1983). *Tests in print: III. An index to tests, test reviews, and the literature on specific tests.* Lincoln, NE: Buros Institute of Mental Measurement.

Mosher, D. L. (1961). The development and validation of a sentence completion measure of guilt. (Doctoral dissertation, Ohio State University, 1961). *Dissertation Abstracts, 22,* 2468.

Murray, H. A. (1938). *Explorations in personality: A clinical and experimental study of 50 men of college age.* New York: Oxford University Press.

Murray, H. A., & MacKinnon, D. W. (1946). Assessment of OSS personnel. *Journal of Consulting Psychology, 10,* 76–80.

Murstein, B. I. (Ed.). (1965). *Handbook of projective techniques.* New York: Basic Books.

Neuringer, C., & Orwick, P. O. (1968). The measurement of anxiety on the sentence completion test. *Journal of General Psychology, 78,* 197–207.

Payne, A. F. (1930). Experiment in human engineering at the College of the City of New York. *School and Society, 32,* 292–294.

Piotrowski, C., & Keller, J. W. (1984). Psychodiagnostic testing in APA-approved clinical psychology programs. *Professional Psychology, 15,* 450–456.

Renner, K. E., Maher, B. A., & Campbell, D. T. (1962). The validity of a method for scoring sentence-completion responses for anxiety, dependency and hostility. *Journal of Applied Psychology, 46,* 285–290.

Rohde, A. R. (1946). Explorations in personality by the sentence completion method. *Journal of Applied Psychology, 30,* 169–181.

Rohde, A. R. (1948). A note regarding the use of the sentence completion test in military installations since the beginning of World War II. *Journal of Consulting Psychology, 12,* 190–193.

Rohde, A. R. (1957). *The sentence completion method.* New York: Ronald Press.

Rotter, J. B. (1946). Thematic apperception tests: Suggestions for administration and interpretation. *Journal of Personality, 15,* 70–92.

Rotter, J. B. (1950a). *Incomplete Sentences Blank—Adult Form* [Test]. New York: Psychological Corporation.

Rotter, J. B. (1950b). *Incomplete Sentences Blank—College Form* [Test]. New York: Psychological Corporation.

Rotter, J. B. (1950c). *Incomplete Sentences Blank—High School Form* [Test]. New York: Psychological Corporation.

Rotter, J. B. (1951). Word association and sentence completion methods. In H. H. Anderson & G. L. Anderson (Eds.), *An introduction to projective techniques and other devices for understanding the dynamics of human behavior* (pp. 279–311). Englewood Cliffs, NJ: Prentice-Hall.

Rotter, J. B. (1973). *Social learning and clinical psychology.* New York: Johnson Reprint Corporation. (Reprinted from *Social learning and clinical psychology,* 1954, Englewood Cliffs, NJ: Prentice-Hall.)

Rotter, J. B. (1982). *The development and applications of social learning theory: Selected papers.* New York: Praeger.

Rotter, J. B., & Rafferty, J. E. (1950). *Manual for the Rotter Incomplete Sentences Blank: College form.* New York: Psychological Corporation.

Rotter, J. B., Rafferty, J. E., & Schachtitz, E. (1949). Validation of the Rotter Incomplete Sentences Blank for college screening. *Journal of Consulting Psychology, 13,* 348–356.

Rotter, J. B., & Willerman, B. (1947). The Incomplete Sentences Test as a method of studying personality. *Journal of Consulting Psychology, 11,* 43–48.

Sacks, J. M. (1949). The relative effect upon projective responses of stimuli referring to the subject and of stimuli referring to other persons. *Journal of Consulting Psychology, 13,* 12–21.

Sacks, J. M., & Levy, S. (1950). The sentence completion test. In L. E. Abt & L. Bellak (Eds.), *Projective psychology: Clinical approaches to the total personality* (pp. 357–402). New York: Knopf.

Sanford, R. N., Adkins, M. M., Miller, R. B., & Cobb, E. A. (1943). Physique, personality and scholarship: A cooperative study of school children. *Monographs of the Society for Research in Child Development, 8*(1, Serial No. 34). Washington, DC: National Research Council.

Shor, J. M. (1946). Report on a verbal projective technique. *Journal of Clinical Psychology, 2,* 279–282.

Stein, M. I. (1947). The use of a sentence completion test for the diagnosis of personality. *Journal of Clinical Psychology, 3,* 45–56.

Stein, M. I. (1949). The record and a sentence completion test. *Journal of Consulting Psychology, 13,* 448–449.

Stotsky, B. A., & Weinberg, H. (1956). The prediction of the psychiatric patient's work adjustment. *Journal of Counseling Psychology, 3,* 3–7.

Sundberg, N. D. (1961). The practice of psychological testing in clinical services in the United States. *American Psychologist, 16,* 79–83.

Symonds, P. M. (1947). The sentence completion test as a projective technique. *Journal of Abnormal and Social Psychology, 42,* 320–329.

Tendler, A. D. (1930). A preliminary report on a test for emotional insight. *Journal of Applied Psychology, 14,* 122–136.

Terman, L. M. (1916). *The measurement of intelligence: An explanation of and a complete guide for the use of the Stanford revision and extension of the Binet-Simon Intelligence Scale.* Boston: Houghton Mifflin.

Terman, L. M., & Merrill, M. A. (1973). *Stanford-Binet Intelligence Scale: Manual for the third revision Form L-M.* Boston: Houghton Mifflin.

Trabue, M. R. (1916). Completion-test language scales. *Contributions to Education,* No. 77. New York: Columbia University, Teachers College.

Watson, R. I., Jr. (1978). The sentence completion method. In B. Wolman (Ed.), *Clinical diagnosis of mental disorders: A handbook* (pp. 255–279). New York: Plenum Press.

Wells, F. J. (1954). [Foreward]. In J. Q. Holsopple & F. R. Miale, *Sentence completion: A projective method for the study of personality* (pp. vii—ix). Springfield, IL: Thomas.

Wertheimer, M. (1979). *A brief history of psychology* (rev. ed.). New York: Holt, Rinehart & Winston.

Wischner, G. J., Rotter, J. B., & Gillman, R. D. (1947). Projective techniques. In S. W. Bijou (Ed.), *The psychology program in AAF convalescent hospitals* (pp. 144–157). Army Air Forces Aviation Psychology Program Research Reports, No. 15. Washington, DC: U. S. Government Printing Office.

7

The Luria-Nebraska Neuropsychological Battery

Charles J. Golden

The Luria-Nebraska Neuropsychological Battery (LNNB) was formally introduced in 1978. Since that time, it has become one of the most widely used and discussed tests within neuropsychology, with both defenders extolling its virtues and detractors criticizing its usefulness. This chapter is an attempt to review the administration, interpretation, and research issues that affect the LNNB.

The LNNB was designed to cover, generally, the major areas of dysfunction that are likely to be seen in a case of brain damage. Covering a broad range of areas, it does not purport to present a detailed statistical analysis of each area but, rather, offers a sampling of the major skills whose performance is reflected in both quantitative and qualitative indices. The major scales of the test include Motor, Rhythm, Tactile, Visual, Receptive, Expressive, Writing, Reading, Arithmetic, Memory, and Intelligence. The test overall includes 269 items, chosen from the work of Luria (e.g., 1966) and formally standardized.

ADMINISTRATION

Administration and scoring procedures of the LNNB are both simple and complex. On the one hand, the procedures are simple because each item measures only a limited area and is accompanied by detailed instructions. Scoring is generally highly objective and easy to use. On the other hand, the battery is complicated by the large number of items. Finally, much of the richness of the qualitative observations comes from watching the client carefully, a task that can be quite difficult. Experience has shown that it takes a minimum of ten administrations before an individual becomes proficient. The test is also somewhat complicated by the flexibility allowed the examiner. This flexibility ensures that items end up measuring what they purport to measure.

General Guidelines for Administration

It is usually recommended that the administration of the LNNB be preceded by information about the client. See Luria (1980) for a discussion of the "preliminary conversation."

Test Materials

The materials necessary for the two forms of the test battery are similar but not identical. Both forms require a small portable tape recorder capable of administering the items on the C2 (Rhythm) scale. Both forms also use the Patient Response Booklet for items that require the client to provide written responses, such as drawings of figures or writing samples.

The set of test materials contains all the stimulus cards needed for the test and a tape cassette used in administering the C2 scale. A number of common household objects are also required for the administration and must be supplied by the user.

Test Setting

The battery can be administered at bedside with the client in a reclining position. It is preferable, however, for the client to be seated upright, with a hard surface available for presenting materials and for written responses. The examiner should be seated opposite the client and should present visual materials in the midline of the client's visual field.

The battery may be given in a series of sessions, and the examiner may vary the length of these sessions as necessary depending on the ability of the client to concentrate and the buildup of fatigue in the individual. By careful observation of the ways in which the client is able to handle the testing situation, a great deal of important qualitative information can be gained, some of which is scored within the qualitative scoring system of the LNNB.

Repeating or Paraphrasing Items

Item instructions may be repeated or paraphrased as necessary to allow the client to understand them. Instructions generally are not repeated more than twice unless the examiner judges that this will improve client performance. When instructions are paraphrased, changes should reflect such factors as the client's cultural language background, as well as any impairment in understanding that may have been caused by brain damage. On most items, item instructions can be written or communicated in a system other than oral speech. Where appropriate, the examiner may demonstrate what is requested of the client in order to ensure that the client understands the task; the demonstrations should not use the items actually employed in the battery. For all scales except C2 (Rhythm), C5 (Receptive Speech), and C10 (Memory), the item stimuli may also be repeated as necessary, unless prohibited by specific item directions. It is permissible to readminister any item in the battery, with the exception of specific C5 (Receptive Speech) and C10 (Memory) items. In these cases, the entire item, not just subsections, is to be readministered.

Encouraging, Questioning, and Instructing the Client

It is the goal of the LNNB to get the maximum possible performance out of the client. Thus, before initiating testing, the client should be informed that he or she will be asked to do a number of things and answer a number of questions, some of which may be very simple and seem silly, while others may be very difficult. Despite the fact that some items may seem silly and meaningless to the client, it is important that the client try to do his or her best, responding to the task as quickly as possible while at the same time making sure that accuracy and quality are maintained. This may take constant encouragement on the part of the examiner, who should exhort the client as necessary. In those cases in which the client does not seem to be exerting full effort, the examiner should discover the reason for this and aid the client in whatever way is necessary to allow the client to perform maximally. It is very important that the examiner be familiar and skilled in dealing with clients from the diagnostic group being seen. It is especially important that the examiner be skilled in working with clients who either have emotional problems or suffer from acute neurological disorders, as these groups tend to be the most difficult to test in an adult population.

When the client gives an answer that is inadequate but not wrong to any item on the battery, the examiner may further query the client (e.g., "Can you tell me more?") until the examiner is clear that the client's intent was clearly right or wrong. Leading questions are not permissible for the objective scoring. In addition, for the qualitative scoring, the examiner may add questions when necessary to clarify the nature of any errors or unusual behavior on the part of the client.

SCORING

Quantitative Scoring

During administration, the examiner scores each item either 0, 1, or 2 on the basis of the criteria listed for each item. A score of 0 indicates normal performance, a score of 1 indicates weak evidence of brain disorder, and a score of 2 indicates strong evidence of brain disorder.

The most general scoring dimension used on the battery is the total number of errors within an item or subitem. To ensure consistency with this general approach, in which a higher raw score indicates a poorer response, items in which there is qualitative judgment are scored in a similar manner: higher scores mean poorer performance. This general technique is carried over to both the scale scores and the derived T-scores, as will be discussed.

Determining Scale Scores

After the individual responses to each item have been converted into item scores (0, 1, or 2), the item scores are summed within each scale to yield summary scale indices. For all scales, one simply adds together the scores of the items that make up each scale. With the addition of the summary, localization, and factor scales, items may each be on multiple scales. Raw scores are converted into T-scores, with a mean of 50 and a standard deviation of 10, using the appropriate tables in the manual. As with such tests as the MMPI, high scores reflect more pathology.

Qualitative Scoring

Those who have had experience with the LNNB items, as well as those aware of Luria's basic theory, notice early in the use of the battery that all items can be missed for multiple reasons. A score of an error on the LNNB (as with all quantitative tests) may arise from a wide range of difficulties: the client may fail to understand the instructions, may perseverate, may ignore the left side of the stimulus, and so forth. In addition, clients may get an answer correct and still show signs of brain dysfunction. For instance, the client may give the correct answer to an intelligence item but may show signs of dysarthria in giving the answer.

Similarly, a client may understand instructions for motor items only after several repetitions and demonstrations.

In the earlier versions of the LNNB, users were admonished to keep track of such material and related observations and to use this information in interpretation, as is generally done with many standardized tests. This procedure, however, made this valuable information unavailable both for quantitative description of the basic deficit and for scientific study. Therefore, in addition to the quantitative scoring system, a qualitative scoring system is now available. The qualitative scoring categories catalog the client's "test behavior." Comparisons may then be made between the frequency of the client's qualitative signs in each category and the frequency of these qualitative signs for normals and various groups of brain-damaged clients. The purpose of the qualitative scoring is to provide a systematic method of reporting the major categories of behavior not regularly scored on the battery, enabling the examiner to better describe the nature of a client's deficits and to make users more sensitive to these categories of behavior. In preliminary use, the scores have been useful in further heightening the ability of the battery to specify the nature of a client's disorder, as well as to classify cases correctly as brain dysfunctional that may have been previously missed.

In the actual scoring of qualitative errors, there is, of course, a nearly infinite range of possibilities aimed at gaining a better understanding of the "why" behind a given error on the battery. It is the ability to make these qualitative observations with some reliability that makes the Luria-type items used on the LNNB especially useful. Integrating the qualitative and quantitative information generates a more definitive and clearer understanding of the client.

The qualitative scoring also allows for the analysis of behavior not directly associated with performance on any single item. For example, a client who, between items, continues to repeat stimuli from the previous items may be scored for Perseveration. Using only the quantitative scoring system, there would be no way to indicate that the client was engaging in this type of behavior.

There are 66 basic qualitative categories that may be scored on the LNNB. These categories have been divided into eleven conceptual groupings or areas: Motor, Sustained Performance, Self-Monitoring, Self-Cuing, Visual-Spatial, Peripheral Impairment, Expressive Language, Dysarthria, Receptive Language, Speed, and Option Card.

INTERPRETATION

In interpreting the LNNB, little confidence is placed in formal interpretations of elevations on individual scales alone. The test is intended to be given as a whole, with pattern analysis, item analysis, and qualitative analysis as the major interpretive steps.

Levels of Interpretation

When interpreting the LNNB or other similar batteries, it is important to be aware that the many levels on which the battery can be interpreted depend on the user's needs, skill, and knowledge. On the first level, concerned primarily with ascertaining whether significant brain injury exists in a given client, the LNNB is a screening procedure to differentiate neuropsychological from other possible disorders. The second level of interpretation involves simple description of what the client can and cannot do, without drawing any conclusions or reaching any integrative statements.

The third level of interpretation takes the second level to the next logical step: identification of the probable underlying causes of the client's overall behavior. Finally, the fourth level of interpretation involves the integration of all the findings and conclusions into a description of how the individual's brain is functioning. In most cases, this is a difficult task since the result of brain damage is determined by a variety of factors.

Identifying Brain Damage

Use of the Critical Level   The first step in identifying a profile that is statistically abnormal and likely to indicate brain damage is based on establishing a valid critical level for the client. The critical level represents the highest LNNB score that can be considered normal for the battery. With the LNNB, unlike some other tests, this cutoff level is variable and is adjusted for both age and education, in an attempt to recognize that individuals with different backgrounds have different premorbid levels of functioning.

The next step is identifying deviant scores. Once the critical level has been established accurately, determining the likelihood of brain damage is relatively simple. The number of scales on the battery that exceed the critical level is counted, yielding the number of abnormal scores. The scores that are considered at this point are the basic clinical scales (C1 through C12) and the S1 (Pathognomonic) scale. In general, three or more scores above the critical level are thought to be indicative of brain damage, whereas no elevated scales, or only one, suggests the absence of brain damage. Two elevated scales are considered borderline. If the critical level has been chosen correctly, the accuracy of this decision is about 85 to 90 percent. The accuracy increases with the accuracy of the critical level.

As noted before, use of these procedures will misidentify 10 to 15 percent of brain-damaged individuals as normal. Other techniques may be used to identify some of these clients. These are detailed in the test manual.

Interpreting Scale and Item Patterns: Clinical Scales

C1 (Motor Functions)   The C1 scale is one of the most complex scales on the LNNB. A wide variety of motor skills reflects both right- and left-hemisphere performance. The first four items involve simple movements of the hands. These items are especially sensitive to disorders in or near the posterior frontal lobe.

Items 5 through 8 are fairly simple motor movements that are performed when the patient is blindfolded. Correct responses require kinesthetic and tactile feedback. Consequently, this section of the scale tends to be more sensitive to injuries in the parietal lobes. Items 9 through 20 are again simple motor movements, but with spatial organization required. These items are sensitive to both frontal lobe disorders and disorders of the right hemisphere, especially those that interfere greatly with optic spatial organization. Items 21 through 27 require complex movements of various kinds. These items are very sensitive to injury to both the motor area of the frontal lobes and the prefrontal areas that are concerned with the organization of behavior. They can also be affected strongly by lesions of the premotor area.

Items 28 through 35 concern oral movements organized in much the same way as the previous sections on hand movements. Items 28 and 29 reflect simple oral movements; items 30 and 31 involve oral movements on the basis of kinesthetic feedback; and items 32 and 33 measure complex oral skills. These are sensitive to disruption of the frontal lobe areas and the parietal areas in the same way as movements of the hand. However, they are also sensitive to disorders of some of the cranial nerves and may therefore reflect problems in the brain stem or problems of generalized cerebral dysfunction. Items 34 and 35 show the client's ability to perform simple oral movements on the basis of verbal instructions. These items can be affected both by impairment to the motor areas and by impairment in understanding of speech, as reflected in the temporal-parietal areas of the brain.

Items 36 through 47 assess construction dyspraxia. Items that are performed very poorly often reflect severe spatial disorganization characteristic of injuries to the right hemisphere or to the left parietal area. Drawings that are accurate but done slowly may simply reflect motor dysfunction of the dominant hand and the opposite cerebral hemisphere (or, sometimes, compulsiveness). Items 48 through 51 measure the ability of the client to respond to speech regulation of the motor act. In each of these items, the client must keep in mind the instructions given, interpret them, and then respond appropriately. These items require involvement of the temporal-parietal areas of the left hemisphere, basic to the understanding of what is required, and of the frontal lobes that are responsible for the verbal command of motor movements. Individuals with frontal disorders can often understand what is supposed to be done but are unable to execute the proper motor movements to respond to the request.

Elevations on the C1 scale are best interpreted in comparison to elevations on the C3 (Tactile Functions), S2 (Left Hemisphere), and S3 (Right Hemisphere) scales. When C1 is elevated but C3, S2, and S3 are not, this is suggestive of difficulties with complex motor tasks. Usually these deficits are caused by injuries to the right hemisphere or in the frontal lobe of either hemisphere. This comparison can be very useful in initially localizing a deficit in the anterior-posterior dimension. Clients displaying pure parietal lobe dysfunction will rarely achieve a C1 score above 60T, although specific items involving kinesthetic feedback will be most frequently missed. On examination, the items on the battery will usually show a clear pattern in these posterior injuries that is highly effective in localizing a given disorder.

When all four of these scales (C1, C3, S2, and S3) are highly elevated, generalized impairment of motor and sensory areas is suggested, but this is often in the context of diffuse deficits. If only these four scales are affected, then peripheral disorders affecting motor and sensory skills need to be considered, as well as the possibility of subcortical diseases such as multiple sclerosis, which may leave cognitive skills intact.

If C1 is greatly elevated over C3, combined with elevation on the S2 or S3 scale, there is a suggestion of an anterior lesion in the hemisphere indicated by the higher of the S2 and S3 scales. For such an elevation to be considered significant, one of the two hemisphere scales must be at least 10 points above the other; the larger the difference, the more likely the result is meaningful (assuming that there are not peripheral disorders). If C1, C3, and one of the hemisphere scales are elevated, especially if the difference is 20 points or greater between the lateralization scales, this is highly suggestive of strong involvement of the sensorimotor area in the brain (around the central sulcus) or its related subcortical area, although the pattern disappears if the motor symptoms remit over time. The scale is not sensitive to motor deficits limited to the lower limbs, nor is it particularly sensitive to those subcortical disorders that do not generally affect voluntary motor behavior.

C2 (Rhythm)   The C2 scale is much more simply organized than the C1 scale. Items 52 through 54 involve the analysis of groups of tones. The client must compare two groups of tones and say whether one is higher or lower. Items 55 through 57 require the client to reproduce tones. Although the initial items involve the perception of tonal qualities—an ability usually localized in the temporal lobe of the right hemisphere or, in some cases, in the temporal lobe of the left hemisphere—these latter items involve the expression of tonal relationships, an ability assigned by some to the frontal lobe of the right hemisphere. It is not unusual for clients with right frontal disorders to show specific deficits on these expressive items. Items 58 through 61 involve the evaluation of acoustic signals. The client must identify the number of beeps in groups of sounds.

The last two items in the C2 scale deal with the perception and repro-
duction of rhythm. Item 62 measures the client's ability to reproduce
rhythmic patterns. This item requires both the perception of rhythmic
patterns, a function localized in the right temporal area, and the repro-
duction of sounds, usually using the dominant hand. Thus, the item can
be missed by individuals with deficits in either hemisphere. Item 63 asks
the client to make a series of rhythms from verbal commands. The combination of verbal and rhythmic content on this item also makes it sensitive to injuries in either hemisphere.

C2 is the most sensitive of all the basic clinical scales to disorders
of attention and concentration. Performance of items 52, 54, 58, 59, 60,
61, and 62 is especially diagnostic for individuals who have difficulty in
attention and concentration. When elevations of the C2 scale are the
highest in the profile, they are most often associated with right-hemisphere injuries, which are usually more anterior. This is especially true
when the highest scales are some combination of C2, C9 (Arithmetic),
C10 (Memory), and C11 (Intellectual Processes). This same pattern, however, may be seen in left anterior lesions as well, although in those cases
it is accompanied by at least subtle, if not gross, deficits in some form of
verbal skills. When the C2 deficit is combined with C4 (Visual Functions)
scale elevation, then the lesion may be either anterior or posterior, with
a more posterior lesion becoming more likely with higher elevations on
C4. In the case where the S3 (Right Hemisphere) scale is quite high over
the S2 (Left Hemisphere) scale, the possibility of a lesion straddling the
sensorimotor area and involving both the anterior and posterior areas of
the hemisphere must be strongly considered. C2 elevations, generally
below those of other scales, are not unusual in left-hemisphere injuries.
Very good scores on the C2 scale are generally inconsistent with severe
right-hemisphere damage outside the sensorimotor areas.

C3 (Tactile Functions)   This scale is the most sensitive of the LNNB
scales to injuries in the anterior parietal lobe of either hemisphere. Items
66 through 79 involve different levels of cutaneous sensation. Individuals
must identify where they are touched, how hard they are touched, and
so forth. Injuries to the anterior parietal area will cause significant elevations on this scale, as will injuries to the middle parietal areas that
Luria (1973) designates as the "secondary areas" of the parietal lobe.
Individuals with damage in and around the angular gyrus may have
particular problems with items 74 and 79. Items 80 and 81 are directly
concerned with muscle and joint sensations. They are sensitive to injuries
not only in the anterior but in the posterior parietal lobe as well. If these
items are the only ones missed on the C3 scale, one should also look for
specific errors on the kinesthetic items of the C1 (Motor Functions) scale.
The last four items on the C3 scale involve the stereognostic perception.
These items are scored both for the number of errors and for time. In-

dividuals who have had old injuries to the parietal lobe on either side may have difficulty in meeting the time requirements. One should be careful in analysis of these items as they are highly sensitive to the residual effects of brain injury even when other skills have improved.

The items on the C3 scale, along with the first 20 items on the C1 scale, make up the S2 (Left Hemisphere) and S3 (Right Hemisphere) scales. A difference in performance between the left and right hands on either the C3 scale, and C1 scale, or both combined is highly indicative of lateralized brain dysfunction. Injuries that tend to be located in the posterior parietal or anterior prefrontal areas will typically not show extreme differences between the S2 and S3 scales.

Profiles with the highest scores on the C3 scale are interpreted in conjunction with the relative standings on the S2, S3, and C1 scales. If C3 is greatly elevated over C1 and one of the hemisphere scales is elevated significantly over the other, then this points to a posterior lesion in the hemisphere indicated by the elevated hemisphere scale. This generally remains true even when the C1 scale is equal to the C3 scale, especially if the C1 deficits arise from construction difficulty and sequencing rather than from motor paralysis. Since all items of the C3 scale are included in the hemisphere scales, it is impossible (if the battery is scored correctly) to get a C3 elevation without elevations in one or both of the hemisphere scales. If both hemisphere scales are elevated, however, then either a bilateral injury or a severe left hemisphere injury must be considered. The deficit may be due to an inability to concentrate, which should also result in inconsistent behavior, or to an inability to integrate and identify all stimuli. When the deficit is purely spatial, as in profiles with C3 and C4 (Visual Functions) elevations, the injury is likely to be right parietal-occipital, although this pattern may also reflect subcortical involvement of one or both hemispheres. When naming is strongly involved, left parietal deficits should be considered. All such hypothesized localizations assume a normally dominant left hemisphere.

C4 (Visual Functions)   The C4 scale evaluates a range of visual functions. Items 86 and 87 ask the client to identify objects by viewing either an object itself or a picture of an object. Since naming is a significant component of these items, they are extremely sensitive to left-hemisphere disorders, especially in the temporal-parietal region. These items are included to provide a measure of the client's ability to name. If the client is not able to do these items, later items on the battery that are more sensitive to right-hemisphere function may be missed simply because of left-hemisphere involvement.

Later items require a great deal more visual-spatial perception than do these first two items, although naming is still required. Item 88 presents pictures that are difficult to perceive, item 89 presents only the shading of a picture, which the person must integrate into the picture, and items 90 and 91 present objects that overlap one another and that the client with poor visual-spatial skills has difficulty identifying. Item 92 is a modification of items from the Raven Progressive Matrices (Raven, 1960). It is also a strong measure of visual-spatial organization and right-hemisphere function. Items 94 through 96 involve spatial orientation— the ability to tell time and to recognize directions. These items tend to be specifically related to right-hemisphere function as long as the client is able to perceive the questions. Item 97 requires the client to do three-dimensional analyses of pictures. This item is especially sensitive to right-hemisphere functions, although deficits may also be seen in more moderate-to-severe left-hemisphere injuries. Item 99 involves spatial rotation without any speech components. Individuals may point to the correct answer or circle it as necessary (or may say it if this is not possible). This item is highly sensitive to visual-spatial skills. It is a very simple task, and normal subjects rarely make more than one mistake on it.

Profiles in which the C4 scale is highest, in combination with any secondary scale, generally reflect impairment in the right hemisphere or in the occipital areas of the left hemisphere. The C4 scale can be elevated in other left-hemisphere injuries, but rarely will it be the highest scale overall. In right-hemisphere injuries, deficits on only more complex visual tasks suggest either a mild parietal involvement or injury to anterior areas. These lesions are usually accompanied by elevation on the C1 (Motor Functions) scale suggestive of right-hemisphere lesions. Subcortical lesions that interfere with visual processing can also cause patterns suggestive of right-hemisphere injury, as can severe peripheral visual problems.

C5 (Receptive Speech)   C5 items evaluate the client's ability to understand receptive speech, from simple phonemic analysis to the understanding of complex sentences with inverted English grammar. Items 100 through 107 concern the understanding of simple phonemes. For items 100 through 105, the individual hears simple phonemes and must then repeat or write them. It is important to note if individuals are able either to say or to write phonemes but not to do both. The ability to repeat phonemes but not to write them suggests impairment in the area of the angular gyrus, whereas the ability to write phonemes but not to say them suggests a disorder of expressive speech rather than of receptive speech.

Items 108 through 116 involve the understanding of simple words and sentences. The client must do relatively simple tasks of naming, pointing, and identification, and must define simple words. The intent of these items is simply to ensure that the client is hearing correctly and interpreting correctly what is said to him or her.

Beginning with item 117 and continuing through the end of this scale to item 132, the individual is given increasingly more difficult instructions. These items assess the client's ability to understand and to perform or answer as requested. All these items can be affected by damage to the left hemisphere, but several items can also be affected by right-hemisphere dysfunction. For example, items 118 through 120 require some spatial orientation on the part of the client. If the client appears to understand the sentence but disrupts the spatial requests made, then the possibility of right-hemisphere dysfunction must be suspected. Similarly, spatial orientation is required by item 123.

Items in the set that require comparisons (items 121, 122, 125, 126, 127, 128, 129, 130, and 131) are especially sensitive to damage in the parietal-occipital areas of the left hemisphere, although they may also be affected by a simple lack of understanding by the client caused by injuries to the temporal lobe or the angular gyrus. None of the items on the C5 scale requires any reading skills, so receptive speech ability can be measured independently of the client's level of education and reading readiness. Good performance on this scale with poor performance on the C8 (Reading) scale is suggestive of damage to the occipital or temporal-occipital areas of the left hemisphere.

Overall, the C5 scale is much more easily elevated by damage to the left hemisphere. The scale may also be elevated by damage to the right hemisphere, especially the anterior temporal-frontal areas. There is evidence that this anterior damage in the right hemisphere does cause specific elevations on the C5 scale. It is possible that this elevation is due to the fact that the right frontal areas may play some role in understanding speech.

When this scale is highest, as well as significantly elevated above the critical level by at least 15 points, deficits are usually associated with left-hemisphere injury. Lesser elevations, caused by difficulty with the more complex items, can appear as the highest scale in right anterior injuries. This can be especially true in mild elevation combinations of C5 and C10 (Memory); C5 and C2 (Rhythm); C5 and C4 (Visual Functions); or C5, C11 (Intellectual Processes), and C9 (Arithmetic). In the most significant elevations, however, left-hemisphere involvement is generally indicated.

C6 (Expressive Speech) The C6 scale evaluates the individual's ability to repeat simple phonemes and words and to generate automatic as well as more complex speech forms. Initial items (items 133 through 142) simply require the repetition of sounds or words spoken by the examiner. Beginning with item 143, the client must repeat the same list of words and sounds by reading them rather than hearing them.

Beginning with item 154, the client must repeat increasingly more difficult sentences. Item 157 requires simple naming of objects, and item 158 requires the naming of body parts. Item 159 examines the ability to name from a description rather than from a visual presentation of the object. Items 160 through 163 ask individuals to count and say the days of the week, first forwards and then backwards—all a form of automatic speech. Items 164 through 169 evaluate the ability to produce speech spontaneously under three conditions: (1) after looking at a picture, (2) after hearing a story, and (3) after being given a topic to discuss. If other items on this scale are performed without difficulty, and yet the client experiences problems with these items, there is the possibility of either low intelligence or damage to the frontal lobe area, usually in the left hemisphere. The final section involves complex systems of grammatical expression; the client must fill in words that are missing in a sentence or make up a sentence from words that are given to the client.

In general, C6 scores are sensitive to injuries in the left hemisphere only. It is rare to see a high C6 score in individuals with unilateral right-hemisphere injuries. Exceptions to this are individuals who had difficulty with reading prior to their injury, or whose disorders have somehow interfered with auditory perception or have had generalized effects (e.g., pressure effects from a tumor). However, with regard to the individual client, examination of the patterns of the items on the battery can easily eliminate these possibilities. In the absence of these types of conditions, elevation on the C6 scale, especially above a score of 70T, is almost always indicative of a left-hemisphere injury. In general, the left-hemisphere injury involves the temporal-frontal area, especially the posterior two-thirds of the frontal lobe. However, if the client is basically able to say the words but has difficulty changing sounds or tends to slur speech, then the possibility of kinesthetic damage must be considered. In these cases, the damage is to the parietal lobe; but such individuals will also show significant kinesthetic and tactile deficits on the C3 (Tactile Functions) scale and can easily be evaluated from that scale and from the kinesthetic items on the C1 (Motor Functions) scale. If the high scores are confined to the more complex items on the battery, then the likely focus of damage is in the prefrontal area of the brain rather than in the more posterior areas represented by other patterns of deficits.

Interpretation of this scale is generally similar to that for C5 (Receptive Speech). When the scale is well elevated over the critical level, some left-hemisphere involvement is generally indicated. Very mild C6 elevations may be associated with right-hemisphere lesions, with the major errors occurring in the last items of the scale (spontaneous speech, sequencing, and fill-in items).

C7 (Writing)   The C7 scale involves an evaluation of the ability to analyze words phonetically in English and then to do copying of increasing difficulty. Initially clients are asked to copy simple letters, next to copy combinations of letters and words, and then to write their first and last names. They are then asked to write sounds, words, and phrases from dictation. The final items on the scale require the client to write sentences about a given topic.

In general, disorders of writing localize to the temporal-parietal-occipital area, especially in and around the angular gyrus of the left hemisphere. Specific disorders, however, may indicate problems in other areas. For example, the ability to write from written material but not from auditory material suggests a specific lesion in the temporal lobe. Conversely, the ability to write from dictation but not from written material suggests a lesion in the occipital or occipital-parietal areas of the cerebral cortex. If the client is, in general, able to write but has difficulty forming letters and changing from one letter to another, there could be a problem in kinesthetic feedback in which the client mixes up letters that are formed by similar motor movements. If the client is simply unable to write at all because of paralysis, this, of course, is suggestive of a lesion in the motor strip area of the posterior frontal lobe. Finally, if the client writes at an angle to the page, suggesting some spatial problems, but has no other writing disorders, this can be related to right-hemisphere dysfunction. Lack of the ability to read or write one's name is often indicative of a general dementia or, in some cases, a disorder of automatic writing that may occur with injuries in both hemispheres.

Deficits in which the concept of spelling is completely lost (e.g., "CAT" is spelled "DBG") are most likely associated with injuries to the left hemisphere, especially in the parietal or temporal areas. Deficits in which the correct letters are retained but are placed in the wrong order have been seen in patients with a wide variety of injuries. Motor writing errors (02) are generally associated with the hemisphere opposite the client's normal writing hand, although care must be taken in injuries that cause the client to change writing hands. In these cases, writing may remain poor but reflects an injury in the ipsilateral hemisphere. Motor writing problems may arise simply as a result of motor problems reflecting the functions of the motor areas of the brain, but they may also arise in injuries involving kinesthetic and tactile feedback. See Luria (1966) for an extensive discussion of the specific qualitative behaviors associated with each of these conditions. Motor writing deficits in which the writing itself is motorically intact but spatially disrupted (at large angles to the horizontal, or with words written over one another) may reflect injuries to the right (or spatially dominant) hemisphere.

C8 (Reading)   The C8 scale closely parallels the C7 scale. The client is asked to generate sounds from letters that the examiner reads aloud. This generally measures the client's ability to show integration of letters and the auditory analysis functions of the temporal and parietal areas of the left hemisphere. The client is then asked to name simple letters, read simple sounds, and read simple words and letter combinations that have meaning. Generally, disruption of these skills implies lesions in the temporal-occipital area of the brain or in the temporal-parietal area of the left hemisphere. Finally, the client must read entire sentences as well as paragraphs. If the client is able to read simple words but not entire sentences or paragraphs, possible injuries include disorders of visual scanning that make it impossible for the client to grasp more than one word at a time. This is usually due to injuries in the secondary visual areas of the occipital lobe.

Generally, deficits on the C8 scale, in a client who could read prior to an injury, are almost always associated with a left-hemisphere injury, usually posterior. Mild deficit with complex words, however, may appear in highly educated individuals with left frontal lesions. The exceptions to this are deficits that occur because of spatial disruption (inability to follow a line, which shows most clearly in the paragraph reading) or neglect of the left side (which should be corrected by the examiner if the test is administered correctly). Both suggest right-hemisphere dysfunction.

C9 (Arithmetic)   The C9 scale is the most sensitive of all the LNNB scales to educational deficits. Even in normally educated individuals, this is the scale most likely to appear in a severely pathological range when there is, in fact, no problem.

The scale starts with the client simply writing down numbers from dictation in both Arabic and Roman numerals. Several items have been employed to get somewhat closer to the spatial dysfunctions that are possible. The Roman numerals IV and VI, for example, can easily be reversed to read VI and IV. Similarly, in Arabic numerals, the client is asked to write 17 and 71, 69 and 96. It is not unusual in a person with a subtle dysfunction to be more likely to show the reversal in the Roman numerals because of less overall familiarity with these numbers. Thereafter, the scale asks the person to write down numbers of increasing complexity. As the numbers become more complex, it is possible to see whether the client places the numbers in the correct sequence, again looking for possible spatial deficits that can be caused by right-hemisphere or left occipital-parietal dysfunction. In the next section of the scale, beginning with item 210, the client is asked to compare numbers with each other, an operation that is basic to the left occipital-parietal area. In items 212 through 214, the client is asked to do simple arithmetic problems. These are problems that most individuals can probably do from memory. Dysfunction in this area is suggestive of serious inability to understand what is being asked or of severe left-hemisphere damage, especially in the parietal areas.

In items 215 through 217, the client is asked to do more complex addition and subtraction problems that cannot be done from memory. Items 218, 219, and 220 deal with more difficult manipulations. The client must fill in a missing number or sign, or do a series of more difficult addition problems. Deficits here are often seen in people with low levels of education and are not considered as serious as deficits in other parts of the battery. An individual with higher educational attainment, however, should be able to do these. Often a left parietal dysfunction in a highly educated person will not show up until this section.

The last section includes presentation of classic serial 7s and serial 13s. Concentration difficulties that may show up on these items can be associated with left frontal lobe dysfunction in the presence of normal arithmetic skills.

The C9 scale appears to be potentially sensitive to lesions in all parts of the brain, as well as to preexisting deficits. The scale has no localizing value except in the combinations indicated already, until an item analysis is done. In cases where the person cannot read or write simple numbers, left-hemisphere injury is indicated; problems with only the spatial aspects of arithmetic suggest, but are not necessarily limited to, right-hemisphere injury.

C10 (Memory)   The C10 scale is basically involved with short-term and intermediate memory. For Form II only, a separate score (C12) is available that specifically assesses intermediate memory. No attempt is made to assess long-term memory functions. The first items on C10 look at the client's ability to memorize a list of seven simple words and to predict his or her performance. The inability to predict is often seen in clients with frontal lobe dysfunction; therefore, these items can be significant, especially if the scores are extremely deviant. In the second section of the scale, item 226 measures visual memory with interference. The client is asked to remember a card under the condition of having to count up to 100 aloud between acquisition and retrieval. Items 227 through 230 involve immediate sensory trace recall. The items test visual memory, rhythmic memory, and tactile visual memory. These items can be affected by both left- and right-hemisphere dysfunction but are more sensitive to right-hemisphere dysfunction. This is especially true when these items are missed while the more verbal items on the test are performed without difficulty.

Items 231 through 234 are measures of verbal memory. Items 231 and 232 involve simple verbal memory under two conditions of interference, while items 233 and 234 are similar in that interference is supplied by additional material that the client must memorize. Several difficulties in short-term memory, especially due to injuries to the left hemisphere, are seen in these items. Injuries to the bilateral hippocampal area, which cause a loss of long-term memory coding, will show up on the items involving interference. Finally, item 235 is a measure of the individual's ability to associate the verbal stimulus with a picture. This item can be interfered with by either left- or right-hemisphere dysfunction and is sensitive to high-level disturbances in memory skills.

Overall, the C10 scale is most sensitive to verbal dysfunction because of its importance in a majority of the items. However, nonverbal dysfunction caused by right-hemisphere lesions will show up in a moderately elevated C10 score of about 60T, with a specific pattern of items missed, as described earlier. It is important to look at the pattern of items missed before venturing the hypothesis of a possible lateralization for the elevation in this scale. Extremely high elevations of 80T or more are nevertheless almost always associated with either left-hemisphere or bilateral dysfunction.

Along with the C2 (Rhythm) scale, this scale is quite sensitive to subcortical dysfunction. Indeed, subtle subcortical dysfunction, especially of the temporal lobes, is often accompanied by deficits on this scale. Very high error scores generally point to involvement of the left hemisphere, whereas lower scores may reflect either hemisphere.

C11 (Intellectual Processes)   Initial items in the scale involve the understanding of thematic pictures. The first two items ask the client to interpret a picture in his or her own words, whereas items 238 through 241 ask the individual to put pictures into a series that makes sense, similar to the items in Picture Arrangement on the WAIS. Items 242 and 243 ask the client to tell what is comical or absurd about certain pictures. These items are often missed entirely by individuals with frontal lobe dysfunction and by those with right-hemisphere dysfunction that interferes with interpretation of verbal schemes. Deficits of visual scanning can also be seen in individuals who are not able to appreciate the complexity of a picture and who therefore tend to focus in one area. Luria (1966) presented a detailed analysis of the type of visual movements present in various kinds of brain disorders, such as injuries to the premotor area of the frontal lobes and injuries to the occipital cortex. In the second section, item 244 asks for interpretation of a story; item 245 asks for interpretation of expressions; and items 246 and 247 ask for interpretation of a proverb. Note that item 247 allows multiple-choice answers, whereas item 246 requires a verbal response. If the client succeeds on item 247 while missing item 246, there is a possibility that the individual's intellectual processes are intact but that expressive language functions have been impaired. Such individuals should be able to show a relatively normal performance on the C5 (Receptive Speech) items requiring little verbal output while missing the items on the C6 (Expressive Speech) scale.

Item 248 involves simple concept formations and definitions, whereas items 249 and 250 ask for comparisons and differences between objects in much the same way as do items on the Similarities subtest of the WAIS. Performance in this area is further evaluated by items 251 through 254, in which the client must find the logical relationships between specific objects and the groups to which they belong. Item 255 evaluates the ability to determine opposites, and items 256 and 257 investigate the ability to form analogies. The last items on the scale, items 258 through 269, all involve simple arithmetic problems very similar to those seen on the WAIS Arithmetic subtest.

Overall, the C11 scale is highly sensitive to disorders in both hemispheres, but it is most sensitive to disorders in the left hemisphere. Injuries in either the parietal lobe or the frontal lobe will cause maximum dysfunction. Poor performance on the C11 scale, in the absence of poor performance on the C5 and C6 scales and in the absence of any significant psychiatric thought disorder, is generally associated with prefrontal dysfunction. The determination of laterality, however, must be made by investigating specific items to judge whether those initial items that are right-hemisphere-oriented suggest adequate visual interpretation skills. If these skills appear to be intact, then the scale is likely to be reflecting a left-hemisphere dysfunction alone. If these are the only items missed on the scale, the possibility of isolated right frontal dysfunction must be seriously considered.

Although the scale can reflect impairment in either hemisphere, a high elevation combined with C2 (Rhythm), C4 (Visual Functions), C10 (Memory), and C9 (Arithmetic) generally points to right-hemisphere dysfunction, whereas elevations combined with C6 (Expressive Speech), C8 (Reading), and C7 (Writing) indicate left-hemisphere damage. This scale is generally more affected by posterior rather than anterior injuries, but it is affected by both.

Interpreting Scale and Item Patterns: Summary Scales

S1 (Pathognomonic)   This scale is most useful as a measure of the degree of compensation that has occurred since an injury. *Compensation* refers to those processes that allow the brain-injured patient to recover from the effects of a brain injury. This includes functional reorganization of the brain, in which the patient uses intact areas of the brain to find alternative ways of doing tasks, as well as actual physical recovery, in which the effects of the brain injury diminish and psychological functions return more closely to normal.

The S1 scale is interpreted by both its overall elevation and its relationship to other scores. In cases where the S1 scale is quite high (usually at least 20 points over the critical level) and is the highest scale overall, the injury is likely to be uncompensated. This pattern is most often seen in acute, severe brain injuries. It may also be seen in a chronic injury of such severity that further compensation does not occur. When S1 is quite high but at about the average of the other scores, compensation has probably taken place and the patient has shown some recovery. If S1 is high but remains the lowest score in the profile, the injury is likely chronic and the patient has generally recovered to the degree that can be expected.

In cases where S1 is elevated but not extremely high (less than 20 points above the critical level), and where it is the highest score overall, the injury may be recent and just beginning to recover. Alternatively, this may reflect a long-term injury in which there has been a general recovery but where there still remains one or more areas of function in which compensation did not take place (usually reflecting severe injury to a limited area). If S1 is elevated but not highly, and is at the same level as other scores, this generally reflects an injury that has partially recovered but still shows some dysfunction, which is generally more diffuse than focal. An elevated S1 that is not extremely elevated and is the lowest score overall is reflective of an injury that is compensated but not recovered, though less serious than the same pattern mentioned earlier when S1 is very elevated.

S2 (Left Hemisphere) and S3 (Right Hemisphere)   These two scales were constructed to give initial measures of lateralization. The S2 scale consists of all items reflecting left-hand sensory and motor performance; the S3 scale consists of all items reflecting right-hand sensory and motor performance. These items are drawn from the C1 (Motor Functions) and C3 (Tactile Functions) scales. The scores on these scales are sensitive to lateralizing disorders that involve the sensorimotor strip in the central part of the brain or those areas directly adjacent to the sensorimotor strip. Lesions that do not affect the sensorimotor area may not show up as a lateralized discrepancy on the S2 and S3 scales. Thus, lesions that are more posterior or more anterior tend to look as if they were nonlateralized.

Extreme differences between the S2 and S3 scales almost always indicate a lateralized disorder involving the sensorimotor areas of the brain. In general, right-hemisphere injuries involving the sensorimotor area will produce an elevation on the S3 scale, but the S2 scale will remain within normal limits (i.e., a T-score of less than 60). In left-hemisphere injuries, however, both these scales will often be elevated above a score of 60T. The S2 scale will, moreover, be 10 to 20 or more points higher than the S3 scale. Bilateral injuries, as a rule, will elevate both scales, but with the scales within 10 to 20 T-score points of each other.

Both these scales reflect sensorimotor operations in the brain and only incidentally reflect some cognitive functions. In general, they are interpreted with respect to the C1 and C3 scales, as discussed previously. Differences between the scales of at least 10 T-score points are necessary before one should begin to take any lateralization suggested by the scales as more than a hypothesis to be investigated. Large differences (in excess of 20 points), in the absence of peripheral problems, generally suggest a lesion involving the sensorimotor area of the brain.

Localization Scales

The localization scales are an empirically developed set of scales designed to aid in generating hypotheses about the nature of a cortical injury. Although the availability of these scales can lead to the temptation to generate statements regarding the areas that have been injured by simply looking at which scales are elevated over the critical level, this is not the correct use of these scales. Rather, as with the clinical scales, the patterns of the scales are more important. Multiple scales are likely to be elevated even in a localized lesion, so that simple elevation cannot be interpreted in isolation.

Factor Scales

Although the items of the original clinical scales were chosen to measure specific basic skills, they represent a heterogeneous set of items that differ markedly from one another in order to allow for the item pattern analysis of a skill within a given broad area, such as motor skills. Analysis of these scales is based on looking at items in different parts of the scale and comparing the performance within each section of the scale, using one's clinical judgment. In order to make this process more objective, a decision was made to determine which items within each scale went together on an empirical basis and to form scale factors that might be useful in breaking down the scale into subscales.

Despite some statistical problems, the factor scales are a useful adjunct to the other profiles. Unlike the other profiles, however, the factor scale profile is used to confirm or disprove hypotheses formed by the integration of the clinical and localization scales rather than to generate entirely new hypotheses or to determine the likelihood of brain damage or lateralization. In general, the factor scales act as an intermediary between the steps of the basic clinical scale analysis and the item analysis; they allow useful modification of the hypotheses that have been formed before the more time-consuming step of item analysis is attempted.

Interpretation of Individual Items and Item Patterns

The next step in the analysis of the objective data is the comparison of the item patterns on the battery with the final hypothesis generated from the integration of the three scale patterns (clinical/summary, localization, and factor). The basic strategy is a review of the performance on the items across the battery for consistency or inconsistency with the hypothesis. Thus, instead of attempting to judge how each item was missed or answered correctly, which is impossible simply by observing a single score, the item score is checked to see if it fits in with the hypothesis that has been generated. If the scores are inconsistent, then the hypothesis must be changed to take into account the discrepancies found. After new hypotheses have been formed, these must then be tested until a single hypothesis or set of hypotheses has been generated that accounts for the data.

Qualitative Analysis

The LNNB lends itself to a qualitative analysis along with the quantitative analysis discussed in this chapter. Consideration of the qualitative factors is the next step in the diagnostic process. Here, the interest is not in whether a client got a certain score on a certain item but, rather, how that score was achieved. One of the great advantages of this battery (inherent in its design as well as in the administration and testing-the-limits techniques suggested) is that the same test procedures lend themselves to both quantitative and qualitative analyses. The two approaches complement each other and allow the user of the LNNB to enjoy the best of both methods, avoiding that continuing, yet ultimately futile, argument over which approach is better or which should be the one employed.

In scoring qualitative errors, there is a wide range of possibilities aimed at gaining a better understanding of the "why" behind a client's error. Qualitative analysis can also aid in evaluating responses that are correct in terms of the quantitative scoring but are still unusual—for example, the client who reads a word on the C8 scale but stutters in pronouncing it, or the client who can describe an object and its uses on the C4 scale but is unable to give its name.

After a qualitative analysis has been made, it should be integrated with the quantitative analysis. It is our strong belief that neither form of data is inherently "superior" in any given case. We know from our own studies that quantitative indices do not have 100 percent hit rates. We also know that clinicians make errors and frequently disagree in their qualitative interpretations of behavior, as demonstrated by the wide range of theories in neuropsychology to explain the same phenomena. In some cases, the qualitative data help to explain inconsistencies that cannot be resolved in the quantitative results. In other cases, the quantitative data suggest an alternative approach to an observation that clears up the interpretation of a qualitative aspect of behavior. Only when the two sets of data have been integrated has a fully effective initial evaluation been completed.

Prior History

Even at this point, there still remains another step in the diagnostic process—the reconciliation of the conclusions of the foregoing techniques with the history. Historical information and the conclusions made available by others prior to the neuropsychological assessment may be right or wrong. A lesion may exist as reported, or it may not. The client's developmental history may be accurate or may contain serious errors. The relative accuracy of information does depend on the source of that information as well as on its nature. In all cases, however, it is important to double-check all such information.

PSYCHOMETRIC PROPERTIES

Reliability

The reliability of the LNNB has been examined from a number of perspectives, including interrater agreement, split-half, internal consistency, and test–retest reliability.

Interrater Reliability   An initial study (Golden, Hammeke, & Purisch, 1978) examined the interrater reliability of the LNNB. The battery was administered to five separate clients who were simultaneously scored by five independent pairs of examiners. The resulting 1,345 comparisons were then examined for level of agreement. Over 95 percent of the comparisons were identical, indicating a high level of interrater agreement.

In a follow-up study, Bach, Harowski, Kirby, Peterson, and Schulein (1981) examined interrater agreement among five raters under two conditions: (1) a normal range of responses and (2) responses that were deliberately vague and difficult to score. To control for the level of agreement due to chance, coefficient kappa (Cohen, 1960) was used. This provides a lower-bound estimate of interrater reliability. The kappa coefficients averaged over .80, well within acceptable limits for comparable tests. Predictably, lower levels of reliability were obtained for the condition in which the answers were intentionally vague.

Split-Half Reliability   Golden, Fross, and Graber (1981) examined the split-half reliability of the LNNB using odd–even comparisons. The sample consisted of 74 normal subjects, 83 psychiatric patients, and 181 neurological patients (N = 338). The resulting reliabilities ranged from .89 on scale C10 to .95 on scale C8.

Internal Consistency   Several recent studies have assessed internal consistency rather than split-half reliability. Mikula (1981) obtained internal consistency estimates (alpha) ranging from .82 (on C2) to 0.94 (on C1) for the original 14 clinical/summary scales on a sample of 146 brain-damaged patients and 74 medical controls. Moses, Johnson, and Lewis (1983) calculated internal consistency for each of the major clinical scales. Based on a mixed sample of 285 patients (88 alcoholic, 101 schizophrenic or schizoaffective, and 89 brain-damaged), they found average alpha coefficients in the mid-.80s (range of .78 to .88).

More recently, Sawicki, Maruish, and Golden (1983) examined the internal consistency of the original 14 scales in a mixed sample of normal and brain-injured patients (n = 559), as well as separate brain-damaged (n = 451), schizophrenic (n = 414), mixed psychiatric patient (n = 128), and normative (n = 108) samples. The correlations are generally quite high, with the lowest reliabilities occurring in the normal sample, probably because of the range restriction within this subgroup.

Test–Retest Reliability An initial study of test–retest reliability was conducted by Golden, Berg, and Graber (1982). For this study, the investigators chose 27 patients exhibiting chronic, relatively stable head injuries whose initial test performances fell into the middle range of the normative distribution for the LNNB. The patients included neurological and psychiatric cases, with testing done after resolution of any acute psychiatric symptoms. Intervals between test and retest averaged 167 days (S.D. = 134 days), with a range from 10 to 469 days.

The lowest reliabilities were found on C3 (.78) and S3 (.77). Other reliabilities ranged from .84 for C10 to a high of .96 for C9. Parceling out the variance contributed by the test–retest interval yielded little change in the resulting correlations, suggesting that the variable range of this interval was of little importance in chronic, static cases.

A further study of test–retest reliability was reported by Plaisted and Golden (1982). Test–retest reliability was calculated for the 14 original scales, the localization scales, and the factor scales. The data were based on a sample of 30 patients with an average test–retest interval of 8.1 months (S.D. = 6 months). All the patients had emotional difficulties but did not show evidence of neurological problems. Test–retest reliabilities for the 14 original scales ranged from .83 to .96, with a mean of .89. For the eight localization scales, the reliabilities ranged from .78 to .95, with a mean of .89. The factor scale test–retest reliability coefficients ranged more widely (from .01 to .96) with an overall mean of .81 across the 30 scales. All the factor scales except two showed acceptable levels of correlation significant at the .001 level.

Validity

Estimates of criterion-related, concurrent, and construct validity of the LNNB have been obtained from a number of empirical studies. These studies have used a variety of approaches, such as classification of brain-damaged versus other criterion groups, comparison of profile patterns for individuals with localized brain impairments and across different diagnostic groups, and comparison of the LNNB to other tests designed to measure similar constructs.

Classification of Brain-Damaged versus Other Criterion Groups An initial study (Golden, Hammeke, & Purisch, 1978) examined the diagnostic efficiency of the test items in discriminating between brain-damaged and normal subjects. Of the 269 items in Form I, 252 discriminated significantly between the neurologically impaired and nonimpaired criterion groups at the .05 level or better.

Hammeke, Golden, and Purisch (1978) reported the first study evaluating the ability of the original 14 scales to differentiate brain-damaged from normal controls. The study found significant differences ($p < .001$)

in the performances of the neurological and control groups on all 14 original scales.

In order to cross-validate the results of the initial studies, Moses, and Golden (1979) compared an additional sample of 50 neurological and 50 control patients, using Form I of the LNNB. The results of the study were almost identical to those reported previously by Hammeke, Golden, and Purisch (1978). Using the cutoff scores determined by Hammeke and his associates, Moses and Golden found hit rates ranging from 62 to 80 percent for the brain-injured groups and from 72 to 98 percent for the control group. Overall hit rates for the original 14 scales did not differ by more than 6 percent from the results in the original study.

Several additional studies have generally supported these earlier results. In a dissertation, Duffala (1979) compared a group of 20 head trauma patients to a younger control group, finding a hit rate exceeding 90 percent. Golden, Purisch, and Hammeke (1980) noted the necessity of establishing formal decision rules as a further aid to discriminating between brain-damaged and non-brain-damaged individuals. In doing so, they cited the importance of a study by Marvel, Golden, Hammeke, Purisch, and Osmon (1979) documenting the extent to which age and education affect performance on the LNNB. Golden, Moses, Graber, and Berg (1981) investigated the use of objective rules for the discrimination of brain-damaged versus normal subjects. The intent was to develop an index similar to the impairment index used with the Halstead-Reitan. The authors, in an initial population of 60 normals, developed a formula for predicting LNNB scores from age and education, which was used to develop the formula for the critical level discussed earlier. The second part of the study compared the efficacy of using the critical level as a standard cutoff point. Overall, a hit rate of 87 percent was obtained.

Malloy and Webster (1981) replicated the initial validation studies, but used neurological and control subjects with initially equivocal neurological results. Using the classification rules developed by Golden, Moses, Graber, and Berg (1981), 80 percent of the subjects were correctly classified into the three diagnostic groups.

MacInnes and co-workers (1983) compared the results of a "healthy" geriatric sample (with a mean age of seventy-two years) and a group of brain-damaged elderly adults (with a mean age of sixty-eight years). Significant differences ($p < .001$) were found between the two groups in a multivariate analysis of covariance on 11 clinical scales, using age, sex, and education as covariates. The classification rules resulted in a hit rate of 92 percent for the healthy group, 86 percent for the brain-damaged group, and 88 percent for the total sample.

Sawicki and Golden (1984) sought to validate two decision rules (three or more scales above the critical level and range of T-scores, excluding both the S2 and the S3 scale, indicating impairment) for classification of brain function with a large, heterogeneous sample of 1,037 normal, psychiatric, and brain-damaged subjects. Use of the number of scales above the critical level accurately classified 73 percent of the normals and 80 percent of the brain-impaired, for a total hit rate of 77 percent.

Classification of Focal Brain Impairments   Validity research has also focused on studies involving patients with localized or lateralized disorders. Osmon, Golden, Purisch, Hammeke, and Blume (1979) examined the ability of the battery to discriminate among lateralized and diffusely injured patients. A discriminant analysis using the original 14 scales of the LNNB correctly classified 59 to 60 patients. By simply subtracting the S2 T-score from the S3 score, the authors achieved a hit rate of 75 percent accuracy in lateralization.

Lewis et al. (1979) examined the ability of the LNNB to localize brain injury to the frontal regions, sensorimotor areas, temporal lobe, and occipital-parietal lobes in each hemisphere. Substantial differences on the clinical scales were found among the groups, as were scale patterns characteristic of each group. In follow-up to this study, Golden, Moses, Fishburne, et al. (1981) compared the scores of 87 patients with localized brain damage and 30 patients who served as normal controls. Using the highest localization scale to determine the side of the lesion (e.g., if L5—Right Frontal was the highest scale, then the case was classified as a right-hemisphere lesion), 92 percent of the brain-injured cases were correctly classified as to side of lesion. For localization, using the highest localization scales as the criterion, 84 percent of the patients were correctly classified by quadrant and the correct hemisphere; using the CT scan as the validation criterion, 74 percent of the cases were assessed correctly in terms of localization. In addition, a multivariate analysis of variance showed that either the localization or clinical scale could discriminate at a high level among the localized and normal groups.

Comparisons with Other Tests

In the development of any test, an important research aspect is the correlation of the battery with other tests. By theoretical predictions of the hypothesized relationships, construct validity may be ascertained, or the data can be used simply to establish concurrent validity.

Halstead-Reitan Comparisons   The introduction of a new test battery generally requires comparison studies to older test batteries that were designed to measure the same underlying traits or abilities. In an initial comparison made by Kane, Sweet, Golden, Parsons, and Moses (1981), the authors compared diagnostic accuracy of the LNNB and Halstead-Reitan in classifying as brain-damaged or non-brain-damaged 45 difficult-to-diagnose individuals. The authors found that the batteries (interpreted by an expert at each procedure) agreed on 37 of the cases.

Golden, Kane, Sweet, et al. (1981) examined 108 subjects who had taken both the LNNB and the Halstead-Reitan. The 14 major LNNB scores were compared against the 15 major Halstead-Reitan scores as selected from Russell, Neuringer, and Goldstein (1970). Multiple correlations were then run between each test and all the tests of the other battery. The multiple *R*s ranged from .67 to .95, with a median in the .80s. The lowest multiple correlation was Finger Tapping (dominant hand). Shelly and Goldstein (1982b) examined the same intercorrelations in an independent sample of 125 brain-injured patients. Their results were generally comparable to those reported in the previous study. In addition, the authors reported a correlation of .82 between impairment level from the Halstead-Reitan and the LNNB average T-scores. A more recent study (Kane, Parsons, Goldstein, & Moses, 1983) found that the two batteries were essentially identical in ability to discriminate between a sample of 50 brain-injured and 50 normal subjects.

Comparisons to the WAIS and WAIS-R   McKay, Golden, Moses, Fishburne, and Wisniewski (1981) compared the intercorrelations between the WAIS and the LNNB in a sample of 280 mixed psychiatric, neurological, and normal subjects. Correlations with the WAIS summary IQ measures were −.84 for Verbal IQ, −.74 for Performance IQ, and −.84 for Full Scale IQ for the C11 scale. Picker and Schlottman (1982) reported LNNB–WAIS correlations in a study employing only normal individuals. In this case, the higher correlations were only in the mid-.70s, somewhat lower than in the previous study.

Preliminary work with the WAIS-R suggests similarly high correlations with the LNNB, with some minor differences in the correlations for specific subtests. Dill and Golden (1988) recently investigated the relationship of the original 14 LNNB scales for Form II with the 14 subtest and IQ scores for the WAIS-R. Of particular interest are the correlations between C11 and the Verbal, Performance, and Full Scale IQs (−.86, −.88, and −.89, respectively). When age and education were partialed out, the correlations decreased to some extent. After correcting for age and education level, IQ accounted for about 35 percent of the overall variance of the LNNB scale scores.

In an ambitious study, Shelly and Goldstein (1982a) attempted to confirm the previous findings of Prifitera and Ryan (1981) and compare the LNNB, the WAIS, and the WRAT. They administered all three measures to 150 neuropsychiatric patients. Using selected T-scores for the 11 basic clinical scales of the LNNB, correlations with the WAIS and WRAT subtests were computed. Correlations with the WAIS subtests ranged from −.38 between C8 and Digit Symbol to −.73 between the two arithmetic measures. In general, the correlations were somewhat higher than those obtained by McKay, Golden, Moses, et al. (1981).

Comparisons with Other Tests   Ryan and Prifitera (1982), in a population of 32 psychiatric patients, found a correlation of −.65 between the Wechsler Memory Scale (Wechsler, 1945) and the LNNB C10 scale. McKay and Ramsey (1983) found a similar correlation between the two measures of memory with a slightly older and less educated group of alcoholics. However, the correlation between the raw scores for C10 and the WMS was much higher ($-.82, p < .001$). In addition to the concurrent validity studies reported earlier, preliminary correlations between the LNNB and several other measures also suggest generally high correlations of the various LNNB scales with the Peabody Individual Achievement Test (PIAT; Dunn & Markwardt, 1970), the Benton Visual Retention Test (Benton, 1955), the Wide Range Achievement Test (WRAT; Jastak, Jastak, & Bijou, 1965), the Boston Aphasia Examination (Goodglass & Kaplan, 1972), and the Peabody Picture Vocabulary Test (Dunn, 1970). These correlations are generally maximum in the range of .70 to .90 and follow the expected pattern of results, with PIAT and WRAT scores maximally correlated with the similar scales on the LNNB (e.g., Spelling with C7, Reading Recognition with C8, Arithmetic with C9, General Information with C11, and Reading Comprehension with C8 and C11). The Benton correlated highest with C4, and the Boston Aphasia Examination with C6 and C5.

CASE EXAMPLE

To demonstrate the basic use of the test, a case example will be employed. This patient is TT, a fifty-six-year-old married right-handed male with four years of graduate school. He suffered two strokes in the right hemisphere prior to an evaluation with the LNNB. Using the age and education tables in the test manual, he was given a critical level of 51. His scores on the basic clinical and summary scales are given in Table 7–1.

Several facts are immediately obvious when examining this profile. First, the Right Hemisphere scale (S3) is more than 40 points higher than the Left Hemisphere scale (S2), pointing to a clear lateralization to the right hemisphere. The highest scales are C1 (Motor), C2 (Rhythm), C3 (Tactile), and C4 (Visual). This pattern suggests severe sensorimotor involvement, with involvement of cognitive areas in both the anterior and posterior areas of the hemisphere. The elevation of Motor suggests the presence of motor-spatial problems (as in drawing), which may be more impaired than pure spatial skills. The understanding of language is intact (C5), as is intelligence generally (C11); but both reading and writing show mild dysfunction (C7 and C8), as does memory (C10), especially in nonverbal areas. Examination of the specific errors on Scales C5 through C11 shows that 74 percent of the errors involve vision. This is usually associated in such lesions with left unilateral neglect, in which the left side of visual stimuli (such as words or sentences) are ignored by the patient. Observation of the patient's qualitative behavior is consistent

Table 7–1 Scores for TT

Scale	T-Score
C1 (Motor)	99
C2 (Rhythm)	92
C3 (Tactile)	92
C4 (Visual)	85
C5 (Receptive)	39
C6 (Expressive)	40
C7 (Writing)	60
C8 (Reading)	60
C9 (Arithmetic)	45
C10 (Memory)	65
C11 (Intelligence)	53
S1 (Pathognomonic)	75
S2 (Left)	81
S3 (Right)	124

with this conclusion, as is analysis of the quantitative item patterns and the factor scales.

The localization scales showed the highest elevations on scales L7 (Right Parietal-Occipital) and L5 (Right Frontal). This is a common pattern in disorders involving the middle cerebral artery (as this one did) on the right side of the brain. The scales point to a right-hemisphere, central focus, with greatest injury in and around the sensorimotor areas of the brain.

A deeper analysis can identify patterns of item errors on each scale that further describe the detail of the patient's injury. Though an obvious and easy case, this patient illustrates the kinds of things that can be seen with scale pattern analysis.

CRITICISMS

A reviewer of an earlier version of this chapter suggested the need to address those criticisms that others have made of the LNNB. Although the author believes that the research and publications to date have already done this, and is well aware that his replies to these criticisms may be deemed by some as biased, I will attempt to cover the major criticisms that arose in the development of this test. In most cases, we have already covered the material that is the basis of these responses. Further data and material in more detail may be found in the test manual (Golden, Purisch, & Hammeke, 1985).

These criticisms arose in a handful of articles (Adams, 1980; Crosson & Warren, 1982; Delis & Kaplan, 1982, 1983; Spiers, 1981), some of which simply repeated the points made in earlier articles. More detailed replies to these articles can be found in a series of articles (Golden, 1980; Bryant, Maruisch, Sawicki, & Golden, 1984; Golden, Ariel, McKay, et al. 1982; Golden, Ariel, Moses, et al., 1982), as well as in the data and procedures discussed in this chapter and in the test manual (Golden, Purisch, & Hammeke, 1986).

The criticisms were also interesting in that none of them were based on actual data. For example, the complaints that the LNNB had poor content validity, poor internal reliability, or poor item scale correlations were all made after "inspection" of the test items rather than experimental data. In every case, actual data have contradicted these criticisms. Indeed, more at the heart of these arguments, once one gets past the detail, is that the authors of these articles have very different theoretical views on neuropsychology. The critiques are more along the lines of the disagreement between a behaviorist and a psychoanalyst on proper therapeutic approaches: one is very unlikely to reach agreement despite any amount of discussion or data. It is the author's firm belief that there is room for many different approaches to neuropsychology, all of which can be used properly, just as many different schools of psychotherapy have helped patients despite the belief of many in one true way. Unfortunately, some in neuropsychology also believe they have found the one truth. Beyond this fundamental disagreement, the major critical points from these articles and a discussion of each follows.

1. *It is inappropriate to use a 0, 1, 2 (normal, borderline, abnormal) scoring criterion.* This is confusing, because the most widely used psychometric tests in the world (the Wechsler Intelligence scales) use exactly the same scoring system without any difficulty, as do other procedures.

2. *There is insufficient research on the LNNB.* This comment was initially written after only the first two articles on the battery had been published. Although it was true then, since that date there have been well over two hundred published articles using the LNNB. The breadth of this literature rivals that for any other major neuropsychological test, and indeed is far more than exists for any other test that is only ten years old. The original criticisms went on to mention specific areas that were missing (internal reliability, item scale consistency, content validity, correlational evidence with other tests, etc.). These can all be found now, as covered in this chapter and elsewhere.

3. *Literal interpretation of the LNNB scales and items may be misleading in some populations, such as severe aphasics.* This, though true, is hardly a criticism, although it was presented as one. All tests may be missed for numerous reasons (hence our emphasis on including qualitative and process variables in the analysis.) This was recognized from the conception of the test. Severe aphasics, for example, may miss items

because they fail to understand the directions. Although the procedure for administration attempts to reduce this factor (which was not discussed in the criticisms) there is no question that such factors need to be understood when giving any procedure. It was also noted that the LNNB scales are multifactorial, which is indeed true and is discussed in detail in the test manual.

4. *The LNNB is interpreted simply by looking at the clinical scales.* This is an interesting comment, generated apparently by psychometric research on the instrument and a failure to read the test manual adequately. As is evident in the summary presented here, interpretation of scale elevations is only one approach to interpreting the test within a much wider variety of techniques (including qualitative and historical variables) that are used in clinical work. Although the test scores do receive prominence in research work (since they are more amenable to statistical manipulation), this work forms only one of the foundations for test interpretation.

5. *The authors were wrong to use Luria's name in the test title.* This is an odd complaint, which seems to suggest that the authors were attempting to capitalize on Luria's name in some way so as to sell more tests. This criticism, though more personally insulting to the authors than meaningful for the user, seems to have more impact than the others for many. In fact, Luria's name was used in order to acknowledge the source of many of the ideas that inspired the test. Luria's ideas, though not responsible for all aspects of the test, certainly are responsible for most of its theoretical underpinnings. In using the name, we sought to honor Luria. The user of the test will have to decide if we did what we intended.

6. *The use of psychometric test batteries is bad because (1) psychometric tests are no good in themselves and (2) they make neuropsychological assessment more accessible to more psychologists.* This is an interesting argument. Obviously, there is a split within the field on the use of psychometric versus more individualized, less standardized procedures. I have discussed this in detail elsewhere (e.g., Golden, 1980) and will not repeat those arguments except to note that there are indeed two camps. We believe that proper use of procedures like the LNNB can take advantage of the positive contributions of both sides, which has placed us at odds with individuals who hold either polarized position.

The second argument is also interesting in that it suggests that neuropsychology should be as obscure as possible so as to keep "unqualified" people out. A similar argument could be made against using CAT scans and other new medical techniques, where computers increasingly do much of the work. Such changes in fields do allow people to misuse the new techniques. The answer, however, is not to criticize the techniques but, rather, to increase our efforts at professional education to avoid misuse.

CONCLUSIONS

This chapter has presented a brief introduction to the structure, administration, interpretation, and research available on the Luria-Nebraska Neuropsychological Battery. Because of space limitations, much material has been omitted that can be found in the test manual (Golden, Purisch, & Hammeke, 1986) and in other referenced publications. It has been my intention to give the reader a general introduction and basic information so as to provide familiarity with the battery. Interested readers are referred to the test manual as a first source of additional information on the battery.

REFERENCES

Adams, K. (1980). In search of Luria's battery: A false start. *Journal of Consulting and Clinical Psychology, 48,* 511–516.

Bach, P. J., Harowski, K., Kirby, K., Peterson, P., & Schulein, M. (1981). The interrater reliability of the Luria-Nebraska Neuropsychological Battery. *Clinical Neuropsychology, 3*(3), 19–21.

Benton, A. L. (1955). *Benton Visual Retention Test.* New York: Psychological Corporation.

Bryant, E., Maruisch, M., Sawicki, R., & Golden, C. (1984). Validity of the Luria-Nebraska Neuropsychological Battery. *Journal of Consulting and Clinical Psychology, 52,* 445–448.

Cohen, J. (1960). A coefficient of agreement for nominal scales. *Educational and Psychological Measurement, 20*(1), 37–46.

Crosson, B., & Warren, R. L. (1982). Use of the Luria-Nebraska Neuropsychological Battery. *Journal of Consulting and Clinical Psychology, 50,* 22–31.

Delis, D., & Kaplan, E. (1982). The assessment of aphasia with the Luria-Nebraska Neuropsychological Battery. *Journal of Consulting and Clinical Psychology, 50,* 32–39.

Delis, D., & Kaplan, E. (1983). Hazards of a standardized neuropsychological test with low content validity. *Journal of Consulting and Clinical Psychology, 51,* 396–398.

Dill, R. A., & Golden, C. J. (1988). *WAIS-R and Luria-Nebraska intercorrelations.* Manuscript submitted for publication.

Duffala, D. (1979). Validity of the Luria-South Dakota Neuropsychological Battery for brain-injured persons (Doctoral dissertation, California School of Professional Psychology, Berkeley, 1978). *Dissertation Abstracts International, 39,* 4439B.

Dunn, L. M. (1970). *Peabody Picture Vocabulary Test.* Circle Pines, MN: American Guidance Service.

Dunn, L. M., & Markwardt, F. C. (1970). *Peabody Individual Achievement Test.* Circle Pines, MN: American Guidance Service.

Golden, C. J. (1980). In reply to Adams. *Journal of Consulting and Clinical Psychology, 48,* 517–521.

Golden, C. J., Ariel, R., McKay, S., Wilkening, G., Wolf, B., MacInnes, W. (1982). The Luria-Nebraska Neuropsychological Battery: Theoretical orientation and comment. *Journal of Consulting and Clinical Psychology, 50,* 291–300.

Golden, C. J., Ariel, R., Moses, J., Wilkening, G., McKay, S., & MacInnes, W. (1982). Analytic techniques in the interpretation of the Luria-Nebraska Neuropsychological Battery. *Journal of Consulting and Clinical Psychology, 50,* 40–48.

Golden, C. J., Berg, R. A., & Graber, B. (1982). Test–retest reliability of the Luria-Nebraska Neuropsychological Battery in stable, chronically impaired patients. *Journal of Consulting and Clinical Psychology, 50,* 452–454.

Golden, C. J., Fross, K. H., & Graber, B. (1981). Split-half reliability of the Luria-Nebraska Neuropsychological Battery. *Journal of Consulting and Clinical Psychology, 49,* 304–305.

Golden, C. J., Hammeke, T. A., & Purisch, A. D. (1978). Diagnostic validity of a standardized neuropsychological battery derived from Luria's neuropsychological tests. *Journal of Consulting and Clinical Psychology, 46,* 1258–1265.

Golden, C. J., Kane, R., Sweet, J., Moses, J. A., Cardellino, J. P., Templeton, R., Vicente, P., & Graber, B. (1981). Relationship of the Halstead-Reitan Neuropsychological Battery to the Luria-Nebraska Neuropsychological Battery. *Journal of Consulting and Clinical Psychology, 49,* 410–417.

Golden, C. J., Moses, J. A., Fishburne, F. J., Engum, E., Lewis, G. P., Wisniewski, A. M., Conley, F. K., Berg, R. A., & Graber, B. (1981). Cross-validation of the Luria-Nebraska Neuropsychological Battery for the presence, lateralization and localization of brain damage. *Journal of Consulting and Clinical Psychology, 49,* 491–507.

Golden, C. J., Moses, J. A., Graber, B., & Berg, R. A. (1981). Objective clinical rules for interpreting the Luria-Nebraska Neuropsychological Battery: Derivation, effectiveness, and validation. *Journal of Consulting and Clinical Psychology, 49,* 616–618.

Golden, C. J., Purisch, A. D., & Hammeke, T. A. (1980). *Luria-Nebraska Neuropsychological Battery: Manual.* Los Angeles: Western Psychological Services.

Golden, C. J., Purisch, A. D., & Hammeke, T. A. (1986). *Luria-Nebraska Neuropsychological Battery: Forms I and II.* Los Angeles: Western Psychological Services.

Goodglass, H., & Kaplan, E. (1972). *Boston Diagnostic Aphasia Examination.* Philadelphia: Lea & Febiger.

Hammeke, T. A., Golden, C. J., & Purisch, A. D. (1978). A standardized, short, and comprehensive neuropsychological test battery based on the Luria neuropsychological evaluation. *International Journal of Neuroscience, 8,* 135–141.

Jastak, J. F., Jastak, S. R., & Bijou, S. W. (1965). *Wide Range Achievement Test.* Wilmington: Guidance Associates of Delaware.

Kane, R. L., Parsons, O. A., Goldstein, G., & Moses, J. A., Jr. (1983). *Further comparisons of the relative diagnostic accuracy of the Halstead-Reitan and Luria-Nebraska Neuropsychological Test batteries.* Paper presented at the meeting of the International Neuropsychological Society, Mexico City.

Kane, R. L., Sweet, J. J., Golden, C. J., Parsons, O. A., & Moses, J. A. (1981). Comparative diagnostic accuracy of the Halstead-Reitan and standardized Luria-Nebraska Neuropsychological Batteries in a mixed psychiatric and brain-damaged population. *Journal of Consulting and Clinical Psychology, 49,* 484–485.

Lewis, G. P., Golden, C. J., Moses, J. A., Osmon, D. C., Purisch, A. D., & Hammeke, T. A. (1979). Localization of cerebral dysfunction with a standardized version of Luria's neuropsychological battery. *Journal of Consulting and Clinical Psychology, 47,* 1003–1019.

Luria, A. R. (1966). *Higher cortical functions in man.* New York: Basic Books.

Luria, A. R. (1973). *The working brain.* New York: Basic Books.

Luria, A. R. (1980). *Higher cortical functions in man.* (2nd ed.). New York: Basic Books.

MacInnes, W. D., Gillen, R. W., Golden, C. J., Graber, B., Cole, J. K., Uhl, H. S., & Greenhouse, A. H. (1983). Aging and performance on the Luria-Nebraska Neuropsychological Battery. *International Journal of Neuroscience, 19,* 179–190.

Malloy, P. F., & Webster, J. S. (1981). Detecting mild brain impairment using the Luria-Nebraska Neuropsychological Battery. *Journal of Consulting and Clinical Psychology, 49,* 768–770.

Marvel, G. A., Golden, C. J., Hammeke, T., Purisch, A., & Osmon, D. (1979). Relationship of age and education to performance on a standardized version of Luria's neuropsychological tests in different populations. *International Journal of Neuroscience, 9,* 63–70.

McKay, S. E., Golden, C. J., Moses, J. A., Fishburne, F., & Wisniewski, A. (1981). Correlation of the Luria-Nebraska Neuropsychological Battery with the WAIS. *Journal of Consulting and Clinical Psychology, 49,* 940–946.

McKay, S., & Ramsey, R. (1983). Correlation of the Wechsler Memory Scale and the Luria-Nebraska Memory scale. *Clinical Neuropsychology, 5,* 168–170.

Mikula, J. A. (1981). The development of a short form of the standardized version of Luria's neuropsychological assessment (Doctoral dissertation, Southern Illinois University, Carbondale, 1979). *Dissertation Abstracts International, 41,* 3189B.

Moses, J. A., & Golden, C. J. (1979). Cross validation of the discriminative effectiveness of the standardized Luria Neuropsychological Battery. *International Journal of Neuroscience, 9,* 149–155.

Moses, J. A., Johnson, G. L., & Lewis, G. P. (1983). Reliability analyses of the Luria-Nebraska Neuropsychological Battery factor scales by diagnostic group: A follow-up study. *International Journal of Neuroscience, 21,* 107–112.

Osmon, D. C., Golden, C. J., Purisch, A. D., Hammeke, T. A., & Blume, H. G. (1979). The use of a standardized battery of Luria's tests in the diagnosis of lateralized cerebral dysfunction. *International Journal of Neuroscience, 9,* 1–9.

Picker, W. R., & Schlottmann, R. S. (1982). An investigation of the Intellectual Processes scale of the Luria-Nebraska Neuropsychological Battery. *Clinical Neuropsychology, 4*(3), 120–124.

Plaisted, J. R., & Golden, C. J. (1982). Test–retest reliability of the clinical, factor and localization scales of the Luria-Nebraska Neuropsychological Battery. *International Journal of Neuroscience, 17,* 163–167.

Prifitera, A., & Ryan, J. J. (1981). Validity of the Luria-Nebraska Intellectual Processes scale as a measure of adult intelligence. *Journal of Consulting and Clinical Psychology, 49,* 755–756.

Raven, I. C. (1960). *Guide to the Standard Progressive Matrices.* London: A. K. Lewis.

Russell, E. W., Neuringer, C., & Goldstein, G. (1970). *Assessment of brain damage: A neuropsychological key approach.* New York: Wiley-Interscience.

Ryan, J. J., & Prifitera, A. (1982). Concurrent validity of the Luria-Nebraska Memory scale. *Journal of Clinical Psychology, 38,* 378–379.

Sawicki, R. F., & Golden, C. J. (1984). Examination of two decision rules for the global interpretation of the Luria-Nebraska Neuropsychological Battery summary profile. *International Journal of Neuroscience, 22,* 209.

Sawicki, R. F., Maruish, M. E., & Golden, C. J. (1983). *Comparison of alpha reliabilities of the Luria-Nebraska Neuropsychological Battery.* Manuscript submitted for publication.

Shelly, C., & Goldstein, G. (1982a). Intelligence, achievement, and the Luria-

Nebraska Battery in a neuropsychiatric population: A factor analytic study. *Clinical Neuropsychology, 4*(4), 164–169.

Shelly, C., & Goldstein, G. (1982b). Psychometric relations between the Luria-Nebraska and Halstead-Reitan Neuropsychological Test batteries in a neuropsychiatric setting. *Clinical Neuropsychology, 4*(3), 128–133.

Wechsler, D. (1945). A standardized memory scale for clinical use. *Journal of Psychology, 19,* 87–93.

8

The Vineland Adaptive Behavior Scales

Sara S. Sparrow
Domenic V. Cicchetti

The Vineland Adaptive Behavior Scales represent a revision of the Vineland Social Maturity Scale (Doll, 1935), which, over the last sixty years, has made major contributions to our knowledge of adaptive behavior assessment and our understanding of mental retardation. In fact, it is to the field of mental retardation that we owe the major development of the constructs of adaptive behavior and its applicability not only to the retarded individual but to many other clinical groups as well. Today the use of adaptive behavior in diagnosing mental retardation is mandated not only by the American Association for Mental Deficiency (AAMD), but also by the American Psychiatric Association (APA), the American Medical Association (AMA), and many federal and state laws.

Portions of this manuscript were reproduced or adapted from materials published and copyrighted by American Guidance Service, Circle Pines, Minnesota (specifically, the Survey, Expanded, or Classroom versions of *The Vineland Adaptive Behavior Scales* by S. S. Sparrow, D. A. Balla, and D. V. Cicchetti, 1984a, 1984b, 1985, Circle Pines, Minnesota: American Guidance Service. This material is presented in this chapter with the permission of the publisher.

Before the early 1900s mental retardation was generally defined in terms of social and personal competence, or the ability of the individual to take care of himself or herself. Needless to say, the grounds on which such judgments were made were very subjective and were not based on scientific principles. In the early 1900s, however, a monumental event in the history of psychology and psychological assessment took place with the introduction of individually administered intelligence scales—essentially, the Stanford-Binet, published originally in the United States in 1916 (Terman, 1916). With the advent of a more scientific way to judge a person's intellectual ability, it increasingly became the practice to define mental retardation entirely on the basis of an individual's performance on intelligence tests. The use of this single criterion for classifying mental retardation led to many abuses; large numbers of people were labeled as mentally retarded who today would not be so classified. For example, intelligence tests were administered to people whose primary language was not English, and who, when they were unable to score in the average range, were classified as retarded. It became clear to many psychologists that the use of a sole criterion for classifying mental retardation was exceedingly problematic and at times very detrimental.

One person who found this method of classification exceedingly inappropriate was Edgar Doll, who was at the Vineland Training Center in Vineland, New Jersey, during the 1930s. Doll began his pioneering work in adaptive behavior assessment with the development of the Vineland Social Maturity Scale (1935, 1965). Doll was particularly interested in studying the relationship between low intellectual ability and social competence, which he defined as "the functional ability of the human organism for exercising personal independence and social responsibility" (Doll, 1953, p. 10). In a 1940 article, Doll listed six criteria for mental deficiency, with social incompetence as the first and most important.

The contributions of Edgar Doll were increasingly apparent as psychologists and educators grew more concerned about classification and treatment of the mentally retarded. It was some years, however, before the role of adaptive behavior in assessing mental retardation would be officially proposed by the American Association on Mental Deficiency (AAMD), when that organization published the first official manual stating that, in addition to subaverage intelligence, an important aspect in the classification of mental retardation was demonstration of deficits in adaptive behavior (Heber, 1959, 1961). The AAMD defined *adaptive behavior* as the following: (1) the degree to which the individual is able to function and maintain himself or herself independently and (2) the degree to which he or she meets satisfactorily the culturally imposed demands of personal and social responsibility (Heber, 1961, p. 61). Later editions of the AAMD manuals reemphasized the significance of the use of adaptive behavior in the classification of mental retardation (Crossman, 1973, 1977, 1983).

Some years after the AAMD took its original position on the importance of adaptive behavior in defining mental retardation, the federal government passed a law (Education for All Handicapped Children's Act of 1975, [P.L. 94–142]) that required states seeking financial assistance from the federal government to provide free and appropriate public education for all children, regardless of their handicap. P.L. 94–142 emphasizes that adaptive behavior should be assessed in all handicapping conditions in children and, furthermore, that a deficit in adaptive behavior must be demonstrated before a child may be classified as mentally retarded. Since the passage of P.L. 94–142, most states have developed guidelines to conform to the law's mandate. It is interesting to note that neither AAMD, P.L. 94–142, nor most state guidelines specify how one assesses adaptive behavior and provides guidelines for the quantification of deficits in adaptive behavior.

In the wake of the federal mandate to provide assessment of adaptive behavior for all handicapping conditions and the requirement that adaptive behavior deficits be demonstrated to classify a child as mentally retarded, a host of adaptive behavior measures have been developed since 1975.

Given the lack of appropriate guidelines, as well as appropriate instruments for assessing adaptive behavior, the revision of the Vineland Social Maturity Scale was begun in the late 1970s. Many similarities exist between the Vineland Social Maturity Scale and the Vineland Adaptive Behavior Scales. Like the old Vineland, the Vineland Adaptive Behavior Scales assess the personal and social sufficiency of individuals from birth to adulthood, and are applicable to both handicapped and nonhandicapped individuals. Again, like the old Vineland, the new Vineland is based on an interview with a person who is familiar with the behavior of the individual being assessed; it does not require direct administration of the items to the individual being evaluated. Finally, like the old Vineland, the new Vineland is based on developmental theory and thus looks at a person's development of personal and social sufficiency in a positive developmental perspective, rather than being based on a deficit model.

CHARACTERISTICS OF ADAPTIVE BEHAVIOR

Several important principles are part of a definition of the performance of daily activities required for personal and social self-sufficiency. First, adaptive behavior is age-related. Thus, adaptive behavior becomes more and more complex as an individual gets older, and we measure different adaptive behaviors at different ages. For example, when we talk about adaptive functioning in young children, we speak of things such as dressing, toileting, make-believe play, and vocabulary. If we are talking about adaptive behavior in adolescents, however, we are talking more about pre-job skills, management of money, and the like. Second, adaptive behavior is defined by the expectations or standards of other people. Thus, although many areas of adaptive behavior are universal, some cultures may judge adaptive behaviors differently. Those with whom we work and interact are the people for whom our behavior must be adaptive. Third, adaptive behavior is defined by typical performance, not ability. This is in direct contrast to assessment of cognitive behavior, for which ability is the prime concern. In adaptive behavior, a person may be well able to perform an adaptive activity, but for some reason, such as lack of motivation or lack of opportunity, does not perform that activity. Thus, a child might be very familiar with safety rules about crossing the street, but not obey those particular rules when crossing the street. Fourth, adaptive behavior is modifiable. Thus, for most individuals, deficits in adaptive behavior are amenable to remediation and modifiability.

CONSTRUCTION OF THE VINELAND ADAPTIVE BEHAVIOR SCALES

Components

There are three versions of the revised Vineland, which differ in the number of items, the materials used, and the method of administration, as well as in the specific information that is required.

The Interview Edition, Survey Form   The Survey Form consists of 297 items and provides the interviewer with an overall assessment of the individual's adaptive functioning. It is useful for determining strengths and weaknesses and for deciding issues of diagnosis and placement. The Survey Form is administered to a parent or other primary caregiver who is very familiar with the individual being assessed. The interview is semistructured; requires a well-trained and experienced interviewer; lasts approximately 20 to 45 minutes, depending on the age and functioning level of the individual being assessed; and is appropriate for persons between birth and eighteen years of age, and for low-functioning adults.

The Interview Edition, Expanded Form   The Expanded Form contains 577 items, including the 297 that are also in the Survey Form. The Expanded Form provides a more comprehensive view of the individual's adaptive functioning and is used primarily for program planning and as a systematic basis for preparing educational, habilitative, or treatment programs. The Expanded Form also uses a semistructured interview with a primary caregiver who is familiar with the individual being assessed.

It is also appropriate for those from birth to 18 years, 11 months, or for low-functioning adults. Administration of the Expanded Form takes from 60 to 90 minutes, although if the administration of the Expanded Form follows the administration of the Survey Form, it is possible that only part of the Expanded Form will need to be administered. Supplementary materials are provided with the Expanded Form for profiling Vineland performance and writing individual educational (IEP) or habilitative (IHP) programs.

Classroom Edition   The Classroom Edition, which is completed by the individual's teacher, looks at adaptive behavior in the classroom. It includes items from both the Survey Form and the Expanded Form, plus several items that have to do with adaptive skills learned in the classroom. The Classroom Edition is not an interview but is a questionnaire completed independently by the teacher about students from 3 years of age to 12 years, 11 months. For assessing most children, it requires approximately 20 minutes for the teacher to complete the questionnaire.

For all three forms of the Vineland, Report to Parent Forms are available in both English and Spanish. This report explains the Vineland and each child's scores. In addition, the record form for the Survey Form is available in both English and Spanish.

Content of the Vineland Adaptive Behavior Scales

All three forms of the Vineland Adaptive Behavior Scales consist of four adaptive domains: Communication, Daily Living Skills, Socialization and Motor Skills. The Motor Skills domain is administered only to children less than six years of age or if the individual being assessed has or is suspected of having a motor deficit. The first three domains each have three subdomains, and Motor Skills has two subdomains (see Table 8–1 for a description of Vineland content). The four adaptive domains for children under 5 years, 11 months, 30 days, provide the data for the Adaptive Behavior Composite. For children over 5–11–30, only Communication, Daily Living Skills, and Socialization make up the Adaptive Behavior Composite. The two interview editions, Survey and Expanded, also have an optional maladaptive behavior domain, which is administered only above the age of five.

Scores Derived from the Vineland Adaptive Behavior Scales

There are several scores available for this norm-referenced test, which is based on the standardization sample of 3,000 individuals from birth to adulthood for the Survey and Expanded forms. The same scores

Table 8–1 Numbers of Items and Content Descriptions of Each Version of the Vineland Adaptive Behavior Scales

Domain and Subdomain	Numbers of Items			Content
	Survey Form	Expanded Form	Classroom Edition	
Communication	67	133	63	
Receptive	13	23	10	What the individual understands
Expressive	31	76	29	What the individual says
Written	23	34	24	What the individual reads and writes
Daily Living Skills	92	201	99	
Personal	39	90	36	How the individual eats, dresses, and practices personal hygiene
Domestic	21	45	21	What household tasks the individual performs
Community	32	66	42	How the individual uses time, money, the telephone, and job skills
Socialization	66	134	53	
Interpersonal Relationships	28	50	17	How the individual interacts with others
Play and Leisure Time	20	48	18	How the individual plays and uses leisure time
Coping Skills	18	36	18	How the individual demonstrates responsibility and sensitivity to others
Motor Skills	36	73	29	
Gross	20	42	16	How the individual uses arms and legs for movement and coordination
Fine	16	31	13	How the individual uses hands and fingers to manipulate objects
Adaptive Behavior Composite	261	541	244	A composite of Communication, Daily Living Skills, Socialization, and Motor Skills domains
Maladaptive Behavior* (no subdomains)	36	36	0	Undesirable behaviors that may interfere with the individual's adaptive functioning

*The Maladaptive Behavior domain is included in both the Survey Form and the Expanded Form for optional use; it is not included in the Classroom Edition.

are available for the Classroom Edition, but for children aged 3 years to 12 years, 11 months. For the four adaptive behavior domains and the Adaptive Behavior Composite, standard scores are available (mean = 100; S.D. = 15). Also available are percentile ranks, stanines, adaptive levels, and age equivalents. Age equivalents and adaptive levels are also available for each of the subdomains. In addition, adaptive levels, percentile ranks, and age equivalents are available for the domains and Adaptive Behavior Composite for a number of supplementary norm groups. Thus, a user can obtain a percentile rank for a handicapped individual that shows the relative standing of that individual in comparison with others with the same handicap. In addition, the optional maladaptive behavior domain yields adaptive levels that can be compared to the normal standardization sample or the supplementary sample groups. Maladaptive levels indicate whether a person exhibits a significant, intermediate, or nonsignificant number of maladaptive behaviors.

Standardization Samples for the Vineland Adaptive Behavior Scales

Survey Form and Expanded Form Samples Following the development and national tryout of the first version of the Vineland Adaptive Behavior Scales, a process that required two years of intensive effort, two versions—the Survey Form and the Expanded Form— were developed. A representative nationwide sample of 3,000 persons, with 100 individuals in each of thirty age groups (between birth and 18 years, 11 months) made up the basic normative data for both the Survey and Expanded forms. To ensure adequate representation of the United States population, based on the 1980 U.S. Census, the sample was further stratified on the basis of sex, race or ethnic group, size of community, region of the country, and level of parental education. The resulting standardization sample closely matched the U.S. population based on the 1980 census. For specific details see Sparrow, Balla, and Cicchetti (1984a, 1984b, pp. 9–18).

Classroom Edition The standardization sample for the Classroom Edition contained 2,984 children ranging in age between 3 years and 12 years, 11 months. As was true of the Survey and Expanded forms, an attempt was also made to ensure adequate representation of the population, based again on the 1980 U.S. Census, for the same variables: sex, race or ethnic group, size of community, region of the country, and level of education. The random selection of children for the Classroom standardization sample did not match the U.S. Census data as closely as did the selection of children for the standardization of the Survey and Expanded forms of the Vineland. In general, however, the Classroom sample is considered an adequate representation. For further specific details, see Sparrow, Balla, and Cicchetti (1985, pp. 9–17).

Both the Survey and Expanded forms of the Vineland were administered to two additional classes of standardization subjects. They have been referred to, broadly, as *overlap* and supplementary samples.

Overlap Samples

The overlap samples were two in number: the first comprised 719 subjects, randomly selected from the Kaufman Assessment Battery for Children (K-ABC) standardization sample, and ranging in age between 2 years, 6 months, and 12 years, 11 months. This group was administered both the Vineland and the K-ABC (Kaufman & Kaufman, 1983). The second group comprised 2,018 subjects between the ages of 2 years, 6 months, and 18 years, 11 months. This group, randomly drawn from another larger standardization sample, was administered both the Vineland and the Peabody Picture Vocabulary Test—Revised (PPVT-R; Dunn & Dunn, 1981).

The importance of these overlap samples is that they contain, for the first time, subjects who have been administered both major cognitive and adaptive behavior assessment instruments. This makes it possible to make direct comparisons of cognitive (K-ABC or PPVT-R) and adaptive levels of functioning in the *same* individual.

Supplementary Groups Samples

In addition to the large national samples of nonhandicapped individuals who took part in the Vineland standardization program, a number of handicapped groups of subjects served to provide what we have referred to as supplementary standardization norms. The clinical importance of these groups is that they provide norms that test assessors can use in order to compare the relative ranking of a given person with a specific disorder, with that of other individuals afflicted with the same handicap. The national supplementary standardization groups can be briefly described as, approximately:

1. 800 residential ambulatory mentally retarded adults (18 years and older);
2. 250 residential nonambulatory mentally retarded adults (18 years and older);
3. 100 mentally retarded adults (18 years and older) who are in nonresidential facilities;
4. 150 residential emotionally disturbed children (9 years through 15 years, 6 months);

5. 200 residential visually handicapped children (6 years through 12 years, 11 months); and

6. 300 residential hearing-impaired children (6 years through 12 years, 11 months).

We are currently in the process of obtaining Vineland Survey norms on a projected sample of approximately 1,000 nonresidential, mentally retarded children (with mild to moderate levels of functioning), who are of school age (3 years to 18 years old).

Reliability Assessments of the Vineland Adaptive Behavior Scales

Definitions/Types of Assessments The purpose of this section is to answer three very important questions pertaining to the reliability of the Vineland Adaptive Behavior Scales:

1. How consistent are two *repeated* assessments made by the same examiner (test–retest reliability)?
2. How consistent are two *independent* assessments made by different examiners (interrater reliability)?
3. How consistent are *Survey* and *Classroom* assessments made on the same individuals?

Samples *Test–retest reliability* assessments were obtained for 484 nonhandicapped individuals, ages 6 months through 18 years, 11 months, who were part of the larger national standardization sample. The same examiner administered the entire Vineland Survey Edition (including the optional maladaptive domain) to the same parent (or other primary caregiver) with a two- to four-week test–retest interval period (average about 17 days).

Interrater reliability assessments were obtained on 160 nonhandicapped individuals, who were also participating in the Vineland National Standardization Program, and who also ranged in age from 6 months to 18 years, 11 months. Pairs of different examiners were used to interview each parent or other primary caregiver independently. The intertest interval ranged from 1 to 14 days, with the average being approximately 8 days. Again, the entire Vineland Survey Form was administered on both testing occasions.

Subjects participating in the project measuring agreement levels between the Survey Form and the Classroom Edition of the Vineland were 420 children who: (1) took part in the Vineland National Standardization program; (2) ranged in age from 3 years to 12 years, 11 months, 15 days; and (3) were assessed on both the Survey Form (with the mother or other primary caregiver as the informant) and the Classroom Edition (in which classroom teachers made the Vineland assessment on the basis of their knowledge of the adaptive behavior levels of their students in the classroom). Although there are 261 items in the Vineland Survey Form, 162 items (common to both Survey Form and Classroom Edition) were appropriate to the age range of the Classroom Edition: 39 items made up the Communication domain, 60 the Daily Living Skills domain, 44 the Socialization domain, and 19 the Motor Skills domain.

It was decided not to use the Motor Skills domain because (1) it is only relevant for children up to 6 years of age, in a nonhandicapped sample; (2) the overlapping age range for Motor items between the Survey Form and the Classroom Editions would, therefore, be only between 3 and 6 years of age; (3) the resulting sample is too small to be usable in calculating the Vineland Adaptive Behavior Composite. Therefore, using the procedure by which the Vineland Adaptive Behavior Composite score (ABC) is formed for any individual beyond 6 years, we derived ABC performance levels of each child based on Communication, Daily Living Skills, and Socialization scores.

Selecting Appropriate Reliability Assessment Statistics

In selecting an appropriate statistic for measuring the reliability of the Vineland Adaptive Behavior Scales, we sought a statistic having the following desirable qualities: that it would (1) differentiate paired assessments that were made by the same two examiners from those made by varying pairs of examiners; (2) differentiate pairs of examiners who merely ranked subjects in the same order (say, examiner 1 ranks 3 subjects as 1, 2, and 3, whereas examiner 2 scores the same subjects as 2, 3, and 4) from pairs of examiners who were in complete agreement (e.g., *both* scored the same 3 subjects as 1, 2, and 3); and (3) would adjust or correct for the amount of agreement expected on the basis of chance alone.

Fortunately, there is a statistic that does possess these three desirable qualities. It is known as the *intraclass correlation coefficient* (R_I) (e.g., Bartko, 1966, 1974; Bartko & Carpenter, 1976; Cicchetti & Sparrow, 1981; Fleiss, 1975, 1981) and was applied for each of the three types of Vineland reliability assessments.

Differentiating between Statistical and Clinical Significance

It is well known to biostatistical workers in the field that levels of reliability that may be trivially low (e.g., close to zero) can nonetheless be highly statistically significant providing only that the number of cases on which they are based is sufficiently large (e.g., Fleiss, 1981). Because of this undesirable phenomenon, a number of investigators have developed guidelines for determining levels of practical, substantive, or clinical significance that already assume a minimal level of statistical significance (at or beyond the conventional .05 level) (e.g., Cicchetti & Sparrow, 1981; Fleiss, 1981; Landis & Koch, 1977). The system reported by Cicchetti and Sparrow (1981) closely resembles the one developed by Fleiss (1981) and is a simplified version of the set of guidelines introduced by Landis and Koch (1977). It can be expressed as:

Level of Reliability Coefficient	*Level of Clinical Significance*
Less than .40	Poor
.40–.59	Fair
.60–.74	Good
.75–1.00	Excellent

Results/Discussion of Reliability Assessments

Test–retest reliability assessments produced R_I coefficients in the upper end of the excellent category for each Vineland domain and subdomain (ranging from .95 to .99) and for the Adaptive Behavior Composite (.99). R_I for the optional maladaptive behavior domain was still at the excellent level of clinical significance (.87) but was somewhat lower than R_I for the domains and subdomains. Finally, R_Is performed on the individual Vineland items, comprising the subdomains and domains, indicated that the great majority of items ranged between .80 and the high .90s. For a small number of items, 100 percent agreement occurred between the two testings (these were items pertaining to adaptive behaviors relevant to the very early ages). Since all these infants and children were assigned to the *same* category of classification at both testings (i.e., a score of 2, indicating that the adaptive behavior was usually or almost always performed), no variability was produced in the two sets of ratings, and therefore no appropriate reliability assessment statistic could be applied to the data. For more detailed information on this subject, see Cicchetti and Prusoff (1983) and Kraemer (1979).

Interrater Reliability Assessments   In general, and as expected, R_I results for interrater reliability were slightly lower than for the aforementioned test–retest estimates. The range of subdomain and domain R_I values was between .93 and .99; the R_I for the optional maladaptive domain, .73, placed it at the upper end of good reliability (recall that the corresponding test–retest R_I was .87).

As was true for test–retest assessments of individual items, there were some items that also did not permit enough variability to produce valid estimates of interrater reliability. In one instance (a Communication item), the category 2 was applied to 156 of the 160 individuals in the first assessment and to 155 of the 160 subjects in the second assessment.

Of those items that did permit a valid interrater reliability assessment (87 percent), the great majority (75 percent) of R_Is ranged between the .80s and the high .90s. Another 20 percent ranged between .60 and .74, and the final 5 percent produced R_Is between .43 and .59.

Agreement between the Survey and Classroom Editions Agreement levels, on a domain basis, were: $R_I = .87$, or excellent, for Communication; $R_I = .76$, or excellent, for Daily Living Skills; $R_I = .53$, or fair (moderate), for the Socialization domain; and $R_I = .79$, or excellent, for the Adaptive Behavior Composite.

With respect to individual items making up Vineland domains (or subdomains), however, some items were scored very similarly on both the Survey Form and the Classroom Edition of the Vineland. No consistent patterns emerged, however. Specifically, some items fell into the excellent range, others into the good, fair, or poor range. Unlike the test–retest or interrater reliability assessments, the low R_I values were caused by low levels of agreement rather than by almost perfect agreement, with no or very little variation in scores. Again, see Cicchetti and Prusoff (1983) and Kraemer (1979) for more specific information on the meaning of this important phenomenon.

These results indicate that the Classroom Edition of the Vineland can be reliably used for quick assessments at both the Adaptive Behavior Composite and the domains level of functioning. The Classroom Edition, however, should *never* be used as a substitute for either the Survey or the Expanded Form, when specific information is required based on individual Vineland item assessments. This would mean that the Vineland Classroom Edition would serve primarily as a quick screening instrument that would be followed by either the Survey and/or the Expanded Form if detailed information is required on an item-by-item basis. The Classroom Edition, however, can be used in its own right for assessing functioning at the domain or Adaptive Behavior Composite levels, if this is the only assessment information that is required.

Some Additional Caveats

Implicit in some of the preceding paragraphs is the notion that, in order for reliability assessment to be meaningful, the data need to exhibit a range of scores (in the best case, in fact, to run the gamut of possible scores). With respect to the Vineland, the gamut would go from adaptive behavior, which is scored as 0 (almost never occurs) to 1 (occurs from time to time, but not consistently) to 2 (occurs usually or most of the time). We have already seen that when two examiners place nearly all the subjects in a single category (say, category 2, for easy adaptive behavior items), we obtain a very high percentage of agreement, but the data do not lend themselves to a meaningful assessment of reliability. A corollary of this principle is that, to the extent that the range of possible scores is limited for one or both assessments, the resulting reliability coefficient will be attenuated.

The second rather explicit caveat expressed in this section is that the standard Pearson product moment correlation (Pearson *r*), for several reasons, is simply inadequate as a measure of reliability (e.g., measures similarity in orderings rather than levels of agreement).

In several recent evaluations of the Vineland Adaptive Behavior Scales, the reviewers were not knowledgeable about either of these two biostatistical facts (e.g., Campbell, 1985; Oakland & Houchins, 1985; Reschly, 1987). These reviewers focused on assessments made with the Pearson *r rather* than those made with the appropriate model of the intraclass *r*. Second, they focused on assessments using standard scores (with more restricted ranges) rather than on assessments using raw scores. This is an important distinction to make because the same standard score can reflect a range of possible raw scores. Finally, this phenomenon is *not* uniform along the range of possible scores. Thus, although standard scores are quite valuable for making clinical decisions, they can *artifactually* lower reliability coefficients. Therefore, raw scores, which do not have this undesirable property, should be used for making reliability assessments (see also Sparrow, Balla, & Cicchetti, 1984a, pp. 34–38).

VALIDITY ASSESSMENTS OF THE VINELAND ADAPTIVE BEHAVIOR SCALES

In the most fundamental sense of the word, *validity* answers the question of whether a test does, in fact, measure what it purports to measure. (In this case, of course, the measurement is of adaptive behavior.) There are several types of validity assessment (e.g., face, content, discriminant, factorial, construct). Messick (1980) presents a convincing argument that all forms of validity can be subsumed under the concept of construct validity, or the extent to which the underlying construct of a test is being measured by that test.

Face Validity

The items on the Vineland do have high *face validity;* that is, they look as though they measure what they purport to measure. For example, it is most unlikely that one would confuse items pertaining to how the individual uses arms and legs for movement and coordination (gross motor items) with items pertaining to how the individual interacts with others (socialization items).

Content Validity

The concept of *content* (or *content-related validity;* see Fitzpatrck, 1983) relates to the extent to which a given test appropriately and adequately samples the universe of items (behaviors, other content) that define the constructs measured by that test. A careful review of the child development literature and extant adaptive behavior scales, as well as clinical experience and judgment, resulted in an initial pool of about 3,000 Vineland items that were arranged hierarchically in developmentally ordered clusters. The later application of very specific criteria—combined with local, state, and national field testing; national item tryout; and the national standardization program—resulted in the three versions of the Vineland (Survey Form, Expanded Form, and Classroom Edition) previously described.

Discriminant Validity

Discriminant validity addresses the validity question by asking the extent to which the relevant criterion is performed differentially, by specially selected samples, in accordance with expectations. For example, consistent with our expectations, *visually handicapped,* residential children showed the most extensive deficits in Adaptive Behavior; residential *hearing-impaired* children showed their greatest deficits on the Communication domain; and residential *emotionally disturbed* children (by DSM-III criteria) manifested their most serious deficits in the Socialization domain. They also displayed appreciably more maladaptive behaviors than did their nonhandicapped peers in the standardization program.

Factorial Validity

Two types of factor analyses (principal component, principal factor) were performed on Vineland standardization data, using the nonhandicapped as the sample. In general, the fitting of subdomains into their respective domains was quite successful. Moreover, the developmental quality of the subdomains was also confirmed. As one example, for children aged two to three, the *written* subdomain did not correlate significantly with the factor labeled Communication. Consistent with this finding, for children aged eight and nine, the *receptive* subdomain did not fit the Communication (or any other domain) to any significant degree. The remaining results were also generally confirmatory. For the younger (two- to three-year-old) and older (eight- to nine-year-old) children, the fitting of subdomains into their respective domains was highly significant. Thus, interpersonal relationships, play and leisure time, and coping skills were the most highly correlated with the Socialization factor (for further details, see Sparrow, Balla, & Cicchetti, 1984b).

Construct Validity

Construct validity addresses the validity question by answering the extent to which a new test purportedly measuring a given construct (e.g., adaptive behavior) is correlated with another test thought to be measuring the same construct. It should be noted here that the correlation should be neither too low nor too high. To the extent that the correlation approaches zero, one would wonder whether the sought-after construct is indeed being measured by the new test. Conversely, a correlation approaching +1 would strongly suggest that the new test is so similar to the older one that the question would be why the new test is required at all. The Vineland Adaptive Behavior Scales are considered a revision of the Vineland Social Maturity Scale (Doll, 1935, 1965), although there are a number of differences between the two instruments in both content and standardization. Therefore, we elected to correlate scores obtained on the two scales, with the expectation that the resulting correlation would approach neither one nor zero. We obtained a correlation of .55, which is substantial enough to indicate a moderate relationship between the two instruments (e.g., see the criteria of Horwitz, Cicchetti, & Horwitz, 1984), but indicated that there were, on the other hand, also some real differences between the two scales. This correlation nicely fits the recommendations of Anastasi (1982, p. 145), who notes that "correlations of a new test with an already existing test should be moderately high but not too high. If the test correlates too highly with an already available test, without such added advantages as brevity or ease of administration, then the new test represents needless duplication."

In this section we have presented data on the validity (face, content, discriminant, factorial, criterion-related, and construct) of the Vineland Adaptive Behavior Scales. The weight of the evidence indicates that the Vineland Adaptive Behavior Scales are both highly reliable and valid for the uses for which they have been intended by their authors.

ADMINISTRATION

General Information

Like the old Vineland, the Vineland Adaptive Behavior Scales (both the Survey and the Expanded Form) use a semistructured interview method that requires specific training and experience. Administration of the Survey and Expanded forms of the Vineland Adaptive Behavior Scales requires a trained professional with a background and experience in individual assessment and test interpretation. Those professionals already well versed in standard assessment procedures will find learning this method, though time-consuming, a valuable asset to their assessment techniques.

The Vineland Interview Method

The Vineland interview method is thoroughly described in the manuals for both the Survey Form and the Expanded Form. However, several general characteristics will be presented here. The Vineland interview method is a general conversation with the parent or primary caregiver and does not consist of reading the items to the respondent or allowing the respondent to read any of the items. The interview begins with very general questions; then, probes are used when necessary to elicit specific information about an individual's activities. The items in the Survey Form are ordered according to difficulty level; therefore, content areas are not grouped together. For example, the five grooming items under Daily Living Skills are found on three separate pages of the Record Form. Therefore, a major task for the interviewer is to be familiar enough with all of the items in each domain so that in the semistructured interview the items that logically are related to each other are probed at the same time. Thus, when the interviewer is discussing telephone skills, he or she should be familiar with all six items that relate to the use of the telephone and ask those at the same time. Since the Vineland interviewer is conversational and flexible, however, exact recall of all exams is not necessary. The interviewer may always go back to items that are not covered in earlier parts of the interview.

In addition, for the Survey Form and the Classroom Edition, there are 25 and 50 pages of scoring criteria, respectively. The interviewer must be familiar with the scoring criteria and have them close at hand during the interview. Immediately following the interview, any questionable answers should be reviewed by examining the scoring criteria and scoring at that time. In general, prior to conducting the interview, the interviewer should complete as much of the front page of the Record Form as possible, review the items expected to be asked, review the criteria for those items, and establish starting points for the interview. In addition, basal and ceiling rules are available so that all items in each domain do not need to be administered (see Survey Form Manual, pp. 27–28; Expanded Form Manual, pp. 27–28). Upon completion of the regular interview, there are a series of questions to which the interviewer should respond that shed further light on the interview. At this time, the interviewer estimates the respondent's rapport accuracy, and other items about the interviewer and the individual being assessed.

SCORING

Scoring of each item on the Vineland Survey and Expanded forms is carried out during the interview, and only questionable items that need further review of the criteria are scored after the completion of the interview. There are five possible scores for the adaptive portions of the Survey and Expanded forms, and these are listed on each page of the record booklet. Possible scores are as follows: 2, which denotes that the person usually or habitually completes a given task; 1, meaning that the person sometimes or partially performs the task; and 0, meaning that the person never completes the task. An additional option is "no opportunity (N)," which may only be scored when allowed as noted in the record booklet. For example, item 63 on page 3 under Communication may be scored "N." At no time may "N" be used unless allowed and so noted in the record booklet. Finally, there is a category of "don't know," which means that the respondent was unable to answer the questions because he or she was not familiar with whether or not the individual being assessed performed that behavior. For a more thorough discussion of scoring and the regulation for using each possible score, see pages 77–79 of the Survey Form Manual and pages 73–75 of the Expanded Form Manual.

INTERPRETATION

Chapter 6 in the Survey Form, the Expanded Form, and the Classroom Edition gives detailed information for interpreting performance on the Vineland Adaptive Behavior Scales as well as for integrating Vineland data with other test data. Chapter 5 in all three editions provides details for obtaining raw scores and derived scores and for completing the Score Summary Sheet. Instructions are also available for investigating differences between domain standard scores, including domain strengths and weaknesses, pairwise comparisons, and ranges of domain standard scores. The investigation of differences between domain standard scores is a crucial aspect of test interpretation. Instructions are given for determining statistical significance and unusual differences. Tables for looking up domain differences are found in the appendix, and forms for computing the differences are found in Chapter 5 and may be reproduced by the user. Finally, special optional scoring procedures are described, which are appropriate for special samples. Methods for prorating, producing estimated scores, and estimating adaptive levels are also provided.

Interpretation of Vineland performance may be done for many purposes, including the following:

1. to diagnose mental retardation, in which case the Vineland is used with a standardized intelligence test and in conjunction with the recommendations by the AAMD and P.L. 94–142;

2. to help plan for educational placement;

3. to be part of a comprehensive assessment of a child's or other individual's total intelligence; achievement; and motor, language, and adaptive development when planning for some type of intervention;

4. to investigate an individual's strengths or weaknesses in particular domains or subdomains;

5. to develop individual education, habilitative, and treatment programs (the Expanded Form is particularly well suited to this use);

6. to measure changes in adaptive behavior over time, such as before and after treatment intervention;

7. to help decide if further assessment or diagnostic procedures are indicated.

Interpretation must always take into account both the content (global functioning or more specific functioning in domains, subdomains, or item clusters) and derived scores (standard scores, national percentile ranks, and stanines), adaptive levels, age equivalents, and maladaptive levels. At times, however, complete interpretation of performance is not necessary. For example, if an investigator in a research project is interested only in comparing socialization between various groups, then Socialization may be the only domain administered, or the only one for which derived scores and content are interpreted.

In general, the first step in interpreting Vineland performance, after completing the Score Summary Sheet and completing domain differences, is to compare the individual's scores with the national standardization sample. The guidelines for this interpretation proceed from the most global (or molar) to the most molecular. Thus, the first step is reporting and interpreting the Adaptive Behavior Composite and associated derived scores, including the bands of errors selected and, if desired, percentile ranks, stanines, adaptive levels, and age equivalents. After the description of general adaptive functioning, it is important to describe performance in the Adaptive Behavior domains. The same scores are available for the domains as for the Adaptive Behavior Composite. The third step is to interpret the differences between domain standard scores, to discuss domain strengths and weaknesses, and to compare the statistical and the clinical significance of adaptive behavior performance. Subsequently, the performance on subdomains can be described using both adaptive levels and, when appropriate, age equivalents. Note, however, that one should always be cautious about the use of age equivalents, which may be misleading to the person who is being informed about the evaluation. (See page 119 of the Survey Form, page 113 of the Expanded Form, and page 82 of the Classroom Edition for additional relevant caveats.)

Similar steps are made when interpreting Vineland performance for supplementary (handicapped) samples and comparing these samples to the normal standardization group. When comparing respondents to specific supplementary samples to their peer group, only percentile ranks and adaptive levels are available.

The next procedure is to generate hypotheses about profile fluctuations. While, in many respects, the most significant information yielded by the Vineland Adaptive Behavior Scales is its empirical data, the Expanded Form goes even further in its statistical treatment of data by pinpointing, through the use of program planning profiles and the score summary and profile booklet, which clusters of items suggest deficits. In addition to investigating the empirical results, however, clinical skill and knowledge of normal and deviant behavior across the developmental spectrum are very useful in generating hypotheses about Vineland results. In fact, when generating hypotheses and making clinical use of the Vineland, all levels of the tests are important, including reviewing individual items and looking at their content.

Finally, the last area to be described about Vineland interpretation pertains to the optional maladaptive behavior domain. If performance on the maladaptive level is either intermediate or significant, it becomes useful to look at individual items and the frequency of specific behaviors when making an interpretation.

CASE EXAMPLES

Case Example 1

Elizabeth, a six-year-old Caucasian girl, has been in kindergarten for a second year. There is a question of her cognitive ability and whether or not she should be placed in a special program for mentally retarded children. In Table 8–2 one can see that Elizabeth performed cognitively in the mild range of mental retardation, with a Full Scale IQ of 66 ± 9. The chances that the range of scores from 57 to 75 includes her true IQ are about 90 out of 100. There are no significant differences between any of the global scores. Her standard score of 71 on the PPVT-R is consistent with her WISC-R findings.

On the Vineland, Elizabeth obtained an Adaptive Behavior Composite standard score of 87; at the 90 percent confidence level, her true score is said to fall between 82 and 92. Her standard score corresponds with a national percentile rank of 19 and classifies her general adaptive functioning as adequate. Elizabeth's standard scores on the Adaptive Behavior domains, along with a band of error at the 90 percent level of confidence, were as follows: Communication, 85 ± 7 (78–92); Daily Living Skills, 95 ± 8 (87–103); Socialization, 92 ± 8 (84–100). Her performance

Table 8–2 Adaptive and Cognitive Assessments of Elizabeth, a Six-Year-Old Girl with Possible Mental Retardation

I. Cognitive assessments		
A. *WISC-R scales*		*Standard Scores*
1. Verbal Intelligence (VIQ)		67 ± 7
2. Performance Intelligence (PIQ)		69 ± 8
3. Full Scale Intelligence (FIQ)		66 ± 6
B. *PPVT-R*		71
II. Adaptive assessments		
A. *Vineland domains*		*Standard Scores*
1. Communication		85 ± 7
2. Daily Living Skills		95 ± 8
3. Socialization		92 ± 8
B. *Adaptive Behavior Composite*		87 ± 5
III. Maladaptive assessments*		

*Since maladaptive behaviors are not considered developmental, they are measured in terms of raw rather than standard scores, which are converted to levels. Elizabeth's score of 5 places her in the range considered not significant for level of maladaptive functioning.

on all the adaptive domains is in the adequate range, with no significant differences between domains. Thus, although Elizabeth scores in the mildly retarded range on cognitive ability, her adaptive skills are in the adequate range. This provides ample support for the suggestion that Elizabeth is not mentally retarded; her adequate adaptive behavior precludes her being classified as such.

Case Example 2

The second case presentation (see Table 8–3) is that of an eleven-year-old boy who was referred to a child guidance clinic because of emotional problems. He was having difficulty getting along with both his teachers and his peers, and was frequently sent to see the guidance counselor because of behavior problems. Cognitive testing revealed that Kevin had a Mental Processing Composite at the high end of the average range—that is, 119 ± 6—with a sequential processing score of 115 ± 9 and a simultaneous processing score of 118 ± 7. Kevin's standard score for achievement was 110 ± 4. Thus, all the global scores on the K-ABC were in the average to above-average range, with no significant strengths or weaknesses. Kevin's standard score of 121 on the Peabody Picture Vocabulary Test places him in the superior range for listening vocabulary. The Survey Form of the Vineland was administered to Kevin's mother as a respondent, and the results are summarized in Table 8–3. Kevin obtained a standard score of 79 for the Adaptive Behavior Composite. At the 90 percent confidence level, his true score was said to fall between

Table 8–3 Adaptive and Cognitive Assessments of Kevin, an Eleven-Year-Old Boy, Referred to a Child Guidance Clinic for Emotional Problems

I. Cognitive assessments	
A. *K-ABC scales*	*Standard Scores*
1. Sequential	115 ± 9
2. Simultaneous	118 ± 7
3. Mental Processing Composite	119 ± 6
4. Achievement	110 ± 4
B. *PPVT-R*	121
II. Adaptive assessments	
A. *Vineland domains*	*Standard Scores*
1. Communication	105 ± 11
2. Daily Living Skills	84 ± 11
3. Socialization	65 ± 9
B. *Adaptive Behavior Composite*	79 ± 7
III. Maladaptive assessments*	

*Kevin's raw score of 27 places him in the range considered significant for maladaptive functioning.

72 and 86. This range of standard scores classifies his general adaptive functioning as moderately low. Kevin's domain standard scores and bands of error at the 90 percent level of confidence are Communication, 104 ± 11 (93–115); Daily Living Skills, 84 ± 11 (73–95); and Socialization, 65 ± 9 (56–74). Thus, Kevin exhibits considerable variability in his level of functioning across the various domains. Although his communication skills are adequate and age-appropriate, both his Daily Living Skills and Socialization skills are below expected levels. Socialization is his weakest area. It is a significant weakness, both statistically and clinically. Such a weakness was found in only 2 percent of the standardization population. Kevin's communication domain is a significant strength, both statistically and clinically, when compared with the other domains. Such a comparative strength was found in only 5 percent of the standardization population. On the maladaptive behavior domain, Kevin received a significant raw score of 27, which indicates a significant level of maladaptive functioning. Closer analysis of both daily living skills and socialization revealed that Kevin performed no household tasks, such as cleaning his room, making his bed, or helping with any domestic chores. Kevin also had poorly developed telephone skills and rarely used the telephone appropriately. Kevin's socialization skills were seriously deficient. He has no friends and participates in no group activities. Thus, although Kevin is a boy with above-average intellectual ability and good school achievement, his adaptive functioning lags well behind what one would expect of a boy his age. Given these data, Kevin's emotional functioning, Socialization, and Daily Living Skills performance were further evaluated

using personality assessment measures and administration of those two domains of the Expanded Form of the Vineland. Subsequent to this evaluation, his school, his family, and the child guidance clinic planned a program to assist in remediation of his areas of specific deficit.

USES OF THE VINELAND ADAPTIVE BEHAVIOR SCALES

Three broad areas of application of the Vineland Scales are for diagnostic evaluations, program planning, and research investigations.

Diagnostic Evaluations

As noted on page 4 of the Vineland Survey Manual, it is quite likely that the instrument will be applied primarily as a major or supplementary diagnostic tool. As one example, the question of whether a school-age child is or is not mentally retarded can be answered by using the Vineland as a measure of adaptive functioning and the K-ABC (Kaufman & Kaufman, 1983) as a measure of cognitive functioning. Because of the overlap between Vineland and K-ABC standardization samples (alluded to earlier), valid comparisons can be made between cognitive and adaptive abilities in a given child suspected of being mentally retarded. The dual usage of the Vineland and the K-ABC will facilitate the ruling in or ruling out of a diagnosis of mental retardation.

It should be emphasized that although the Vineland is expected to play a major role in evaluating suspected cases of mental retardation, the instrument is by no means restricted to use with those who are, or may be, suspected of being mentally retarded. Other groups of children and adults for whom the Vineland may prove valuable include those with emotional, hearing, or visual handicaps. In fact, the Vineland may be indicated whenever a given handicap is suspected of interfering with one's level of daily functioning (e.g., self-help skills, socialization skills, or communication skills).

Program Planning

Although program planning to develop specific individual educational programs (IEPs) or individual habilitative programs (IHPs) can be most readily facilitated by using the Vineland Expanded Scales, the other two versions also can play a significant role in certain circumstances. As one example, a teacher may observe that a given seven-year-old child seems to be having difficulty interacting satisfactorily with his classmates. In order to obtain a better understanding of the phenomenon, she decides to use the Classroom Edition to score the child on each of the relevant major Vineland domains. After consulting with the school psychologist, she discovers that her hunches have been supported. John scores in the adequate range for both Communication (standard score or S.S. = 106); and Daily Living Skills (S.S. = 102). His score on the Socialization domain, however, is more than two standard deviations below the mean of 100 (S.S. = 68).

In order to test the extent to which John's adaptive behavior is similar (or different) in other settings or surroundings, the school psychologist interviews the child's mother using the Survey Form of the Vineland. The results, based on the mother's responses, closely parallel those provided by the classroom teacher, namely: for Communication, S.S. = 101; for Daily Living Skills, S.S. = 107; and for Socialization, S.S. = 71.

Through further consultations between the classroom teacher, the psychologist, and John's mother, the decision is reached to develop a comprehensive step-by-step programming plan to increase John's level of socialization skills. A program is developed and implemented by two psychologists and an educator, using the Vineland Expanded Form to develop a specific IEP. As we note (Sparrow, Balla, & Cicchetti, 1984b, p. 4), "The Expanded Form was specifically developed to provide detailed information about the prerequisite skills of adaptive behaviors and offers step-by-step guidelines for preparing an individual program."

Research

The Vineland Scales can be used in many types of research investigations in which the development and functioning of both handicapped and nonhandicapped individuals is the focus of concern. Because the Vineland does not require the presence of the individual being evaluated, it can facilitate research on parent–child relationships, mental and physical handicaps, and infant development.

Our own avenues of research can be broadly dichotomized into clinical case studies, and comparative studies, in which theoretical, developmental, and underlying constructs are brought to bear as we attempt to distinguish both levels and patterns of adaptive and cognitive functioning, as they may vary from one diagnostic group to another.

Clinical Case Studies   Thus far, we have carefully examined a number of individual case studies in order to gain some understanding of how specific handicaps, be they cognitive, adaptive, or emotional, differentially separate one diagnostic category from another.

In one study (Sparrow & Cichetti, 1984), two *hypothetical* case histories (which closely parallel clinical practice) were discussed. In one, a six-year-old boy's levels of adaptive functioning were found to be adequate. Specifically, Richard's Vineland standard scores were 88 for Communication, 85 for Daily Living Skills, 92 for Socialization, and 85 for

Adaptive Behavior Composite. Finally, level of functioning on the Maladaptive Behavior domain fell into the nonsignificant range. However, levels of cognitive functioning were quite low. Thus, K-ABC standard scores were 76 for Sequential Processing, 66 for Simultaneous Processing, 67 for Mental Processing Composite, 71 for Achievement, and 76 for PPVT-R Listening Vocabulary score.. This pattern of adaptive and cognitive functioning provides strong support for the diagnostic conclusion that Richard is *not* mentally retarded. It should also be noted that his PPVT-R standard score of 76 fits the general range of several K-ABC cognitive areas. This finding also parallels that of a number of research investigations that indicate moderate to high correlations between K-ABC and PPVT-R areas of assessment (e.g., Kaufman & Kaufman, 1983, p. 138). In a more general context, the case of Richard is clinically significant because of the fact that scores in each measured area of cognitive ability border around the recent AAMD cutoff range of 70 to 75 for the diagnosis of mental retardation (i.e., Grossman, 1983). Obviously, in such cases, levels of adaptive functioning are crucial for either ruling in or ruling out the diagnosis of mental retardation.

In a second hypothetical clinical case (also closely paralleling some of our cases in clinical practice), cognitive and adaptive assessments were made on a nine-year-old girl, Genevieve, who was initially referred to a pediatric clinic for emotional problems. This case depicts the *reverse* of the phenomenon shown by Richard, namely consistently high levels of cognitive abilities associated with specific deficits in adaptive functioning. With respect to levels of Vineland adaptive functioning, Genevieve's standard scores were 120 for Communication, 86 for Daily Living Skills, 72 for Socialization, and 90 for the Adaptive Behavior Composite; and her level of Maladaptive functioning was significant. For cognitive areas, K-ABC standard scores are 144 for Sequential Processing, 124 for Simultaneous Processing, 138 for the Mental Processing Composite, and 122 for Achievement. Consistent with these cognitive areas of assessment, Genevieve obtained a PPVT-R standard score of 136.

Genevieve's adaptive functioning varies considerably across the various domains. Her Communication score of 120 is classified in the Vineland Survey Manual as moderately high (which encompasses the range of 116 to 130). This finding is consistent with the fact that scores on the Communication domain correlate more highly than those on any other domain with the cognitive areas, as measured by K-ABC and PPVT-R performance. Specifically, Communication items measure reading and writing skills, as well as some verbal skills. While Genevieve's performance on Daily Living Skills items is at the lower end of the adequate range (standard score of 86), her level of adaptive functioning in the area of Socialization would be classified at the low end of the moderately low range (S.S. = 72). The low Socialization score is of diagnostic import because of its relationship to the presenting reason for referral, namely a suspicion of emotional and behavioral disorder. Similarly, the performance on the Maladaptive Behavior domain far exceeded the 85th percentile for the occurrence of maladaptive behaviors exhibited by nine-year-old children participating in the Vineland standardization program. This finding also bears nosologic significance to the reason for referral.

With respect to global scores, it is noteworthy that Genevieve's Adaptive Behavior Composite score of 90 is in the adequate range of functioning (85–115). Nonetheless, the Adaptive Behavior Composite score is significantly *lower* than both her Mental Processing Composite score and her Achievement score (p. < .01 in each case). One might conclude that Genevieve's emotional and behavioral problems seem not to have greatly diminished her performance in either cognitive or achievement areas of functioning. Finally, the Expanded Form of the Vineland could be used to begin to develop a specific educational program for Genevieve. Such an endeavor would probably involve a close collaboration between parent, child, school personnel, and pediatric psychologist.

In a very recent publication (Sparrow & Cicchetti, 1987), five additional selected clinical cases were presented, again varying in diagnosis and/or presenting problem, as follows: (1) anxiety disorder (DSM-III diagnosis), (2) atypical pervasive developmental disorder (DSM-III diagnosis), (3) no psychiatric disturbance (three children ranging in age between 8 years, 7 months, and 9 years, 3 months), (4) mild mental retardation (DSM-III diagnosis), (5) infantile autism (DSM-III diagnosis) (two children, aged 12 years, 5 months, and 12 years, 1 month, respectively).

Our findings with respect to patterns of cognitive and adaptive functioning of the first *three* children were as follows:

1. The specific type of neuropsychiatric diagnosis bore no relationship to level of cognitive ability, as assessed by the Wechsler Intelligence Scale for Children—Revised (WISC-R).

2. Conversely, as the severity of the disorder *increased* from none (free of psychiatric disturbance) to anxiety disorder to atypical pervasive developmental disorder, the pattern of Vineland scores showed progressively *increasing deficits* in *overall* adaptive functioning.

3. The specific patterns of Vineland deficits for both the child with anxiety disorder and the one with atypical pervasive developmental disorder included high deficits in the Socialization domain and evidence of intermediate (for the child with anxiety disorder) to significant (for the child with atypical pervasive developmental disorder) levels of maladaptive behavior.

4. Performance on both the Communication and the Daily Living Skills domains tended to be more idiosyncratic (or less predictable). Our experience to date has been that some

emotionally disturbed children will show significant deficits in one or both of these areas of adaptive assessment, but others will not.

Both the child with an anxiety disorder and the one diagnosed with atypical pervasive developmental disorder are functioning adequately, both cognitively and academically, in regular classrooms. Both are also undergoing psychotherapy for their emotional and behavioral problems. Plans are also being implemented for remediating their specific deficits in adaptive behavior (for more specific details, see Sparrow & Cicchetti, 1987).

The remaining two cases were a child diagnosed as having mild mental retardation, with no emotional disturbance, and another diagnosed as having infantile autism and also functioning cognitively in the mentally retarded range. Findings indicated that:

1. There were no appreciable differences in cognitive functioning between the child with mild mental retardation and the one diagnosed with infantile autism. The K-ABC Mental Processing Composite (MPC) scores were 60 and 61, respectively; the corresponding PPVT-R scores, similarly, were 62 and 65.

2. The autistic child demonstrated a significantly lower level of functioning (Adaptive Behavior Composite = 35) than did the mentally retarded child, whose corresponding score was 60 ($p < .01$).

3. The mentally retarded child showed levels of overall adaptive functioning (60 for the Adaptive Behavior Composite) that were virtually interchangeable with corresponding cognitive levels (K-ABC, MPC = 62; PPVT-R = 60).

4. The autistic child manifested levels of overall adaptive functioning (35) that were appreciably *lower* than corresponding levels of cognitive functioning (K-ABC, MPC = 65; PPVT-R = 61).

5. The mentally retarded child's level of maladaptive behavior is intermediate, whereas that of the autistic child is in the significant range of functioning.

The autistic child attends a special school for autistic children. The mentally retarded child attends a special class in a public school for educable mentally retarded children.

Comparative Studies

A number of studies conducted at the Yale Child Study Center have focused on patterns of adaptive and cognitive behaviors of emotionally disturbed and nonhandicapped groups who were comparable in age and levels of cognitive abilities. Several of these studies have already been published or are scheduled to appear in print soon. Others are in various stages of progress. Children that have been the focus of this research form the following groups: (1) normal, (2) reactive, (3) atypical, 4) developmentally delayed, and (5) autistic children.

Research with Reactive and Atypical Children

In a recently reported study (Sparrow & Cicchetti, 1987; Sparrow et al., 1986), we compared the cognitive and adaptive functioning patterns of three groups of children who had been diagnosed *prior* to the publication of DSM-III criteria as (1) mild atypical personality development, (2) reactive disorder, or (3) normal development.

Briefly, the mild atypical children could be observed as having low thresholds for anxiety, oppositional behavior, marked oddities of thought and language, and a shallow manner of relating to other persons. The reactive disorder group tended to exhibit behavioral and adjustment problems, which were thought to be related to experiential events that had interfered with development or to problems in the parent–child relationship. In stark contrast, the children who made up the normal group displayed what can be described as age-appropriate behaviors—shyness, some obstinacy, occasional flashes of temper, mild anxiety in the testing situation, and even some task refusal—but manifested few if any symptoms suggestive of psychiatric disturbance. Findings were as follows:

1. There were no statistically significant group differences in either cognitive or academic achievement levels (as determined by the WISC-R and the Woodcock Johnson Psychoeducational Battery, respectively).

2. With respect to overall adaptive functioning, and consistent with clinical expectations, mild atypical children showed the lowest levels of adaptive functioning, reactive children were intermediate, and normal children performed best.

3. There were overall statistically significant differences between the three groups ($p < .05$) on the Communication domain, with mild atypical children (standard score of 87) being more than one standard deviation below the normal children (S.S. = 103). Again, reactives were intermediate, with a score of 92.

4. The three groups ordered themselves in Daily Living Skills as they did for both the Adaptive Behavior Composite and the Communication domain. However, there were no overall group differences that even approached statistical significance ($p = .27$).

5. The most striking differences occurred on the Socialization domain, where overall group difference was statistically significant at $p < .0001$. Mild atypical children had a mean score of 74, approximately 1 standard deviation below that of reactive children (mean = 88) and more than 1.5 standard deviations below that of normal children (mean = 98).

6. Finally, with respect to performance on the optional Maladaptive domain, and consistent with the aforementioned findings, mild atypical children performed at or above the 85th percentile in frequency of maladaptive behaviors, reactive children performed between the 51st and 84th percentile, and normal children manifested a nonsignificant number of maladaptive behaviors (mean performance at or less than the 50th percentile).

Research with Autistic and Developmentally Disabled Children

In another recently published study, also conducted at the Yale Child Study Center, we compared the adaptive behavior patterns of low-functioning autistic children to those of nonautistic developmentally delayed children who did not differ significantly from their autistic peers in age, IQ, or gender ratio. Both groups were diagnosed on the basis of DSM-III criteria (Volkmar et al., 1987). Results were as follows:

1. There were no statistically significant group differences on the Communication or Daily Living Skills domain.

2. There were striking differences in adaptive functioning on the Socialization domain. Autistic children showed significantly lower levels of Socialization behavior than did nonautistic developmentally delayed children ($p < .01$).

3. Finally, both groups showed an average frequency of Maladaptive behaviors occurring beyond the 85th percentile, in comparison to nonhandicapped standardization subjects. However, autistic children averaged significantly more Maladaptive behaviors (mean = 23) than did their nonautistic peers (mean = 18; $p < .05$).

In the previously described investigation, we were able to demonstrate that the Vineland, though not designed as such, may have some diagnostic utility for distinguishing disorders characterized by specific deficits in socialization (e.g., the quality of interpersonal relationships). In a follow-up investigation, we correlated Vineland assessments of autistic children with those made by the Autism Behavior Checklist (Krug, Arick, & Almond, 1980), an instrument used diagnostically for differentiating autism from other developmentally disabling disorders (Volkmar et al., 1988).

Comparing the Vineland and the Autism Behavior Checklist as Diagnostic Instruments

In correlating the various components of the Autism Behavior Checklist with the various Vineland domains, Volkmar et al. (1988) showed that a majority of correlations (over 60 percent) were statistically significant and fell into the low (.20) to moderate (.43) range (e.g., the criteria of Horwitz, Cicchetti, & Horwitz, 1984).

These results can be explained in part by the fact that the Vineland and the Autism Behavior Checklist are quite different in content, and also that the Autism Behavior Checklist, when compared to DSM-III clinical estimates of autism, shows an overall diagnostic accuracy of only 77.5 percent, a sensitivity of only 75 percent, and a specificity of 81 percent. The resulting false positive and false negative error rates are high enough to be of concern (Volkmar et al., 1988).

Concluding Comments

To date, our clinical and research findings are consistent with the following hypotheses:

1. The severity of adaptive behavior deficits increases with the severity of a given handicap.

2. Emotionally disturbed children (compared to appropriate comparison groups) show their most severe deficits in socialization and maladaptive areas of functioning.

3. The results based on differential performance on Communication and Daily Living Skills domains are much less predictable. Some disturbed children manifest severe deficiencies in one or both of these two areas, while others do not. The reasons for these phenomena are not yet clear and require further research.

4. These findings can be applied to the development of IEPs and IHPs or, more generally, to intervention planning designed to address problems of emotionally disturbed children.

CONCLUSION

The purpose of this chapter was to provide an overview of the Vineland Adaptive Behavior Scales. Toward that objective, we have provided brief descriptions of the following:

1. the background and history of adaptive behavior;
2. defining features of adaptive behavior;
3. a rationale for the revision of the Edgar Doll Social Maturity Scale;
4. the construction of the Vineland Adaptive Behavior Scales in terms of:
   a. the three components, namely, the Survey Form, the Expanded Form, and the Classroom Edition;
   b. Vineland Content—domains, subdomains, and individual items;
   c. scores derived from the Vineland Scales;
   d. the various Vineland Standardization samples;
   e. the various types of Vineland reliability assessments:
      i. test–retest;
      ii. interrater;
      iii. agreement levels between the Survey Form and the Classroom Edition;
5. Vineland Validity Assessments:
   a. face;
   b. content;
   c. discriminant;
   d. factorial;
   e. construct;
6. administration of the Vineland;
7. scoring and interpreting Vineland performance;
8. uses of the Vineland, namely for:
   a. diagnostic evaluations;
   b. program planning;
   c. research.

In closing, we wish to present our final and most important caveat. Both the Survey and the Expanded Form of the Vineland are assessment instruments that must *not* be administered by novices. Lack of experience may increase the possibility that invalid information will be generated. As we noted on page 61 of the Vineland Survey Form (Sparrow, Balla, & Cicchetti, 1984a), the interview editions

> must be administered and scored by a psychologist, social worker, or other professional with a graduate degree and specific training and experience in individual assessment and test interpretation. It is expected that the professional who administers and scores the Survey Form—(the same applies to the Expanded Form), will have a background in human development and behavior and tests and measurement, and an understanding of handicapped individuals. The interviewer should have training in interview techniques and experience in the administration and interpretation of adaptive behavior scales.

Additional qualifications include practice in administering the two forms of the Vineland, and a thorough understanding of the scoring criteria for each item.

Finally, there are a number of personal qualities that the interviewer must possess, such as a professional, pleasant, and encouraging manner, toward the objective of making the respondent feel comfortable and at ease during the entire semistructured interview. Such personality characteristics greatly increase the probability of establishing rapport with the respondent and producing reliable and valid information about the subject of interest to the interviewer.

REFERENCES

Anastasi, A. (1982). *Psychological testing* (5th ed.). New York: Macmillan.

Bartko, J. J. (1966). The intraclass correlation coefficient as a measure of reliability. *Psychological Reports, 19,* 3–11.

Bartko, J. J. (1974). Corrective note to: "The intraclass correlation coefficient as a measure of reliability." *Psychological Reports, 34,* 1–11.

Bartko, J. J., & Carpenter, W. T. (1976). On the methods and theory of reliability. *Journal of Nervous and Mental Disease, 163,* 307–317.

Campbell, I. O. (1985). Review of Vineland Adaptive Behavior Scales. In J. V. Mitchell (Ed.), *Buros ninth mental measurements yearbook* (2nd ed.), (pp. 1659–1661). Lincoln: University of Nebraska.

Cicchetti, D. V., & Prusoff, B. A. (1983). Reliability of depression and associated clinical symptoms. *Archives of General Psychiatry, 40,* 987–990.

Cicchetti, D. V., & Sparrow, S. S. (1981). Developing criteria for establishing interrater reliability of specific items: Applications to assessment of adaptive behavior. *American Journal of Mental Deficiency, 86,* 127–137.

Doll, E. A. (1935). A genetic scale of social maturity. *American Journal of Orthopsychiatry, 5,* 180–188.

Doll, E. A. (1940). *Measurement of social competence.* Circle Pines, MN: American Guidance Service.

Doll, E. A. (1953). *Vineland Social Maturity Scale.* Circle Pines, MN: American Guidance Service.

Doll E. A. (1965). *Vineland Social Maturity Scale.* Circle Pines, MN: American Guidance Service.

Dunn, L. M., & Dunn, L. M. (1981). *Peabody Picture Vocabulary Test—Revised.* Circle Pines, MN: American Guidance Service.

Educational attainment by age, race and sex. (1983). In *World Almanac and Book of Facts* (p. 205). New York: Newspaper Enterprise Association (published for Doubleday).

Fitzpatrick, A. R. (1983). The meaning of content validity. *Applied Psychological Measurement, 1,* 3–13.

Fleiss, J. L. (1975). Measuring agreement between two judges on the presence or absence of a trait. *Biometrics, 31,* 651–659.

Fleiss, J. L. (1981). *Statistics for rates and proportions.* New York: John Wiley & Sons.

Grossman, H. J. (Ed.). (1973). *Manual on terminology and classification in mental retardation* (revised). Washington, DC: American Association on Mental Deficiency.

Grossman, H. J. (Ed.). (1977). *Manual on terminology and classification in mental retardation* (revised). Washington, DC: American Association on Mental Deficiency.

Grossman, H. J. (Ed.) (1983). *Classification in mental retardation* (revised). Washington, DC: American Association on Mental Deficiency.

Heber, R. F. (1959). A manual on terminology and classification in mental retardation. (Monograph Suppl.). *American Journal of Mental Deficiency.*

Heber, R. F. (1961). A manual on terminology and classification in mental retardation (2nd ed.). (Monograph Suppl.). *American Journal of Mental Deficiency.*

Horwitz, R. I., Cicchetti, D. V., & Horwitz, S. M. (1984). A comparison of the Norris and Killip Coronary Prognostic Indices. *Journal of Chronic Diseases, 37,* 369–375.

Kaufman, A. S., & Kaufman, N. L. (1983). *Kaufman Assessment Battery for Children.* Circle Pines, MN: American Guidance Service.

Kraemer, H. C. (1979). Ramifications of a population model for kappa as a coefficient of reliability. *Psychometrika, 44,* 461–472.

Krug, D. A., Arick, J., & Almond, P. (1980). Behavior checklist for identifying severely handicapped individuals with high levels of autistic behavior. *Journal of Child Psychology and Psychiatry, 21,* 221–229.

Landis, J. R., & Koch, G. G. (1977). The measurement of observer agreement for categorical data. *Biometrics, 33,* 159–174.

Messick, S. (1980). Test validity and the ethics of assessment. *American Psychologist, 35,* 1012–1027.

Oakland, T., & Houchins, S. (1985). A review of the Vineland Adaptive Behavior Scales, Survey Form. *Journal of Counseling and Development, 63,* 585–587.

Public Law 94–142 (1975). The Education for All Handicapped Children Act, *20,* U. S. Congress, 1401–1461.

Reschly, D. J. (1987). *Adaptive behavior in classification and programming with students who are handicapped.* Minneapolis: Minnesota Department of Education. (Monograph).

Sparrow, S. S., Balla, D. A., & Cicchetti, D. V. (1984a). *The Vineland Adaptive Behavior Scales I: A revision of the Vineland Social Maturity Scale by Edgar A. Doll: Survey Form.* Circle Pines, MN: American Guidance Service.

Sparrow, S. S., Balla, D. A., & Cicchetti, D. V. (1984b). *The Vineland Adaptive Behavior Scales II: A revision of the Vineland Social Maturity Scale by Edgar A. Doll. Expanded Form.* Circle Pines, MN: American Guidance Service.

Sparrow, S. S., Balla, D. A., & Cicchetti, D. V. (1985). *The Vineland Adaptive Behavior Scales III: A revision of the Vineland Social Maturity Scale by Edgar A. Doll. Classroom Edition.* Circle Pines, MN: American Guidance Service.

Sparrow, S. S., & Cicchetti, D. V. (1985). Diagnostic uses of the Vineland Adaptive Behavior Scales. *Journal of Pediatric Psychology, 10,* 215–225.

Sparrow, S. S., & Cicchetti, D. V. (1987). Adaptive behavior and the psychologically disturbed child. *Journal of Special Education, 21,* 89–100.

Sparrow, S. S., Rescorla, L. A., Provence, S., Condon, S. O., Goudreau, D., & Cicchetti, D. V. (1986). A follow-up of "Atypical" children. *Journal of the American Academy of Child Psychiatry, 25,* 181–185.

Terman, L. M. (1916). *The measurement of intelligence.* Boston: Houghton Mifflin.

Volkmar, F. R., Cicchetti, D. V., Dykman, E., Sparrow, S. S., Leckman, J. F., & Cohen, D. J. (1988). An evaluation of the Autism Behavior Checklist. *Journal of Autism and Developmental Disorders, 18,* 81–97.

Volkmar, F., Sparrow, S. S., Goudreau, D., Cicchetti, D. V., Paul, R., & Cohen, D. (1987). Social deficits in autism: An operational approach using the Vineland Adaptive Behavior Scales. *Journal of American Academy of Child and Adolescent Psychiatry, 26,* 156–161.

Zigler, E., & Hodapp, R. M. (1986). *Understanding mental retardation.* New York: Cambridge University Press.

9

Wide Range Achievement Test—Revised

Gary S. Wilkinson

The Wide Range Achievement Tests (WRAT; Jastak, 1946; Jastak & Jastak 1965, 1976, 1978; Jastak & Wilkinson, 1984) have been among the most widely used instruments of psychological measurement for over forty years. The first WRAT was standardized by Joseph F. Jastak in 1936 as a convenient tool for the study of the basic school subjects of reading (word recognition and pronunciation), written spelling, and arithmetic computation (Jastak & Jastak, 1965). The current Wide Range Achievement Test—Revised (WRAT-R; Jastak & Wilkinson, 1984) has remained very similar in content and form to the original test. Few other psychological tests can match the longevity and extensive professional use of the WRAT.

The WRAT-R, like the WRAT before it, is actually a set of three tests that permit examiners to identify at which point a child or adult (ages five through seventy-five) functions along a line of increasingly more difficult items for each of the respective skills. The tests, or variable lines, when used by the examiner, can measure an individual's school coding skills in much the same way that a tape measure can give an individual's height or a scale can indicate someone's weight.

The Reading Test (word recognition only) gives the testing professional information as to where on a list of gradually more difficult words an individual is capable of performing. There are 75 words on the Level 1 Reading Test (for ages 5 through 11 years) and 74 words on the Level 2 Reading Test (for ages 12 through 75 years). Similar measures are made of spelling from dictation and written calculations. Although psychological instruments are less reliable than are measures of physical properties, the examiner can establish with a high degree of confidence an individual's degree of word recognition, spelling, and/or calculating skill.

Jastak developed this simple, straightforward measurement of the school subjects to complement the existing measures of cognitive ability available in the 1930s. His formation of the three academic measures was actually intended to add coding subtests to the Wechsler-Bellevue Scales. Jastak preferred the multiple-subtest approach to cognitive measurement that the Wechsler scale offered and wanted to add three more subtests to get a better diagnostic picture of the individuals being measured.

Jastak believed it was necessary to measure multiple behaviors in order to get a more complete description of the individual. Throughout his professional life he believed that individual test scores were more than measures of an individual trait but were, in fact, reflections of many different underlying behavioral factors. He stated that the only way to separate out individual behavioral strengths and weaknesses was to have a collection of individual measures that could be systematically compared with one another.

Jastak's theory of test score meanings (Jastak & Jastak, 1979) postulates that individual scores have multiple variances, which include global, lobal, and obal variances. *Global variance* refers to that part of the test score which is associated with general ability, often referred to as *intelligence*. *Lobal variance* is that part of the test score which, when combined with other related test scores, reflects the existence of a more specific behavioral skill or ability (i.e., language ability, perceptual organization, and focus of attention). *Obal variance* was described as that part of the test score which was attributable to test error and/or unique variance.

In the 1930s there were no clinical measures of school ability that would be convenient enough for inclusion in a standard psychological test battery. The existing achievement tests were prohibitive because of the several hours needed for administration. It was the recognition that more information was needed on individuals to make accurate interpretations of test scores, and the need for a short, simple test of school achievement, that provided the impetus to create the WRAT.

From the beginning Jastak intended to measure only the mechanics of learning. He felt that the codes of reading, writing, and computing were the means of communicating ideas. They were the tools of intellect, not intellect itself. He likened these processes to transportation systems, which entailed the building of the vehicles on the one hand and the operating of them on the other (Jastak, 1939).

With reading, Jastak concentrated on the association between the sounds of the spoken language and the symbols visually perceived. He emphasized that this was a sensorimotor process distinct from the more cognitive process of comprehension. The skill of recognizing and saying the printed word was described as the vehicle for the thought. There was, and is, a need to measure an individual's effectiveness in building these vehicles of communication and thought. Assessment of the operation of these vehicles is quite separate and can be adequately covered in different types of tests, such as cognitive ability measures. Comprehension and communication of meaning are psychologically distinct processes, which were never included in the WRAT assessments.

The WRAT-R, like the earlier WRAT editions, purports to identify the three variable lines and to measure individuals along these scales with accuracy. The variables being measured are the codes of word recognition, written spelling, and arithmetic computation. The goal of this type of measurement instrument is to create a yardstick that examiners can use to assess where an individual falls among the many items that make up these variable lines.

If this measurement can be done reliably, a precise tool is available for the educational, psychological, and counseling professionals that will show the extent of coding skill a particular individual possesses. The assessment professional would be able to identify the individual's level of coding skill and compare this with other measures of intellect or cognitive abilities. Similarities and discrepancies among measures provide objective insights into educational and behavioral normalities and abnormalities. In addition, the three coding scores add to the aggregate information from which individual behavioral measures, such as Jastak's lobal factors, can be extracted (Jastak & Jastak, 1979).

The following sections will describe how this set of so-called school rulers was made, how the WRAT-R can be used, and what the results mean. A case example will be offered and a discussion of strengths and weaknesses will be given.

CONSTRUCTION

The WRAT-R is an updated version of the WRAT, which was first published for public distribution in 1946 (Jastak, 1946). The construction of the WRAT-R is best observed through the historical perspective of the first editions of the test, which actually date back to 1936, when Jastak originally constructed the instrument while attending Columbia University.

Jastak considered the following factors to be of greatest importance during the first construction of the WRAT: (1) low cost, (2) individual standardization, (3) ease and economy of administration, (4) suitability of content, (5) relevance of the functions studied, and (6) comparability of results over the entire range of the skills in question.

Jastak chose the three variables of word recognition, written spelling, and written computation because he felt that most school learning proceeded from the acquisition of the basic coding skills. He believed that the vehicles of thought—the codes—were the important school variables to measure. He proceeded to do this by selecting test content and format that best represented the actual school behavior. By forming a measure of word reading, spelling from dictation, and paper-and-pencil calculating, the examiner would have real-life measures of important behavioral variables.

Jastak went about forming his school rulers by selecting items that were representative of the larger domain of the items being tested. For reading and spelling, he selected words from the dictionary that he felt were spread over a line of difficulty from easy to hard. His first selection of items, containing hundreds of words, was subsequently narrowed by the process of analyzing item difficulty using the percentage-correct method. A similar process was used on the arithmetic section, where Jastak went through arithmetic textbooks and selected items that were representative of the subject area. From these original selections he narrowed the final test to those items that were spread over the difficulty continuum in a uniform fashion (Jastak, 1946).

Because the scales were intended to begin with the youngest of the school-age persons, it became necessary to supplement the items of each scale with other items that were not formal operations of the skill itself. A scale needs to have enough floor for the measurement of the low-abled individual on a particular skill. Jastak therefore decided to include pre-reading, prespelling, and precalculation items to extend the respective scales downward. The prereading items selected were matching similar letters and naming letters. Prespelling consisted of copying letterlike marks. The prearithmetic items consisted of counting, reading numbers, and solving oral math problems.

Jastak intended to have three single scales that could be used to measure an individual according to his or her ability on that specific skill. Whether the individual was young or old, unskilled or proficient, a measure could be obtained on a simple, direct scale of ability that the examiner could use as a frame of reference for behavioral description and analysis. The *wide range* concept can be traced to this beginning.

Subsequent editions of the WRAT followed the same premise. In

1965 the WRAT was divided into a Level 1 (for ages 5 years through 11 years, 11 months) and a Level 2 (for ages 12 years through 65 years, 11 months). New items were added to expand the respective levels, but the concept of direct measurement of a simple, straightforward skill was retained. The 1976 and 1978 editions were revisions of norms without any changes in test content or format.

In 1984 the WRAT-R was published, keeping the ideals of the original WRAT. Item and format changes were minimal. Some modifications reflected more advanced thinking in psychometric theory; others were intended to make the WRAT-R more user-friendly, in the current jargon.

The most sweeping change was a completely new standardization, with norms developed using the stratified sampling technique. The factors of sex, age, race, metropolitan/nonmetropolitan, and geographical region were controlled. Twenty-eight age groups were used, with a sample of 200 individuals in each group. Level 1 was normed on individuals from 5 years to 11 years, 11 months, and Level 2 was normed on individuals from 12 years to 74 years, 11 months.

In previous editions of the WRAT, probability samplings were instrumental in selecting the norm groups. In this method subjects were selected on the basis of the individual's performance on a comprehensive general ability test given concurrently with the WRAT. From the general ability measures a normal distribution of subjects were selected for each age group according to IQ. Jastak believed that this probability sampling would factor out all other pertinent factors that might affect the representativeness of the samples for the general population.

With the use of this probability sampling method, it was thought that the referred status of subjects would not be crucial. In the WRAT-R sampling, all subjects were selected randomly from the general school population. Individuals were selected to meet the stratification variables, which were defined prior to data collection. No subjects were selected from listings of those who had been referred for educational and/or psychological diagnosis. In this way it is thought that the WRAT-R has been made more representative of the general population than were the older editions of the WRAT.

The probability sampling technique used on the earlier WRAT editions probably had an unwanted effect on the norm results. Since there was a large proportion of referred subjects in the earlier norm samples, the mean performance scores would most likely be lower than for a completely random selection of students. The lower means would, therefore, have the effect of increasing the grade equivalents, standard scores, and percentiles.

Test researchers have found strong to moderate correlations on the WRAT with a variety of other achievement measures. They have also discovered that the standard scores and grade equivalents were significantly higher (Alford, Moore, & Simon, 1979; Bradley, 1976; Hollensworth & White, 1981; Prasse, Seiwert, & Breen, 1983; Williamson, 1979). The 1984 revision was decided on, in part, because of these findings.

Scores on the WRAT-R are significantly lower than previous WRAT scores. Grade equivalents at the earlier ages are nearly one full grade lower, and standard scores range, on average, between 8 and 10 points lower. There cannot be any one number representing the difference between the two measures, because there are various differences for the twenty-eight age groups as well as differences within the individual age groups depending on degree of ability. Suffice it to say that the WRAT-R scores are, for the most part, lower than the old WRAT scores, and that this result was both anticipated and desired.

Because of the differences between the WRAT and the WRAT-R, it was decided to terminate the availability of the WRAT upon presentation of the WRAT-R. Primarily, this was done because, otherwise, examiners could choose high or low scores by selecting one instrument over the other. Such a choice is inconsistent with the objective of precise and reliable measurement of coding ability. Possible misuses, unintentional or otherwise, could affect eligibility, selection, and other administrative decisions concerning those individuals with true discrepancies of ability and academic code performance. An individual could, by selecting one test or the other, influence the end result without consideration of the true ability of the individual being tested.

On previous editions of the WRAT, the Reading, Spelling, and Arithmetic sections of both levels were included on one form. Format changes on the WRAT-R allowed each separate level to have its own four-page form. In this way, the Arithmetic section was spread over two pages instead of being confined to one. The Reading words were printed in larger type for ease of reading.

The Spelling and Reading words were left unchanged from WRAT to WRAT-R. There were minor changes on the Arithmetic sections, but no problems were excluded. There were some additional problems on both levels to give the tests more of a floor for low-functioning individuals.

From a technical point of view, the Rasch method of item analysis and internal consistency measurement was used to clarify further the psychometric properties of the individual items as well as the effectiveness of the composite instruments. Item and person separation indices confirm that the WRAT-R is able to measure academic codes reliably and accurately (Jastak & Wilkinson, 1984).

ADMINISTRATION

The WRAT-R can be administered and scored within 20 to 30 minutes, depending on the individual being measured. The Reading subtest (word recognition) needs to be given individually. The Spelling and Arithmetic subtests can be given either individually or in groups as long as there is adequate monitoring on the part of the test giver.

Although the WRAT-R can be used by examiners who are not licensed or certified test givers, there needs to be care and preparation in the use of the WRAT-R. The administrators of the WRAT-R should be experienced in test giving, with particular attention given to correct scoring, standardized procedures, establishing rapport, and informed test interpretation.

The level of difficulty involved in administering the WRAT-R has been frequently underestimated because of the simplicity of the test format. It is vitally important that the examiner be able to recognize the correct pronunciations of the word-recognition words, and to pronounce the spelling words correctly. Specific attention by the examiner to the codes being measured is mandatory for reliable and meaningful test results.

Correct selection of either Level 1 or Level 2 is also important in getting meaningful results. Starting with the 1984 edition, the WRAT-R has a separate form for each level. Level 1 is normed on individuals from age 5 through age 11. Level 2 is for individuals from 12 through 75 years of age. To transform the respective raw scores to standard scores or percentiles, it is necessary to select the appropriate age level.

Certain circumstances might require that the WRAT-R be given using the inappropriate level with respect to age. One such circumstance could arise in research studies where subjects progress to Level 2 during the pre–posttest interval. Another situation could be the measurement of either very talented or very limited individuals, where the examiner wants either a higher ceiling or a lower floor for the test items. In such cases there is a procedure for the examiner to follow in converting the raw scores of a given level to the equated raw scores of the other level. This bridge method allows the examiner to add or subtract a constant for each of the subtests in order to get an equated raw score for the other level (Jastak & Wilkinson, 1984).

In this way, an examiner can find a standard score for a thirteen-year-old when Level 1 was administered. Then, by determining the Level 2 equated raw score from the table in the manual, the examiner can use this raw score in transforming to age-appropriate standard scores and percentiles. This practice is not recommended as a standard procedure, since the equated scores are actually statistical approximations of what the other level's raw score would be. Since measured test scores are only approximations of true ability, this bridge method must be used cautiously. Greater caution is warranted the further the age of the individual being examined is from the cutoff age of 12. Nevertheless, in some situations the desire to have data equated from one level to another outweighs the disadvantages of such a procedure.

SCORING

In keeping with the simplicity that has been a hallmark of the WRAT tests, scoring is straightforward and uncomplicated. The total number correct on each subtest gives a raw score, which can then be converted into grade equivalents, standard scores, and percentiles. The latter two scores are based on age norms, whereas the grade equivalents are based on the norm sample broken down by grade.

To obtain the raw scores, the scorer must count by hand the number correct on each of the three tests. There is no computer scoring service, for two reasons. First, it is a quick and easy task to count the correct responses on the WRAT-R. To offer a computer system of scoring would complicate matters more than ease them. Second, in order for computer scoring to work, the format and the process of the tests would have to change so that the scores could be read by a computer. This would normally entail multiple-choice answers, which are not similar to the type of responses that naturally occur in real-life settings. One advantage of the WRAT-R is that it gives hard-copy examples of an individual's performance, which can then be used for sample behavior in parent and teacher conferences or for further clinical analysis.

Scoring criteria for Reading, Spelling, and Arithmetic are given in the manual. The phonetic guides for each of the Reading and Spelling tests are listed, and the correct answers to the Arithmetic tests are given in a format that resembles the actual problem placement on the respective forms.

INTERPRETATION

In order for most test scores to be interpreted, they must be transformed into meaningful units of measure. Raw scores by themselves offer very little information to the test user because there are no reference points from which to appreciate relative performance. A high or low raw score will tell where on the scale of that variable an individual falls, but to understand the meaning of the score fully it is best to relate that score to some common frame of reference. On the WRAT-R, grade equivalents relate the raw score to average performance by members of each grade from 1 through 12. Standard scores and percentiles relate raw score performance to the average performance of individuals within each person's own age range.

One of the significant differences between the WRAT-R and its predecessors is that the grade equivalents are given on an ordinal scale instead of an interval scale. Previous editions of the WRAT, like most other academic skill tests, use a decimal-type scale, with the whole number representing the grade year and the decimal indicating the month. The use of the decimal score tends to lead test users to add and/or subtract these scores. This is inappropriate, however, since it is not legitimate to perform arithmetic operations on ordinal data.

To solve this frequent misuse of grade equivalent data, the WRAT-R uses an ordinal scale, with the grade given numerically and the place within that grade given verbally as either Beginning, Middle, or End. Thus, the grade equivalent score that was given as 2.9 on the WRAT is now given as 2E, or end of second grade, on the WRAT-R. This prevents an examiner from subtracting two like scores and coming up with a difference, a mathematical procedure that is inappropriate for ordinal data.

The grade equivalents are based on the average performance of those identified individuals from the norm sample at each of the grade levels from one to twelve. From grade to grade the average performance of that particular group was charted. A grade equivalent score then indicates that an individual has received a score that is most similar to that particular group of individuals. There is no intention to indicate at what specific instruction level an individual should be placed. This placement decision must be made with more knowledge of the local curriculum.

For example, if an individual receives a grade equivalent of 4B on the Arithmetic subtest on the WRAT-R, this means that the individual's performance was slightly lower than that of those individuals in the norm group who were actually in the fourth grade. It does not necessarily mean that the individual is doing beginning fourth-grade math as referenced by any specific curriculum. The distinction here is that we are measuring individuals compared to a norm group rather than to a specific curriculum criterion.

This distinction becomes more crucial in the upper grades. High school students who receive tenth- or eleventh-grade scores on the WRAT-R may not be actually doing tenth or eleventh grade curriculum work. In addition to the WRAT-R being a norm referenced test instead of a criterion referenced test, there is also the problem that numerous curricula exist in our schools. It is impossible to describe in specific terms what a tenth-grade instructional level is in math, since there are college preparatory, business, and basic math courses all being taught in the tenth grade. Thus, a 10B score on the WRAT-R Arithmetic section indicates that the individual has performed basic math calculations at a level similar to that of the average beginning 10th grader.

The proper way to treat grade equivalent scores, as well as all other psychometric scores, is to understand that the test scores are only an approximation of the true score—the theoretical, absolute ability of the tested individual. The correct way to use the grade equivalent scores is to develop a range around the test score which is ± 2 standard errors of measurement. The standard error of measurement for raw scores for each test is given on the back of the respective test forms. It is appropriate to conclude that a person's true ability is within 2 standard errors of the test score 95 percent of the time. The true score is within a range of one standard error of the test score 66 percent of the time.

For example, if an individual receives a raw score of 50 on the Reading Test of Level 1, he or she is functioning at the test level of 2M, middle of second grade. The standard error of measurement for Level 1 Reading raw scores is 2. The 95 percent accuracy range for true ability would be a raw score of 46 to 54, or a range of 2B to 2M when the raw scores are converted to grade equivalents. Actual lines can be drawn on the test forms at the $+2$ and -2 standard error of measurement points. This gives a visual representation of the band within which there is a 95 percent chance that the true score is contained.

Grade equivalents are given on the WRAT-R as a convenience to the test user, since most examiners have the grade frame of reference in mind. For use in individual assessment, the standard scores and percentiles are actually superior scores. The standard scores and percentiles are transformed scores from the raw scores based on age norms. There are twenty-eight age groups used in the WRAT-R norms. Intervals are smaller (six months) at the younger years because individuals grow more in academic coding skills during these years than in the adolescent and adult years. During the adult years the age interval increases to ten years. In each of the twenty-eight age groups that make up the norms there are 200 individuals who were selected according to a national, stratified sampling technique. This means that there were 5,800 individuals included in the total norm process.

An individual's raw score is transformed into a standard score on the basis of the comparison of the individual with individuals within the age-appropriate norm group. The standard score is one ranging from 46 to 155, with a group mean of 100 and a standard deviation of 15. Standard scores provide a frame of reference that is commonly understood by testing professionals. Because it is a score based on interval data, it can be added or subtracted without difficulty.

Standard scores are superior to grade equivalents for several very important reasons. It makes logical sense to group individuals by age rather than grade. Age is a lawful and consistent process, whereas grade retention and promotion are frequently at the discretion of individual teachers and school policies that differ widely from grade to grade and from school to school. Therefore, if one school has a strict grading system, the average grade performance will be significantly different than in a school that promotes all students regardless of performance.

Furthermore, other commonly used psychological tests, such as intelligence tests, also use standard scores. WRAT-R and intelligence scores can be compared providing that certain assumptions can be upheld. The first and foremost of these is that the norm samples are adequately drawn on both tests so that one can reasonably expect that the same population of individuals is being measured. Tests cannot be compared if the norm groups differ significantly from one another. Second, standard scores can have different means and standard deviations. When a WRAT-R user wishes to compare the WRAT-R scores with other tests, it is important that the user check to see that the two tests both use the mean of 100 and the standard deviation of 15. If not, then transformations must be made. Third, it is vital to remember that the standard error of measurement is to be taken into account on both tests before significant discrepancies are claimed.

Of key importance is the fact that standard scores are interval data scores and, therefore, can be added and subtracted as well as handled in other arithmetic procedures. Discrepancy scores can be calculated to identify significant differences between academic coding skills and general ability. Treatment effects can be measured more accurately, and post-treatment performance can also be observed in comparison to pretreatment data. Standard scores allow the examiner to treat the data in such a way that appropriate statistical procedures can be used for accurate and reliable educational, clinical, and/or vocational decisions.

Consider this misuse of test scores, which was brought to the publisher's attention by a concerned teacher. A third-grade child who had been retained twice was administered the WRAT-R to assess the academic codes. The grade equivalent scores obtained were 3B, 3E, and 4E for Reading, Spelling, and Arithmetic, respectively. The Reading and Spelling scores were in line with typical third-grade performance, but Arithmetic performance was even better than third-grade performance. The grade equivalents, however, did not tell the whole story. This child was, in fact, two years older than the comparison group that was being used.

Is a ten-year-old child who is performing at the third-grade level equivalent to an eight-year-old child at a similar level? Of course not—any more than a ten-year-old child with a mental age of eight is the same as an eight-year-old child with a similar mental age of eight. The strict use of grade equivalents in this case would hide vital information. In fact, the school district of this child was contending that there were no significant discrepancies in the academic performances of word recognition and spelling.

Standard scores in this case give a much different picture. There was a recent WISC-R score of 109 on this child. His standard scores on the WRAT-R were 80, 87, and 95, respectively, on the Reading, Spelling, and Arithmetic tests. The 29- and 22-point discrepancies on Reading and Spelling in comparison to IQ far exceed even the most conservative discrepancy models. Even when two standard errors of measurement are included on both the general ability and achievement measures, there are still significant differences between the measures. By using the standard scores, the examiner can focus on real learning problems compared to age. This is the key variable in looking at relative performance.

Grade equivalents can then be used as points of reference from which parents, teachers, and counselors can get an idea of the individual's approximate grade performance. In any case, they should not be used to diagnose learning problems. Only through statistically appropriate discrepancy models should such determinations be made. This necessitates the use of the standard scores over the grade equivalents.

There still remains the question of how much discrepancy is significant. This answer remains unclear since various systems and/or professionals will set different levels of significance. Over the years Jastak has recommended that a fifteen-point discrepancy between coding and general ability should be considered significant. There are computer discrepancy models available that give a more statistically precise answer at various levels of significance (Reynolds, 1984).

Whatever level of discrepancy is considered to be significant, there are some crucial concerns that need to be addressed by the testing professional before making any diagnoses of coding deficiency. Jastak (1965; Jastak & Jastak, 1978) has carefully provided specific guidelines that give substance to the clinical decision-making process.

Word recognition, spelling, and numerical calculation, like any other ability, are positively related to general cognitive functioning. It was estimated by Jastak's own research that intelligence contributes approximately 22 percent of the variance of such abilities. This would mean that 78 percent of the variance of these abilities would be attributable to other than intellectual factors. Word recognition scores, as well as other ability scores, will vary in relation to general cognitive ability. High-IQ individuals will sometimes receive low academic code scores. On the other hand, intellectually limited persons can learn these skills at a level higher than would be expected on the basis of IQ alone.

In order to diagnose coding deficiencies correctly, it is necessary to collect data from a wide variety of tests that measure diversified content and process. Only general cognitive tests that have such a diversified base are appropriate for reference points from which to make the diagnosis of learning disability. Certainly tests like the WISC-R and the WAIS-R would meet such a requirement.

Tests that are respectively focused on single abilities, like those in the WRAT-R, are necessary to get a clear picture of those skills. When the tests of academic abilities are combined with seemingly related, but still different, cognitive factors, such as reading comprehension, verbal reasoning, or numerical reasoning, the results are confused and specific diagnoses cannot be made. If these combined measurements were to be used, there would be no clear estimate of the individual skills making up the composite behavior. To obtain clear, concise measurement of an ability, that ability must be examined in an isolated fashion and then compared to the general ability measures that use diversified content and process.

If one were to use only an oral reading paragraph test to diagnose reading disorder, it would not be possible to diagnose whether or not the individual has a coding problem, a comprehension problem, or both. The individual might be able to code well, but not comprehend. On the other hand, he or she might not be able to transfer sight symbols to sound symbols, but might comprehend very nicely when operating in a different medium, such as oral communications. As stated earlier, the WRAT-R is designed to measure the *carriers* of thought—the codes—not the thought itself. To make meaningful decisions, one must measure these processes separately and then compare them to general ability measures.

According to Jastak's theory, individual test scores contain much more information than is commonly appreciated. By examining a variety of test scores and analyzing them systematically, the examiner can objectively learn a great deal about the individual being tested. In such ways, intelligence and achievement tests can be used to assess more behavioral and emotional factors, such as perceptual organization, focus of attention, reasoning, and affect qualities. Although this treatment of data is not the focus of the present chapter, examples of this type of data examination will be given in the case example presented. More specific details on the Jastak Cluster Analysis of test data are presented in *Jastak Cluster Analysis: Meanings and Measures of Mental Tests* (Jastak & Jastak, 1979).

CASE EXAMPLE

Name: Ted   *Sex:* Male   *Age:* 13 years, 6 months

Client is in eighth grade. Has never repeated a grade yet. Behavior at school is said to be terrible. Is an attention-getter. Is easily distracted. Is often put out of the classroom but still finds some way to be distracting. Behavior often depends on the teacher he has. Gets along best with experienced teachers.

Has had problems in school since kindergarten. Was referred to a psychologist in the fifth grade. Parents were told that he had a high IQ—that his behavior problems at school would continue because he is bored and above the level of others.

Is highly resistant to any basics that require repetition or drill. Wants only new material. Does poorly academically. Has recently received two Es as interim marks. Is highly disorganized in his work. Brings home no homework. Handwriting is said to be extremely poor.

Was in a private school from the second to the sixth grade. Did fairly well until the sixth, when he did poorly again. Had a tutor and seemed to do well on a one-to-one basis.

Is said to be good in anything he likes or puts his mind to. Draws well. Can initiate mechanical things. Is good in some sports, when he is not bored or distracted. Is thought to have some talents in music and took piano lessons for one year, but would not practice.

Client is of average height and of stocky build. Speech quality is good. Responds very quickly on most test items. This results in many careless mistakes.

Is verbally and emotionally responsive. Loves to talk at great length about topics he brings up. Is good-natured and likes to joke.

In talking about school, Ted feels that "they should improve how they do stuff." Feels that they "waste your time—do too many unnecessary things." Does not admit to the extent of the behavior problems that are described by parents and teachers. Feels that his main problem is that he "cracks up" when others do something funny or make a mistake. Admits that he likes to joke and "pull things." Feels that his problems are the fault of the teachers. Admits that he frequently does not feel like doing his homework. Says that he can do all the work when he is free to talk about it but cannot put it down on tests. Insists that his handwriting is O.K. except that he makes some letters, especially capitals, "a bit fancy."

Test Results

Mental Ability   The Wechsler Intelligence Scale for Children—Revised (WISC-R) gave the following results:

Scale	Standard Score		Percentile
Verbal	107	Average	82nd
Performance	120	Superior	91st
Full Scale	114	High Average	82nd

Intellectual functioning is high average, as indicated by IQ. Discrepancy between Verbal and Performance scores would indicate more proficiency in the practical and the applied areas of learning, and less proficiency in all language-type activities.

Educational Skills   The Wide Range Achievement Test—Revised (WRAT-R) gave the following results:

Test	Standard Score		Percentile
Reading/Word Recognition	93	Average	32nd
Spelling	89	Low Average	23rd
Arithmetic	87	Low Average	19th

Ratings in these educational skills cluster around a low average level. This would indicate that all ratings are on the low side in comparison to his population age group.

All ratings are more than one standard deviation (more than 15 points) below his WISC-R IQ. This would warrant a diagnosis of generalized learning disability, moderately severe in nature.

Behavior Traits Derived from Jastak Cluster Analysis

The following interpretations come from the analysis of this client's WISC-R and WRAT-R scores. The Jastak Cluster Analysis (Jastak & Jastak, 1979) is an experimental method designed to extract more exact meanings from objective test scores.

Language functions are variable. Makes poor use of his intellect in learning verbal skills and in doing other forms of rote, verbal learning. Uses intellect adequately in verbal expression, in learning through the auditory medium, and in verbal comprehension. High comprehension may actually have served as a handicap in client's learning of the verbal codes.

Client is aggressive in dealing with his physical and social environments. Feels a strong need to be concretely and actively involved with whatever is going on around him. Learns effectively only when allowed to manipulate concrete objects or participate in lab-type situations. Possesses much common sense and practical knowhow. Is adept at manipulating to get his own way. Is highly flexible and adaptable, sometimes too much so for his own good.

Motivation is deficient. Has an extremely low frustration level. Lacks impulse control. Immediately comes out with whatever he thinks or feels. Is unable to engage in sedate behavior that requires close attention or concentration. Is highly rejecting of activities requiring practice, drill, or repetition. Acts with almost total disregard for the consequences of his actions.

Mobilizes physical energy within normal time limits. Is good in perceiving relationships in time and space. Work output per given time period is satisfactory, once he puts his mind to a task at hand and decides to do it. Has good physical stamina but lacks mental stamina.

Deals with his environment with a minimum of emotional involvement. However, this trait may be somewhat obscured as a result of his lack of impulse control and high degree of physical assertiveness. Is relatively indifferent to either success or failure, to praise or criticism. Neither event seems to serve as sufficient incentive to get him working.

Is highly dependent on his environment. Because of low motivation, accomplishes little even in well-structured situations. Accomplishes even less when left on his own. Tends to dawdle, waste time, and fool around. Is prone to make poor and impulsive decisions.

Finds it difficult to reason logically or systematically when faced with a problem. Sees only the steps immediately before him. Engages in much haphazard and random behavior. Loses sight of consequences. Tends to flit from one thing to another without goal, purpose, planning, or organization.

Summary and Recommendations

1. Intellectual ability is high average.

2. Word recognition skills, spelling, and arithmetic tend to be low average. It was indicated that client has a generalized learning disability.

3. The kinesthetic approach is strongly recommended as a remedial approach to his reading and spelling deficits.

4. To improve arithmetic skills, it is recommended that he work fifteen minutes a day simply doing arithmetic calculations at a degree of difficulty appropriate to his grade level.

5. In view of his age, it is somewhat marginal as to whether or not he will be too amenable to the above remedial approaches. As a result, it is recommended that he receive a few counseling sessions to help him get a good start and increase the chances of his cooperation.

6. Since he learns more effectively through doing, it is recommended that he be exposed as much as possible to activity-oriented programs which serve as constructive outlets for his excess energy, which is now being dissipated in a more random and unproductive manner.

7. As soon as age and grade permit, it is felt that a transfer to a vocational or technical high school would be likely to increase his chances of remaining in school and reducing his behavior problems.

8. Personality structure is similar to that of individuals who may benefit from medication. Therefore, it is recommended that this be discussed with the family physician or pediatrician.

9. Training measures should be undertaken that increase motivation and strengthen his willingness to accept responsibility. Needs firm and consistent handling. Also should be required to take full consequences of his actions. Parents should come in for counseling to establish such structure and be provided the support to follow through with it.

10. Little would be gained by having client repeat a grade since this might actually delay vocational training and increase his chances of dropping out of school.

ASSETS AND LIABILITIES

The WRAT-R is an individually administered test of school coding skills, which has been normed on age groups from five years to seventy-five years old. It is a short but accurate measure of school skills.

One of the more popular advantages of the WRAT-R has always been its economy of time. Within approximately 25 minutes, an examiner can have reliable and accurate information regarding three important school skills. In addition to the grade equivalent and age-related standard scores, the examiner also has the opportunity to observe the client performing these skills and can begin to make tentative conclusions about particular strengths and weaknesses within each skill. There is a hard copy of each student's or client's performance, and these can be used as examples of behavior.

In addition to being quick to administer and score, the WRAT-R is also very accurate in separating individuals of varying ability and providing some common reference points to measure them by. It is a simple, straightforward test of three school skills, which gives the examiner a yardstick to use in assessing word recognition, spelling, and arithmetic calculations.

Because of the thoroughness of norming, the results of the WRAT-R can be compared with other measures of specific and general ability. The scores of the WRAT-R and the Wechsler scales can be used together in the Jastak Cluster Analysis to provide objective information on behavioral functioning. Using a collection of tests of adequate norms and structure permits a variety of measures to be used to determine the correct meaning of test scores (Jastak & Jastak, 1979). Such an analysis is shown in the case example given earlier.

One of the greatest criticisms of the WRAT, and later of the WRAT-R, is that the test does not measure either comprehension or arithmetic reasoning. Although the WRAT tests have moderate to strong correlations with these behavioral skills, the WRAT-R was never designed to measure these skills. On the contrary, it has always been intended that the WRAT and WRAT-R measure only the vehicles of thought, the codes.

There are criterion-referenced diagnostic tests that give a closer look at the breakdown of the coding skills. When an examiner wants to perform a closer examination of the word recognition or spelling processes, it may be necessary to use these more comprehensive measures. This does not mean that the WRAT-R is not a more than adequate measure, but it cannot be all things to all people. It cannot be a short, accurate ruler for school codes and still be a measure that closely analyses the individual components of phonetic decoding. While there are many examples on the WRAT-R to draw on, there is not meant to be a systematic breakdown of varying phonetic components so that a specific diagnostic conclusion can be formulated.

CONCLUSION

The Wide Range Achievement Test—Revised is a very popular measurement instrument for the scholastic codes of word recognition, spelling, and arithmetic calculations. It combines ease of administration, economy of time, well-defined age norms, and accurate and reliable results. Its use has been in a variety of settings that need quick assessments of the basic educational skills. Schools, clinics, agencies, and private practitioners have all used the WRAT-R or the WRAT for more than thirty years.

The WRAT-R sets out to be a measurement instrument of the basic school coding skills. It was intended to build a school skills ruler by which we could measure students or adults and increase our understanding of their behavior. This chapter has described the history, administration, and interpretations of this common assessment instrument.

REFERENCES

Alford, D., Moore, M., & Simon, J. (1979). A preliminary assessment of the validity and usefulness of the WRAT with visually handicapped residential school students. *Education of the Visually Handicapped, 11,* 102–108.

Bradley, J. (1976). Evaluating reading achievement for placement in special education. *Journal of Special Education, 10,* 237–245.

Hollensworth, R., & White, R. (1981). Relationship between reading scores on the Wide Range Achievement Test and the Gilmore Oral Reading Test in young children. *Psychological Reports, 49,* 191–193.

Jastak, J. (1939). Understanding the non-reader. *Mental Hygiene, 23,* 228–240.

Jastak, J. (1946). *Wide Range Achievement Test.* Wilmington, DE: C. L. Story Company.

Jastak, J., & Jastak, S. (1965). *Wide Range Achievement Test.* Wilmington: Guidance Associates of Delaware.

Jastak, J., & Jastak, S. (1976). *Wide Range Achievement Test.* Wilmington: Guidance Associates of Delaware.

Jastak, J., & Jastak, S. (1978). *Wide Range Achievement Test.* Wilmington, DE: Jastak Associates.

Jastak, J., & Jastak, S. (1979). *Jastak Cluster Analysis: Meanings and measures of mental tests.* Wilmington, DE: Jastak Associates.

Jastak, S., & Wilkinson, G. (1984). *Wide Range Achievement Test—Revised.* Wilmington, DE: Jastak Associates.

Prasse, D., Siewert, J., & Breen, M. (1983). An analysis of performance on reading subtests from the 1978 Wide Range Achievement Test and Woodcock Reading Mastery Test with the WISC-R for learning disabled and regular education students. *Journal of Learning Disabilities, 16,* 458–461.

Reynolds, C. (1984). Critical measurement issues in learning disabilities. *Journal of Learning Disabilities, 18,* 451–476.

Williamson, W. (1979). The concurrent validity of the 1965 Wide Range Achievement Test with neurologically impaired and emotionally handicapped pupils. *Journal of Learning Disabilities, 12,* 201–203.

10

The Wechsler Preschool and Primary Scales of Intelligence

Patricia O'Brien Towle

The Wechsler Preschool and Primary Scales of Intelligence (WPPSI) is the "youngest" of the Wechsler intelligence tests. Designed for children four to six and a half years of age, it was intended as a downward extension of the Wechsler Intelligence Scale for Children, now revised (WISC-R). The WPPSI consists of eleven subtests, eight of which are either directly continuous with or essentially equivalent to WISC-R subtests, and three of which are unique to the WPPSI. Parallel to the WISC-R, the subtests are organized under separate Verbal and Performance Scales, and the major standard scores yielded are the Full Scale IQ, Verbal IQ, and Performance IQ.

At the time of its publication in 1967, the WPPSI was viewed as an important alternative to the Stanford-Binet Scales of Intelligence, primarily because it permitted analysis of differential abilities in specific areas of functioning. Although several other major tests of preschool cognitive skills have since appeared—and the Stanford-Binet has been reconstructed—the WPPSI remains a useful and very popular instrument. The purpose of this chapter is to review its clinical use: its psychometric properties, features of administration and interpretation, and appropriateness with specific types and ages of children.

CONSTRUCTION

Reviewers of the WPPSI invariably praise its psychometric qualities. It follows the Wechsler tradition of good standardization procedures and high reliability.

Standardization

The WPPSI was standardized on 1,200 children, 100 boys and 100 girls at each of six age groups. Subjects were chosen proportionally from various socioeconomic strata, ethnic groups, and geographic regions according to the 1960 U.S. Census data.

Reliability

Split-half reliability coefficients for the three IQ scores are very high, ranging from .91 to .97 across the age groups. The reliability coefficients for the individual subtests, based primarily on odd-even correlations, are more variable. They range from a low of .62 for Animal House at age four to a high of .91 for Mazes at age five and a half. Most coefficients, however, are in the .80s.

Validity

Concurrent validity was determined by correlating the WPPSI Full Scale IQ with the Stanford-Binet IQ (using the 1960 norms); a median correlation of .82 was obtained (Sattler, 1988). The WPPSI Verbal IQ correlates more highly with the Stanford-Binet than does the Performance IQ. Correlations between the WPPSI and other measures, such as the Peabody Picture Vocabulary Test and the Pictorial Test of Intelligence, were sufficiently high to indicate a significant association, but not high enough to make the standard scores interchangeable.

Carlson and Reynolds (1981) examined the construct validity of the WPPSI through the use of factor analysis. They demonstrated the presence of two main factors that are the same as the Verbal and Performance Scales. The results apply across all age groups and for different ethnic samples (Sattler, 1988). These results are different from those for similar research with the WISC-R, for which factor analysis results in alternative groupings of the subtests besides the Verbal and Performance Scales.

Another feature of construct validity confirmed through factor analysis is that all eleven subtests load sufficiently on a single underlying factor, interpreted as *g,* or general intelligence (Carlson & Reynolds, 1981).

ADMINISTRATION

Working with Young Children

Establishing Rapport   Working effectively with children of the ages covered by the WPPSI—four to six and a half years—requires some experience with and understanding of the age group. These children are no longer babies, are normally quite verbal, and understand the notion of sitting down to work. Yet successful administration remains dependent on establishing good rapport from the outset and maintaining the child's interest and motivation throughout the session(s). In general, the effective examiner is friendly, enthusiastic, and animated without being effusive, and is liberal in applying low-key praise for effort. Given the wide variety of young children's personalities and attitudes toward the testing situation, however, the only valid further guideline is to be vigilantly observant of the child's behavioral cues and to respond accordingly. Thus, the fearful and reticent child may require extra warmup time, during which unstructured and nonthreatening activities are undertaken. In extreme circumstances the parent may begin by remaining in the room with the door open, and slowly move out as the child becomes engaged with the activities and, eventually, with the examiner. In contrast, if the child is overactive or presents a frank management problem (e.g., oppositional or extremely distractible), increased structure and friendly but firm limits are usually in order. Setting clear contingencies and providing tangible rewards (such as stickers or the opportunity to play with an attractive toy) are often very effective when obtaining compliance is an issue.

When the child presents no special problem, or is particularly outgoing and eager to play the offered "games," then the examiner should delve right into cognitive testing in order to catch the child at his or her freshest. Suggestions on ways to introduce the testing and warmup items are provided in the WPPSI manual.

Training in Child Development   The examiner should also have background in qualitative features of the cognitive processes of young children. Piagetian concepts of child perspective, logic, and ability to abstract differ between the preschooler, the school-aged child, and the adult. Moreover, important cognitive-developmental changes take place over the age period covered by the WPPSI. Although the test does not specifically tap the intellectual processes described by Piaget, it is important that the examiner understand the nature of cognitive development in preschoolers to avoid devaluing the reasoning that the child may display during testing.

The Role of Observation   Reynolds and Kaufman (1985) suggest that 50 percent of the information obtained through standardized intelligence testing is based on observation during the testing session. A partial list of what is observed includes: (1) the child's approach to the tasks (impulsive versus reflective); (2) the child's ability to plan or organize responses; (3) the nature and quality of the child's verbalizations, affect, and behavior in response to different tasks and level of demands; (4) the types of errors made; (5) the quality of the child's fine and gross motor movements; and (6) the child's visual-motor accuracy.

General Administration Procedures

Learning to administer the WPPSI requires time and practice. For those experienced in giving the WISC-R, this time will be much reduced because of the similarity in several of the subtests. The WPPSI Block Design and Mazes subtests are sufficiently different from their WISC-R counterparts, however, to warrant study. The subtests that are completely different in the WPPSI are Animal House, Sentences, and Geometric Design.

Administration time ranges from 50 to 90 minutes, with an average of one hour. Two separate sessions can be used if the child becomes too inattentive or tired. The testing situation should be quiet, free from distractions, and well lit, yet comfortable enough to avoid resembling a medical setting. A child's table or desk with a smooth surface and a child's chair should be used.

The materials needed for administration (besides the test kit and manual) are a stopwatch, two short red pencils, and the record forms. On the main test protocol, the face sheet is arranged for recording all totaled raw scores and corresponding standard scores; the remaining four pages provide areas for recording answers and raw scores for each subtest. Two other forms are needed for each testing—a folded sheet printed with Mazes, and sheets designed for the child's drawing on the Geometric Designs subtest.

The preferred order of administration of the subtests, which is the order that they appear in the manual and the record form, is as follows:

1. Information
2. Animal House
3. Vocabulary
4. Picture Completion
5. Arithmetic

6. Mazes
7. Geometric Design
8. Similarities
9. Block Design
10. Comprehension
11. Sentences (Supplementary)
12. (Animal House Retest)

The intention was to alternate verbal with nonverbal tests and challenging with less challenging ones. The order can be changed, however, in consideration of special circumstances, such as the child's motivation for particular activities. Moreover, if a child gives up quickly on an easy item yet demonstrates skills at a higher level, or refuses to do a particular item or subtest, these can be returned to later. The Sentences subtest is a supplementary test. This means that it is optional and is available to be used if another verbal subtest is spoiled. The Animal House Retest procedure is also optional and can be used if the examiner is particularly interested in how a child remembers the task.

All subtest instructions are standardized. For each subtest the manual specifies how much demonstration, inquiry, and specific types of encouragement are permissible. In general, encouragement for the reluctant child takes the form of "just try it once more" or "try a little longer."

Several subtests are strictly timed. If the child gives up before the time limit has been reached, encourage him or her to continue. On the other hand, if the time is up and the child is almost done, it is best to let the child finish while scoring the item as a fail. For the items that are not timed, a guideline of 15 seconds is suggested for the child to begin a response. For Verbal subtests, the examiner must write down responses verbatim. This is important for making scoring judgments later that are sometimes based on subtle criteria. Most examiners develop their own shorthand notations to ease this task (e.g., leaving out vowels; *you = u, because = bc, something = st, to = 2*). Verbatim recording is most important for the Vocabulary and Comprehension subtests.

With the exception of Block Design, subtests begin with item 1 for all children. On Block Design, the exact procedure differs for children under and over six years of age. Each subtest is discontinued after a given number of consecutive items have been failed (referred to as obtaining a ceiling). The guidelines for each are printed on the record form.

Administration Guidelines: The Subtests

1. Information (23 items, 1 point each) Each item consists of a short question requiring a short answer. Acceptable responses are provided in the manual.

2. Animal House (1 procedure, timed)   Materials are a formboard and a box of small wooden cylinders of four different colors. At the top of the formboard are four pictures of animals, each with a cylinder of a different color beneath it. This is the sample that the child must follow. The rest of the formboard consists of rows of animal pictures, with empty holes beneath them. The child's task is to put the correct cylinders in the holes. The examiner's instructions are elaborate and essentially need to be memorized. The child's performance is timed, with five minutes as the limit. The raw score is based on how much time was required for the child to complete the task, as well as errors and omissions made.

An optional feature is the Animal House Retest, whereby the subtest is readministered at the end of the entire test.

3. Vocabulary (22 items, 1–2 points each)   For each item, the child is asked to define a word ("tell me what they mean"). The scoring is complex, requires study, and calls for some judgments to be made. Certain responses should be queried according to guidelines specified in the manual. The examiner must record responses verbatim.

4. Picture Completion (23 items, 1 point each)   Materials are a small spiral-bound book of line drawings, each picture having something missing from it. The child is to name the missing part. Pointing receives credit if what the child intends is clear.

5. Arithmetic (14 items, 1 point each)   The first four items require the use of a spiral-bound book in which there are pictures. An example of an item is: "Here are three apples. Which is the biggest? Point to it." On items 4 through 8, the blocks from Block Design are used for counting problems. Items 9 through 20 are verbal arithmetic problems, starting with very simple problems and proceeding to more complex ones.

6. Mazes (10 items, ranging from 1 to 4 points each, timed)   This subtest requires use of the preprinted sheets that have two types of mazes on them: lengthwise mazes drawn from left to right (for earlier items), and box mazes with increasingly complex labyrinths within them. The instructions are complicated and include demonstrations, first and second trials, and detailed scoring criteria. The examiner demonstrates with a lead pencil, and the child uses a red pencil.

7. Geometric Design (10 items, ranging from 2 to 4 points each)   A spiral-bound book containing the ten designs is used. Each design is presented to the child to copy, using a red pencil on the sheets provided. Scoring criteria, which require study, are in the back of the manual, along with numerous drawn examples.

8. Similarities (16 items, ranging from 1 to 2 points each)   For the first ten items, the child is asked to finish a sentence such as "You draw with a crayon and you also draw with a _____." Acceptable responses are provided in the manual. For the last six items, the child is asked to explain how two objects are alike or the same—for example: *apple–pear* or *dog–cat*. Scoring criteria are given in the manual and require study.

9. Block Design (10 items, 0–2 points each, timed)   Materials are a set of thin red and white wooden blocks, approximately one inch square, and the spiral-bound booklet with red and white designs in it. Younger and older children start with different items. For the first four items, the examiner makes a design with the blocks out of the child's sight (using the manual as a screen), presents it to the child, and demonstrates how to copy it using the same number of blocks. After the demonstration blocks have been scrambled, the child's task is to copy the designs. By item 6 no demonstration is given, and by item 8 a printed design is used. Again, the instructions are complex and should be virtually memorized. Directions for dealing with rotations of designs on the child's part are in the manual.

10. Comprehension (15 items, 1–2 points each)   This subtest consists of questions requiring an explanation on the part of the child. It is similar to Vocabulary in that the scoring criteria demand study beforehand, and involve queries to specific responses, verbatim recording, and judgment on the examiner's part.

11. Sentences (10 items, 1–4 points each)   For each item, the child is to repeat a sentence after the examiner says it. The response must be written verbatim because scoring is determined by counting errors of omission, transposition, addition, and substitution. This subtest is optional, to be given as a substitute for a spoiled subtest, or if the examiner is particularly interested in how a child might perform on this task.

SCORING

After the task of scoring is completed for each subtest according to the guidelines in the manual, some clerical work is required. First of all, the simple arithmetic required for totaling the points on each subtest should be double-checked. The totals are then transferred to the face sheet, where all Verbal subtests are listed together, as are Performance subtests. Errors can be made in the process of transferring, so totals should be checked when finished.

Second, a standard score called a scaled score (mean = 10, S.D. = 3) is obtained for each subtest raw score by using the normative tables arranged by ages in the back of the manual. The child's age is calculated by subtracting the child's birth date from the current date (see page 42 of the manual). The scaled scores, recorded next to the raw scores on the face page of the record form, provide the basis for profile analysis.

Third, the scaled scores are summed for the Verbal subtests and then for the Performance subtests, and these sums are converted to the Verbal and Performance IQs using the tables in the manual. The two sums are also added together and converted to the Full Scale IQ. The three IQs are recorded in the appropriate spaces on the face sheet.

Special Scoring Procedures   The WPPSI IQs can be prorated if only four out of the five subtests have been given on either the Performance or the Verbal Scale. The procedure is to multiply the sum of the four scaled scores obtained by four-fifths. It is easiest, however, to use Table 24 in the manual, which lists the prorated IQs for each sum of four subtests. The Full Scale IQ must be based on at least four Verbal and four Performance subtests. The Full Scale IQ itself is never prorated.

A second issue is that IQs should be calculated only if the child obtained a raw score greater than 0 on at least two subtests per scale. Because of features of the normative tables, even raw scores of 0—meaning the child passed no items on the subtest—can earn scaled scores of up to 4. Therefore, a child who got no items correct on the whole test could hypothetically earn an IQ that is above his or her actual abilities.

INTERPRETATION

General

A great advantage of the WPPSI is that it yields so much material to interpret: global scores, verbal and nonverbal groupings, and individual measures of myriad abilities. Although these features create rich clinical results, they also present the evaluator with considerable responsibility. The responsibility is that of making judgments based on the simultaneous consideration of many details, matching the judgments to observed behavior and reports of behavior from other sources, and at the same time being aware of the "hard facts" from a psychometric point of view.

The first judgment that must be made involves asking the question, "Is it a valid testing?" Were the scores obtained from a motivated, cooperative, relaxed child? If he was hypersensitive to sound, were the noises in the hall a constant distraction? If she needed glasses or hearing aids, was she wearing them? Sometimes a child's behavioral style calls for a disclaimer of some results. For example, the bright but extremely compulsive child may fail many of the timed tests because of being overly methodical, but not from lack of cognitive ability. In such a case it would be necessary to state that several of the Performance tests (and probably the Performance IQ) may be an underestimate of the child's ability. An invalid excuse, however, that beginning evaluators are prone to make is that a child was especially inattentive and distractible. The tester may reason that if she had paid better attention, she would have been able to do it. In fact, children are likely to be increasingly inattentive when faced with tasks they cannot complete successfully; moreover, chronic lack of concentration tends to result in frank deficits in skill and knowledge acquisition. Thus, poor attention may be a result of limited skills rather than the cause of low scores. In any event, the test report should include a statement regarding the examiner's judgment of the validity of the test administration as a measure of the child's ability.

Fortunately, the task of WPPSI interpretation is made very much easier (and more valid) because of the previous work of investigators. Although less empirical research has been done with the WPPSI than with the WISC-R, a fair amount does exist, and much that has been written about the WISC-R is applicable to the WPPSI as well. Therefore, it is essential that the WPPSI be used *in conjunction with* other sources that provide the several necessary tables and guidelines for responsible interpretation. The two that I most recommend are Sattler (1988) and Kaufman (1979). Table 10–1 lists eight of the fifteen tables in Appendix

Table 10–1 Selected Tables in Sattler (1988) Relevant to WPPSI Interpretation

Table Number	Title
C-14	Confidence intervals for WPPSI Scales
C-15	Significant differences between WPPSI scaled scores and between IQs (.05/.01 significance levels)
C-16	Differences required for significance when each WPPSI subtest scaled score is compared to the mean scaled score for any individual child
C-23	WPPSI structure of intellect classifications
C-24	Interpretive rationales and implications of high and low scores for WPPSI subtests
C-41	Percentile ranks and suggested qualitative descriptions for scaled scores on the WISC-R, WPPSI, and WAIS-R
C-42	Interpretive rationales and implications of high and low scores, and instructional implications for Wechsler scales and factor scores
C-43	Suggested remediation activities for combinations of Wechsler subtests

Reproduced with permission from *Assessment of Children* by Jerry Sattler, 1988, J. M. Sattler, Publisher.

C of Sattler (1988) that pertain to the WPPSI. Kaufman's book on the WISC-R is also an excellent source for guiding the detective work necessary to take full advantage of the subtest profile.

Major techniques of interpretation traditionally have been dichotomized into *normative* and *ipsative.* The normative approach relates the child's overall level of skill to that of other children the same age. The ipsative approach evaluates the pattern of strengths and weaknesses of an individual child.

Normative Interpretation

The normative mean and standard deviation of the IQ scores and the individual subtest scaled scores are the major tools used to judge the child's level of functioning in relation to that of his or her peers. For the IQs, the mean is 100, and the standard deviation is 15; it is 10 and 3, respectively, for the subtest scores.

The Hard Facts   When the IQs of a child are reported, the numbers are presented within a context that takes several forms, including confidence intervals, percentile ranks, and categories or levels of functioning.

A confidence interval, or band of error, is derived from the standard error of measurement of the test score. It is the range of scores within which the child's true score will fall, at a given level of confidence—for example, 95 percent of the time. Using confidence intervals is important for two reasons: to reflect the statistical phenomenon of measurement error, and to avoid the notion that an IQ score is a fixed, immutable property or one that can be measured extremely precisely. It is necessary to use a table, such as that in Sattler (1988) (C-14), to obtain the confidence intervals for the WPPSI IQ scores. The table is divided according to six age levels and several levels of confidence. The number listed is actually the standard error, along with a " " sign; the confidence interval is created by first subtracting and then adding the number to the child's obtained score. For example, at the age of six, the confidence interval for the Full Scale IQ at 95 percent confidence is 7. Thus, if a child obtains a Full Scale IQ of 102, the statement can be made that "there is a 95 percent chance that Stephen's true Full Scale IQ is between 95 and 109."

The levels of cognitive functioning and percentile ranks are listed in Table 10–2. Because the language used in the WPPSI manual for several of the levels is outdated, current terminology has been used instead (e.g., *mentally retarded* for *mental defective,* and *low average* for *dull normal*). An example of how to express the IQ results verbally in terms of levels and percentiles is as follows: "Johnny's Full Scale IQ of 105 places his functioning in the Average range of intelligence and at the 63rd percentile." Examples of variations in reporting the three types of information associated with the IQ score are available in Sattler and in Kaufman.

Table 10–2 Levels of Cognitive Functioning

IQ Score	Classification
130+	Very superior
120–129	Superior
110–119	High average
90–109	Average
80–89	Low average
70–79	Borderline
–69	Mentally retarded

Adapted from Table 7 of the manual for the Wechsler Preschool and Primary Scale of Intelligence by special permission. Copyright © 1963, 1967 by The Psychological Corporation. All rights reserved.

The cutoff for mental retardation of 69, or two standard deviations below the mean, is consistent with other well-used typologies such as that of the American Association on Mental Deficiency (AAMD) (Grossman, 1983). The AAMD also has specified that in order for an individual to be diagnosed as mentally retarded, adaptive behavior scores as well as intellectual test scores must be significantly delayed. Below the 69 cutoff, specific levels of mental retardation are determined by the number of standard deviations below the mean that scores fall. An important limitation of the WPPSI when evaluating significantly delayed children is discussed next.

The Insufficient Floor and Ceiling of the WPPSI One criticism justifiably leveled at the WPPSI is that it does not discriminate the full range of functioning at the lower end. The manual specifies that the child must have attained skills at approximately the three-year level for the WPPSI to be usable. Therefore, the child needs to have an IQ of about 75 at age 4, of 60 at age 5, and of 50 at age 6 (Wechsler, 1967). Even a four-year-old child who barely produces a scorable protocol may obtain an IQ as high as 55 because he or she can receive up to four scaled score points for getting a raw score of 0 or 1 (see Sattler, 1988, p. 214). It is clear, then, that the WPPSI is not appropriate for determining the presence or degree of mental retardation in young children. The exception occurs if mild retardation to borderline functioning is suspected in a child at the higher age ranges of the test.

A corresponding problem is the limited ceiling. If a gifted six-year-old child receives the highest possible scaled scores on most or all subtests, the test obviously is not functioning as a fine-tuned measure of his or her skills.

When IQ Scores Should Not Be Interpreted When there is considerable intraindividual variation present in the child's performance, interpretation of the Full Scale IQ, Verbal IQ, and Performance IQ should be done with caution or not at all. For example, if a very large difference exists between the Verbal and Performance IQs, then the Full Scale IQ is a meaningless "average" that does not adequately reflect either the child's strengths or his or her weaknesses. What constitutes a significant amount of variability is discussed in the next section.

Ipsative Interpretation

Evaluation of the pattern of scores the child obtains is referred to as *interpretation of scatter* or as *profile analysis*. A profile is produced when the subtest scores of an individual test are charted on a common scale and then connected with a line. The peaks and valleys that result can reveal much about the child's style of learning.

The Hard Facts   The first step is to compare the Verbal and Performance IQs. In order to determine whether the difference is statistically significant, a table available in the manual (p. 24) should be consulted, since the exact amount varies according to age. A general guideline offered by Sattler (1988) is that a difference of 11 points is significant at the .05 significance level and a difference of 14 points at .01. The main implication of a significant difference is that the Full Scale IQ is not a good summary of the child's abilities. A Verbal–Performance disparity also has other implications, but interpretation should be deferred until patterns within the scales are examined.

The next step is to determine the range of subtest scores. Kaufman (1979) and Reynolds and Kaufman (1985) have emphasized that a certain amount of variability is normal, and that profiles with scatter are actually more common than absolutely flat profiles. Within each scale, a range of up to 10 points between the lowest and highest scaled scores is not uncommon (Reynolds & Gutkin, 1981), and therefore is not usually clinically significant.

Even when the overall range of scatter is not significant, meaningful differences among the individual subtests can still occur. These differences can be identified in two ways. The first is to compare the individual subtest scaled score to the mean of the scaled scores on the same scale (i.e., the Verbal and Performance Scales are treated separately). If the subtest is about 3 points higher or lower than the mean, it can be labeled with an S for strength or a W for weakness, following the technique described by Kaufman (1979) for the WISC-R. The exact number of points needed for a significant difference does vary for each subtest and for different levels of significance (see Sattler, 1988, Table C–16). The second way is to compare pairs of subtests. The number of points necessary to claim a significant difference between any two subtests is 3 to 4 points (.05) and 4 to 5 points (.01). Table C–15 in Sattler (1988) provides precise values.

The Meaning of the Variation   Each of the subtests is associated with unique and shared abilities, which means that the examiner must know what the subtests measure both alone and in various combinations. Many descriptive lists have been compiled by a variety of investigators; a very comprehensive one is available in Sattler (1988, Tables C–23 and C–24). All the Verbal subtests have general verbal comprehension in common, based on factor-analytic findings, but in addition each calls for a particular combination of skills. For example, Information taps long-range memory, whereas Vocabulary measures concept formation and verbal fluency, among other things. On the Performance scale, all subtests measure "perceptual organization." All but Picture Completion also tap visual-motor coordination in some way. In addition to listing the abilities measured by the subtests, Sattler also provides a table of implications of high and low scores.

The major way to make sense out of groupings of high and low scores is to make lists of abilities shared by the subtests clustering together and to generate hypotheses about the child's skills that are consistent with the pattern of scores. At the same time, the absolute level of subtest scores should be noted to gain a perspective about this child's similarity to same-aged boys and girls. Figuring out the meaning of levels and patterns of scores is the core of WPPSI test interpretation, requiring effort and skill. Skill level will be enhanced, of course, by accrued experience and knowledge about children's cognitive and neuropsychological functioning.

Another source of interpretation for combinations of *groups* of high and low scores is Kaufman (1979), which deals specifically with the WISC-R but has implications for the WPPSI as well. On the Verbal Scale, for example, subtests can be grouped according to those requiring reasoning versus recall, long stimuli versus short stimuli, and much expression required versus little expression required. On the Performance Scale, groupings are made on the basis of right-brain processing versus integrated functioning, simultaneous versus successive processing, imitation versus problem solving, visual organization versus visual-motor coordination, and cognition versus convergent production. The meaning of these terms and the methods for determining their relevance for a particular child can be studied in Kaufman (1979).

If a test record's pattern of high and low scores fits one of these groupings or can be attributed to a consistent pattern of shared and unique abilities, the hypotheses generated must be checked against observations of test behavior. If no particular grouping is salient, yet single subtests stand out as strengths and weaknesses, then the subtests can be interpreted alone. A final psychometric consideration then becomes relevant—that of the degree of specificity associated with each subtest. Specificity is determined statistically and reflects the extent to which a subtest measures some quality or qualities that are not covered by one or more other subtests. Subtests with good specificity are Vocabulary,

Similarities, Sentences, Animal House (except at age four), Picture Completion, Mazes, and Block Design. Those with less but still adequate specificity are Arithmetic, Geometric Design, and Animal House (age four). Those having inadequate specificity are Information and Comprehension (from Reynolds & Kaufman, 1985). Thus, if either Information or Comprehension is the only subtest showing significant variation, little should be interpreted from it.

Interpreting Verbal versus Performance IQ strengths as a general attribute of the child can be done with justification when the set of Verbal subtests and Performance subtests do not contain excessive scatter. Implications of general strengths in verbal and performance areas are listed in Sattler (1988, Table C–42). Kaufman (1979) also offers a number of interpretations of a significant differential in Verbal versus Performance IQs. These include fluid versus crystallized ability, psycholinguistic deficiency, coordination problem, field dependence versus field independence, and socioeconomic/ethnic factors.

Summary of Approach to Interpretation   First note the level of the Full Scale IQ, and compare Verbal and Performance IQs. If the Verbal IQ–Performance IQ difference is significant, do not interpret or emphasize the Full Scale IQ. Next inspect the subtests for scatter and patterns, simultaneously noting the absolute level of the subtest scores. Calculate scatter across all subtests as well as for the Verbal and Performance scales. Determine whether individual subtests represent strengths and weaknesses. Study descriptions of abilities measured by each subtest and each group of subtests, and interpret patterns found that are also corroborated by observed test behavior. If no specific patterns are found, interpret individual subtests that stand out if adequate subtest specificity is associated with them. If relatively little scatter is found within each of the Verbal and Performance Scales, interpret any significant difference between these two general areas of skill, again corroborating with observation.

CASE EXAMPLE

Mike N, a five-and-a-half-year-old boy of Korean background, was referred for an evaluation by the staff of the preschool program he attended in a lower-middle-class neighborhood. Concerns involved hyperactivity and impulsivity, poor peer relationships and social skills, and gross and fine motor deficits. Mike was noted to have very good language skills, and used only English. Although his parents' native language was Korean, they spoke only English at home. His social difficulties were not those usually associated with hyperactivity and attentional problems; instead, he was seen as isolated and sometimes bizarre. He often chose to engage in fantasy play involving TV cartoon characters rather than interact with others. His social skills were poorly developed, and he soon alienated the other children. By the end of the year in preschool, however, Mike had made gains in relating to peers, and could successfully participate in some group activities.

Mike had been the product of a full-term, uncomplicated pregnancy. He was of normal birth weight and had no perinatal difficulties. By report, his early developmental milestones were attained on schedule, but he was always overactive. He developed asthma at thirty months of age, creating a constant concern for his well-being on the part of his parents.

Interview with Mother

Mrs. N was asked a number of questions for background information purposes and for administration of the Vineland Adaptive Behavior Scales. She appeared to be torn between her concern for Mike and her need to deny the problems he might have. Mr. and Mrs. N had followed the suggestions of professionals to seek this evaluation, as well as a previous one, but had decided against sending Mike to a special-needs kindergarten. At the time of the evaluation he had been attending a private religious school for two weeks. Since no reports, good or bad, had been received yet from teachers, Mrs. N said that he was doing very well—no problems. When asked if the examiner could contact the teachers for a verbal report, Mrs. N asked that no contact be made since this might give the school the idea that Mike had a problem.

Mrs. N acknowledged that Mike was often a handful because of his overactivity and impulsiveness. She primarily saw him as very bright because of his well-developed fantasy life and because he "talks like an adult." On the advice of her pediatrician, she had sent him to preschool at age three because he had never had any children to play with and appeared undersocialized.

As the conversation continued, it became obvious that Mike was quite overprotected and that his demands were most often indulged by both parents in order to avoid the problems that came with denying him. His asthma appeared to have a significant impact on the family dynamics, and his mother was prone to have him stay at home if he had any respiratory problems, although she acknowledged his need for the educational and socializing experience of day programs. During the Vineland administration, several of the daily living skills items that were age-appropriate were met with, "Oh no, I don't let him do that . . . he's just a baby!"

Mike's Behavior during Testing

Mike was a tall, good-looking boy who separated from his mother very easily and was eager to play some games. Though quite active and distractible, he was nonetheless compliant and cooperative during testing.

He chattered constantly on both related and unrelated topics, and had to be redirected frequently to the task. His attention span was obviously limited. He did put forth effort on all items, even those that were difficult for him, and seemed undaunted that some of his products were of very poor quality. The results of testing were considered valid.

Mike's behavior and affect during testing were remarkable in several other ways. He had a wide-eyed, "spacy" demeanor most of the time, accentuated by his constant chatter while his eyes roamed about the room. The topics of conversation he chose usually started with some relation or association to a test item and were either about his family or about TV characters. He told numerous anecdotes, only some of which were comprehensible. The manner in which he spoke, although he used good vocabulary and sophisticated sentence structure, was quite babyish in its inflections and constant excitement.

Mike was disinhibited in many ways, including his constant conversation that jumped from topic to topic and his physical activity (often standing next to his chair rather than sitting in it, constantly looking around, moving his arms and legs while sitting). He often became excited and physically active when responding to fairly simple questions. For example, when asked to define a *swing,* he said, "A swing is something that you whooooo—swing on!" while gesturing widely with his arms. A bicycle was "something that you zzzzhooom on!" When asked how many legs a dog had, he replied "three" and jumped onto the floor in imitation of a dog.

Mike's behavioral and verbal disorganization could be modified with increased structure imposed by the examiner. On the Animal House subtest, he could perform adequately only when given the maximum guidance allowed in the standardized instructions. Under the structure of telling a well-known story (during a break from testing), Mike's excellent verbal skills came out. His rendition of Little Red Riding Hood was long, detailed, and accurate. He spontaneously and creatively incorporated the plastic "Sesame Street" characters that were in front of him, choosing ones that corresponded well to the wolf, the grandmother, and Little Red Riding Hood.

Mike's difficulty with fine motor coordination was obvious in his pencil grasp, the effort he expended to gain control of his drawing, and the poor quality of his drawings. He has been described by preschool staff as clumsy in gross motor activities as well.

Test Results

The IQ and subtest scores obtained for Mike are shown in Table 10–3. The 17-point difference between Mike's Verbal and Performance IQs is statistically significant at the .001 level, and therefore the Full Scale IQ should not be emphasized in the report. Before interpreting a

Table 10–3 Mike's IQ and Subtest Scores

	IQ	Confidence Interval (95%)	Percentile	Level
Verbal	99	92–106	50	Average
Performance	82	75–89	10	Low average
Full Scale	90	85–95	25	Average

Subtest	Score	Subtest	Score
Information	12	Animal House	9
Vocabulary	12	Picture Completion	10-S
Arithmetic	7-W	Mazes	6
Similarities	11	Geometric Design	6
Comprehension	7-W	Block Design	6

straightforward verbal versus nonverbal pattern, the subtest scatter and patterns need to be examined. Although the amount of scatter was not remarkable in itself (6 points overall, 5 points on the Verbal Scale, 4 points on the Performance Scale), some significant strengths and weaknesses could be identified. On the Verbal Scale, the mean of the scaled scores was 9.8, rounded to 10, so that the 3-point difference between this mean and the scaled scores of 7 on Arithmetic and Comprehension were significant. Similarly, the mean of the Performance subtests was 7.4, rounded to 7, so that the 10 of Picture Completion indicated a strength. On each of the scales, the differences between the lower scores and each of the higher scores were statistically significant as well. In total, sufficient scatter was present to warrant attempting to explain more detailed patterns of abilities than simply Verbal versus Performance skills.

On the Verbal Scale, Mike's abilities in verbal conceptualization were solidly age-appropriate and even slightly above, as shown by his scaled scores of 11 and 12. Since the standard deviation of the scaled scores is 3, it would have taken scores of 13 to conclude that he was significantly ahead of his peers. With reference to the tables in Sattler (1988), Mike's performance on these subtests (Information, Vocabulary, and Similarities) suggests he has good verbal conceptualization, range of knowledge, abstract thinking abilities (verbal), memory, and logic, and has not been culturally deprived. The scores dispel concerns that bilingualism (which did not actually exist) or cultural differences have depressed his language learning.

Mike's pattern of Verbal scores does not fit any particular grouping suggested by Kaufman. Therefore, individual interpretation of the subtests is in order. For Arithmetic, this is not difficult. For one thing, according to both Sattler and Kaufman, this is the single Verbal subtest (except for Sentences) that taps immediate attention and ability to concentrate. This interpretation is relevant for Mike, since behavioral observations indicated problems with attention. Furthermore, even when Mike was paying attention, he showed a paucity of number concepts. He correctly solved two problems requiring him to point out the "biggest" and the "longest" object, and he could count by rote, but he failed items where he had to take time to count and figure. He even failed counting nine blocks because he moved quickly and did not maintain touching one block per number with his finger. As will be seen later, this behavior was consistent with visual-motor problems discerned from the Performance Scale.

Because the Comprehension test shares many abilities with the Verbal tests on which Mike did well, its low score is initially puzzling. Yet any interpretation of the low Comprehension score is contraindicated because, as noted in an earlier section, the test does not have adequate subtest specificity. One cannot help noting, however, how well the "possible indications of a low Comprehension score" presented in Sattler (1988) fit Mike. These include poor social judgment, overdependency, immaturity, and limited involvement with others. Kaufman notes that when interpretation of given patterns cannot be supported statistically, there is nevertheless justification in doing such interpretation very cautiously when a great deal of support from observation and other sources exists.

Moving next to the Performance Scale, a pattern noted in Kaufman did fit Mike's scores—that of visual organization versus visual-motor coordination. Picture Completion calls for visual inspection of details but not for motor coordination as required in Mazes, Block Design, and Geometric Design. Animal House is not included in Kaufman's groupings because it is not a WISC-R subtest, but Sattler indicates that visual-motor dexterity is involved as well. In Mike's case, he appeared to compensate verbally by talking his way through the subtest, and his dexterity was sufficient for him to get the cylinders into the holes fairly quickly. In contrast, on Mazes, Block Design, and Geometric Design, Mike was stymied. His lack of fine motor control, poor visual-motor-spatial integration, and poor planning abilities were obvious, and converged on these tasks to yield scores in striking contrast to his general verbal conceptual abilities.

Integration of WPPSI Results with Other Test Scores

On the Vineland Adaptive Behavior Scales, standard scores (which have a mean of 100 and a standard deviation of 15) were below average in all domains except Motor Skills, which was at the low end of the average range. Mike's Daily Living Skills score was actually in the deficient range (65), resulting from a combination of fine motor deficits, lack of mastery of demands made on him, and social immaturity. That his Communication score (79) was low in contrast to his verbal conceptual potential as measured by the WPPSI is reconciled by the fact that the Vineland measures language use in relation to social competence. Mike's Socialization score of 78 therefore also was probably reflective of his immaturity.

On the Conners Parent Questionnaire, filled out by Mrs. N, Mike received scores one standard deviation above the mean on the subscales of Learning Problems, Impulsivity-Hyperactivity, and the Hyperactivity Index. Elevation on these subscales is consistent with the behavioral observations and other test scores.

Summary and Implications

Mike appeared to be a bright five-year-old with significant difficulties in several areas of learning and behavior. He certainly exhibited the soft signs of developmental/neurological immaturity with his motor incoordination, visual-spatial problems, hyperactivity, and distractibility. He nonetheless was functioning well in verbal expression and in acquiring information from his environment. He exhibited some social immaturities that were of concern. His lack of inhibition and verbal flightiness appeared to be a result both of Mike's intrinsic qualities and of gaps in parental socialization that would foster internalized controls. His intense involvement in fantasy, totally inappropriate peer social skills, and wandering conversations at first created concern about an incipient psychotic process. But hallucinations were not present by observation or report, nor was the content of his fantasy play bizarre with morbid or sexual content. Lack of social skills could be explained in part by his early lack of contact with other children and by his impulsivity. As noted, over a year of nursery school he had made gains in relating to others and joining group activities.

It was recommended that Mike be in a school setting that could accommodate his needs without isolating him from peers of similar intellectual potential. This called for a small, structured classroom situation where noise and distractions could be controlled, and one-to-one attention would be available to him for part of the day. Special attention was warranted in fine and gross motor skills. The degree of deficit he demonstrated in fine motor and visual-spatial skills could have a significant impact on his acquisition of early academic skills such as reading and printing. Extra help and monitoring would undoubtedly be called for. Attention to acquiring peer social skills was also seen as very important. If Mike did not show significant improvement in social skills in a supportive classroom environment, group or individual therapy would be indicated. It was also recommended that Mike's parents become involved in family counseling for guidance in dealing with Mike's behavior at home. Mike should certainly be reevaluated at the end of the current school year to assist in planning for educational placement for first grade.

SUMMARY: ASSETS AND LIABILITIES

The major assets of the WPPSI include its good psychometric properties, its continuity with the widely used WISC-R, and its ability to sample many different skills. The child's strengths and weaknesses can be scrutinized at length, while global scores are also obtained.

The major limitation of the WPPSI, as reviewed herein, is its limited floor and ceiling. This feature restricts the test's usefulness with children of extreme levels of abilities. It should not be used with children suspected of mental retardation, except possibly for children above age five and a half years where the mental retardation is no more than mild (i.e., IQ greater than 55). Conversely, it should not be used for extremely gifted children above age five.

Because the test's norms were developed over twenty years ago, a restandardization was begun in 1987. This revision is expected to be completely different with regard to content, administration, and scoring, and may bear little resemblance to its predecessor. The publication date is not anticipated for at least one year, however, and therefore it will probably be several years after that before the WPPSI-R has sufficient lore to justify its wide use.

In summary, the WPPSI remains a time-honored measure of preschool children's intellectual functioning. Like any such test, it should be used only under the appropriate circumstances and as part of a set of information-gathering techniques. The WPPSI's contribution to a test battery will invariably be valuable and detailed.

REFERENCES

Carlson, L. C., & Reynolds, C. R. (1981). Factor structure and specific variance of the WPPSI subtests at six age levels. *Psychology in the Schools, 18,* 48–54.

Grossman, H. I. (Ed.). (1983). *Manual on terminology and classification in mental retardation.* Washington, DC: American Association on Mental Deficiency.

Kaufman, A. S. (1979). *Intelligent testing with the WISC-R.* New York: John Wiley & Sons.

Reynolds, C. R., & Gutkin, T. B. (1981). Test scatter on the WPPSI: Normative analysis of the standardization sample. *Journal of Learning Disabilities, 14,* 460–464.

Reynolds, C. R., & Kaufman, A. S. (1985). Clinical assessment of children's intelligence with the Wechsler scales. In B. Wolman (Ed.), *Handbook of intelligence: Theories, measurements, and applications* (pp. 89–132). New York: John Wiley & Sons.

Sattler, J. M. (1988). *Assessment of children* (3rd ed.). San Diego, CA: J. M. Sattler.

Wechsler, D. (1967). *Manual for the Wechsler Preschool and Primary Scale of Intelligence.* New York: Psychological Corporation.

11

Peabody Picture Vocabulary Test— Revised

Victoria Shea

The title of the Peabody Picture Vocabulary Test—Revised (PPVT-R; Dunn & Dunn, 1981) describes all the essential elements of this instrument. Its development began at *Peabody* College in Nashville, Tennessee, in the 1950s. It uses *pictures* to assess the client's receptive *vocabulary*. Administration and scoring procedures are standardized, and the client's score is compared to normative data, thus making it a *test*. Finally, the original Peabody Picture Vocabulary Test (Dunn, 1959) was *revised* in 1981, yielding the PPVT-R.

CONSTRUCTION

Test Task

The client is shown a page of four pictures at a time, while the examiner pronounces an English word. The client's task is to indicate which picture best fits the word. This can be done by pointing, by communicating the number of the picture that is chosen, or even by indicating yes or no as the examiner touches each picture in turn. Thus, the PPVT-R does not require any verbal responses on the part of the client.

Test Setting

The PPVT-R manual calls for a standard test setting of privacy, comfortable seating, adequate light and ventilation, and the development of rapport between examiner and client before testing begins. The manual suggests that the examiner and the client sit around the corner of a table from each other, with the test materials directly in front of the client. This arrangement can be modified as necessary; for example, for the sake of rapport the examiner may sit next to an anxious client, or may hold a hyperactive child on his or her lap.

Intended Population

The PPVT-R is designed for use with clients ranging in age from two and a half years through forty years. The test is useful with a variety of populations, including but not limited to children or adults who cannot speak.

Qualifications of the Examiner

The test authors suggest that a variety of professionals, such as teachers, physicians, counselors, and social workers, should be able to administer the PPVT-R, provided they have proper training in behavioral measurement principles and methodology. The manual is designed to be as clear as possible about issues such as accurate scoring, the standard error of measurement, and uses of the test, so that nonpsychologists can administer and interpret the test appropriately. In fact, in many settings the PPVT-R is used mainly by speech/language pathologists or special education teachers, rather than psychologists.

Test Materials

The PPVT-R has two equivalent forms, L and M, each consisting of 175 items and 5 training items. Each form is contained in a spiral-bound book with an easel back, so it can be propped at an angle to the client for easy viewing. The PPVT-R kit also includes test protocols for each client, an administration and scoring manual, and a separate technical supplement that describes in more detail the development of the test and its psychometric properties.

Each test item uses a *plate* or page of four black-and-white drawings, laid out in quadrants. One of the drawings represents the correct answer, and the other three drawings are called *decoys*. A drawing that is a decoy on one plate may be used in a later item as the correct answer. All drawings were developed specifically for the PPVT-R and were designed to be clear representations of their subject, free of unnecessary visual details.

Item Content

The words used for the PPVT-R fall into nineteen categories, according to the manual, as follows:

1. verbs (gerunds);
2. animals and associated items;
3. buildings;
4. clothing and accessories;
5. adjectives and adverbs;
6. foods (produce);
7. foods (nonproduce);
8. items found in households and yards;
9. household utensils;
10. human body parts;
11. people in their work roles;
12. human groups and humanlike forms;
13. mathematical terms;
14. plants;
15. items found in schools and offices;
16. tools and machines;
17. toys, games, and musical equipment;
18. vehicles;
19. items related to weather and geography.

Differences from the PPVT

Some of the words and drawings from the original PPVT are used in the PPVT-R, although most of the words and artwork are new. Other major changes are as follows. The PPVT-R has 175 items in each form, whereas the PPVT had 150. In the development of the PPVT-R, special attention was given to balancing the content in terms of race and gender issues. The standard scores obtained on the PPVT were described as IQs, which is not the case on the PPVT-R.

ADMINISTRATION

Form Administered

Since the PPVT-R is available in two equivalent forms (L and M), either can be administered. There is no need to administer both forms, and no way of combining scores if both forms are given. Usually two forms are used together only for research purposes.

Items Administered

The items on the PPVT-R are arranged in order according to difficulty. Not all items are administered to a client; instead, only items within the "critical range" between the client's basal and ceiling level are administered. Items below the basal level are assumed to be passed, and items above the ceiling are assumed to be failed. For most clients, according to the manual, the number of items actually administered is 35 to 45. Thus, testing usually can be completed in 10 to 20 minutes.

The examiner begins testing at an item assumed to be within the client's ability level. For clients of average intelligence, the test protocol indicates starting points according to chronological age; for developmentally delayed clients, estimates based on mental age or adaptive skills can be used to determine a starting point. Selecting an appropriate starting point is important, according to the manual, so that the client experiences some initial success, without responding to so many easy items that the task becomes boring. From the starting point, the examiner administers consecutive items to determine the client's basal. On the PPVT-R, a *basal* is defined as eight consecutive correct items. Usually, from the starting point the examiner works forward, and eight or more items are answered correctly before the first error. If, however, a client makes an error before obtaining a basal, the examiner immediately works backward from the starting point until a sequence of 8 consecutive correct items has been identified.

After the basal has been established, the examiner works forward until the client reaches a ceiling. The ceiling on the PPVT-R is six errors within eight consecutive responses.

As is the case with many other psychological tests, clients will occasionally obtain multiple basals or ceilings. For example, on the PPVT-R the client may start at item 100, make an error at item 104, obtain a basal at items 96–103, then later answer correctly items 111–118. This would be a double basal. The PPVT-R manual is very clear about scoring procedures under such circumstances. The scoring rule is that items failed below the highest basal are scored as *correct,* and items passed above the lowest ceiling are scored as *incorrect*. The manual includes sample protocols for practice in scoring.

Occasionally, also, clients will not obtain a basal (in the case of mentally retarded or severely language-impaired clients) or a ceiling (in the case of extremely gifted clients). In these situations, test results should be interpreted with caution.

Administration Procedures

Specific wordings of directions are contained in the test manual, in boldface type for easy reference.

For older children and adults, administration procedures are very simple. The examiner explains that the test will involve pictures, or that it is a vocabulary test. A training plate is shown to the client, who is told that each picture is numbered, and that his or her task is to tell the examiner the number of, or point to, the picture that best tells the meaning of the word. The examiner may use as many training plates as needed to establish that the client understands the task and will make a clear response. The examiner corrects mistakes made by the client during the training phase, and demonstrates the correct response. For younger children, and by implication for delayed or handicapped older clients, more intensive explanation and practice are permissible. There is no penalty for guessing, so clients may be encouraged to guess. Clients who answer impulsively, without seeming to consider all the choices, may be encouraged to slow down and look at each picture before responding. Clients may change answers; their final choice is the one recorded and scored.

After the training items, the examiner must be careful not to indicate in any way whether the client's choice is correct. Further, guesses or apparently random answers should be noted by the examiner, who later will make a judgment about the overall validity of the assessment.

The examiner must read each stimulus word exactly as it is presented in the manual (a pronunciation guide is included). Alternative pronunciations should also be given, and words may be repeated as needed, but items cannot be readministered later in the session. It is not permissible to change the stimulus word in any way, for example by using the plural form. Examiners may not allow clients to see the printed words, or give clients the spelling of the words.

SCORING

Test Protocol

The PPVT-R protocol consists of columns of plate numbers with the correct drawing number for each plate and space for recording the subject's choice (drawing 1, 2, 3, or 4). The examiner records all responses so that the client does not receive a differential reaction to correct and incorrect answers. If the response was incorrect, the examiner also draws a line through the item number. This allows the examiner to note where the basal was established and to proceed until the ceiling level of six errors in eight consecutive responses has been reached.

Raw Score

When the basal and the ceiling have been reached, testing is finished. The examiner calculates the client's raw score by subtracting the number of errors from the ceiling item, which is defined as the last item administered. For example, if the client made six errors in items 101 through 108, then 108 is the ceiling item. All errors between the highest basal and item 108 would be subtracted from 108 to obtain the client's raw score.

Derived Scores

Derived scores allow the examiner to compare the client's performance to that of other individuals of the same age, and to determine the significance of the resulting difference. The first step in obtaining derived scores is to calculate the client's age. To do this, the examiner subtracts the client's date of birth from the date of testing. In the result, days above 15 are rounded up to the next month (for example, 8 years, 4 months, 16 days, equals 8 years, 5 months).

The PPVT-R provides the following derived scores: standard score equivalents, percentile ranks, stanines, and age norms. The standard score equivalents of the PPVT-R have a mean of 100 and a standard deviation of 15. Percentile ranks indicate what percentage of chronological-age peers obtained scores below that of the client. Stanines (an abbreviation of standard nines) divide the normal curve of standardized scores into nine broad groupings, with group 5 including the middle 20 percent of scores, groups 4 and 6 including 17 percent on either side of the mean, groups 3 and 7 having the next 12 percent, groups 2 and 8 having the next 7 percent, and groups 1 and 9 having the least common 4 percent of scores. Stanines are frequently used in reporting educational test scores. The age norms on the PPVT-R range from 1 year, 9 months, to 33 years, 8 months. The norms below 2 years, 6 months, are extrapolations from the normative group, which means that children below this age were not actually tested, but scores were estimated based on the data from children in the normative group.

The manual provides all norms according to age groups; norms by grade level are available from the publisher. Standard score equivalents in the manual range from 40 through 160. Extrapolated tables for standard scores below 40 are also available from the publisher.

The manual includes a clear explanation about the standard error of measurement (SEM) on the PPVT-R. Briefly, SEM is an estimate of the effects of chance and error on an individual score. Theoretically, if an individual could take a test many times without practice effects, the individual's score would differ slightly each time because of chance and error. The scores obtained under these circumstances would sometimes be higher and sometimes lower than the individual's obtained score on the single administration. In theory, the scores would be distributed around the obtained score in a normal, bell-shaped curve. The standard deviation of this distribution is called the standard error of measurement. Many psychological test scores are reported as the obtained score plus or minus one or more SEMs.

On the PPVT-R, information is provided about the SEM for each form of the test (L and M) at each age level, and for obtained scores at varying distances from the mean. Further, the protocol provides all the information necessary to determine and graphically display the obtained score and the "true score confidence band." The probability is 68 percent that the individual's true score falls within this range, which is essentially one SEM on either side of the obtained score.

PSYCHOMETRIC INFORMATION

Assumptions

The psychometric foundation of the PPVT-R rests on two assumptions. One is that the hearing vocabulary develops with age in a linear fashion, that is, increasing steadily over time. This assumption was found to be correct in the standardization population up to age 33 years, 8 months. After this time, receptive vocabulary for single words declines with age, which explains why age equivalents are not available above 33 years, 8 months. The second assumption is that the distribution of hearing vocabulary follows a normal or bell-shaped curve. This assumption was also essentially verified in the course of test construction, and so was used in the calibration, or development of item placement and specific scoring rules of the test.

Item Placement

Sophisticated statistical procedures (Rasch-Wright Latent Trait Item Analysis) were used to determine the order of words in the vocabulary list, and to make forms L and M equivalent. The specifics of these procedures are explained in the manual.

Normative sample: The PPVT-R was normed on 4,200 children and 828 adults. The sample of children included 100 males and 100 females at six-month age intervals from 2 years, 6 months, through 6 years, 11 months, and then at yearly age intervals from 7 years through 18 years. This sample was stratified to match the 1970 U.S. Census in terms of geographic area, community size, ethnic background, and parental occupation. The adult standardization sample was significantly smaller and somewhat less representative than the childhood sample. Ages ranged from 19 years to 40 years. Males and females were equally represented, and the occupations of adult subjects were consistent with the 1970 U.S. Census. The major deviation from national patterns was that the majority of the adult sample was from the North Central region of the United States. Another limitation was that no data were gathered on the ethnic background of the adult sample. Therefore, data collected from an adult compared to these norms should be interpreted much more conservatively than data from children. The PPVT-R can be used with adults above age 40, but results must be interpreted with the caution that the individual is being compared to younger adults, rather than to chronological age peers.

Reliability

The internal reliability of the PPVT-R was studied by split-half procedures. The complete statistical procedures used are explained in the manual. Briefly, individuals' scores on odd-numbered items were compared to the same individuals' scores on even-numbered items. The resulting scores were highly correlated, ranging from .61 to .88. Test–retest reliability was established by retesting a subsample of the standardization children 9 to 31 days after their original testing. Correlations ranged from .52 to .90, with a median of .77. The equivalence of Form L and Form M was determined by administering both forms to a subsample of 642 children; coefficients of equivalence ranged from .73 to .91, with a median of .82. Differences between forms generally fell in the direction of slightly higher standard scores on Form M.

Validity

Studies looking at the correlation of the PPVT-R with other measures of cognitive skills have found moderate correlations (generally in the range of .40 to .60) with intelligence tests such as the Stanford-Binet (Form L-M), the Wechsler Intelligence Scale for Children—Revised (WISC-R), and the Wechsler Adult Intelligence Scale—Revised (WAIS-R). These findings indicate that higher scores on one test are usually found with higher scores on the other test (and lower with lower). Even with high correlations, however, the actual scores of an individual on the PPVT-R and another measure may differ. The PPVT-R has been found to yield scores 5 to 15 points lower, on average, than the intelligence tests listed here. This is also the usual difference found between the PPVT-R and the original PPVT. The major exception to this trend appears to be the relationship of the PPVT-R and the McCarthy Scales of Children's Abilities; in the few studies currently available, average scores on these two instruments tend to be equal.

Studies of the relationship between PPVT-R scores and tests of academic achievement yield mixed results, depending on the population studied and the achievement test used. Correlations are generally highest with reading and language skills, and lowest with arithmetic skills. Some studies have found that the PPVT-R correlates more highly with achievement tests than with intelligence tests; other authors disagree. Summaries of this literature are contained in articles by Bracken and Prasse (1984) and D'Amato, Gray, and Dean (1987).

Very little information is currently available on possible differences in test performance of whites and ethnic minorities using the PPVT-R. Bracken and Prasse (1984) cited two small studies indicating lower scores for nonwhites, including one study in which groups of black and Hispanic children scored lower than a group of white children on the PPVT-R even when the children were equated for IQ.

INTERPRETATION

The PPVT-R is well accepted as a reliable test of hearing vocabulary for single English words. If this were its only function, however, it would be an insignificant test indeed. The potential importance of the PPVT-R derives from the relationship of vocabulary to overall human intelligence. The history of intelligence testing is marked by the appreciation of vocabulary as a foundation of general intellectual skills. Vocabulary is a significant part of language, and language skills represent significant tools for human problem solving. Thus, when a test as simple and brief as the original PPVT was shown to be reliable, it was seized on by psychologists, educators, and others. It became a popular tool in clinical assessment, educational screening, research, and many other settings where information about general cognitive skills was needed.

The original PPVT lent itself to these uses because the standard score derived from it was called an IQ score, just as the results of intelligence tests usually are. Thus, the PPVT came to be thought of as an IQ test and was probably misused in certain situations in which the limited nature of the test task (that is, receptive vocabulary for single words) was not understood. This problem has been addressed to some extent in the PPVT-R by the elimination of the term IQ. The test authors describe the PPVT-R as a measure of scholastic aptitude, but not of general intelligence. The extent to which this phrasing clarifies the nature of the test for the average user is uncertain.

As described before, the research literature on the uses and validity of the PPVT-R includes studies looking at the issues of whether the test has more similarities to intelligence tests or to tests of academic achievement. The findings of these studies are contradictory and inconclusive. Probably the answer should be that the PPVT-R is a test of receptive vocabulary, which in certain populations is highly correlated with intelligence, with academic achievement, and with other attributes such as cultural background and educational history.

CASE EXAMPLES

The following case examples are presented to illustrate the many appropriate uses of the PPVT-R, and a typical inappropriate use.

Case Example 1

Dr. Smith was the chief psychologist in the Department of Public Instruction of a southern state. The department had just received funding and authorization to develop a screening program for all children entering kindergarten, in order to identify youngsters who were at risk for school problems.

Dr. Smith recognized that screening procedures needed to be efficient and economical in the use of examiners' time for test administration and scoring. She therefore selected three measures aimed at assessing common areas of developmental/educational problems in early childhood. She decided that the screening battery would consist of a parental rating scale of the child's behavior and activity level, a test of eye-hand coordination, and the PPVT-R. She included the PPVT-R on the assumption that it would pick up many children with specific language difficulties, as well as children with more global developmental delays in intellectual development.

As in any screening program, not all affected children were identified, and not all children identified turned out to be affected. In this case, the PPVT-R did not identify all children with articulation difficulties, specific problems with expressive language, or deficits in the ability to process complex receptive language, as opposed to single words. Nevertheless, the battery of instruments selected turned out to be acceptably effective, and the PPVT-R was a good choice for this purpose of screening for early childhood language delays.

Case Example 2

Roger was a twenty-five-year-old man with Down syndrome who had never received any formal education as a child. At the time of the assessment, he had recently been accepted into a group home for adults with mental retardation and other developmental disabilities. Roger rarely spoke, and when he did his speech was extremely difficult to understand. Prior to admission to the group home, Roger had been tested by a psychologist who administered the Stanford-Binet. Roger had failed all verbal items above the two-and-a-half-year level, so the psychologist had discontinued testing and declared Roger to be profoundly mentally retarded. During Roger's first week at the group home, however, he was very interested in the social interactions around him, and seemed to understand at least some of what was said to him. Reassessment of his intellectual and language skills was requested for programming purposes. The group home's speech/language therapist began by administering the PPVT-R. The results placed Roger's receptive vocabulary at the 8 year, 5 month, level. On the basis of this finding, the psychologist administered an intelligence test that did not depend on oral language; Roger's scores indicated moderate mental retardation. These results were used by the psychologist and speech/language therapist to plan further evaluations of Roger's specific communication skills and needs, and to clarify with other program staff that Roger had much greater potential than his expressive language would suggest.

Case Example 3

Sam was a graduate student in psychology, preparing to conduct his dissertation research. His topic was the effect of Ritalin on hyperactive children in structured or unstructured situations. His plan was to observe children four times: both with and without their usual dosage of Ritalin, in both structured and unstructured situations. In all situations, Sam would observe behaviors such as motor activity, focused attention, and number of extraneous verbalizations. For the unstructured situations, Sam decided to observe the children at free play in a room with some toys. For the structured situation, he decided to have the child sit at a table and take the PPVT-R. The two forms of the PPVT-R were ideal for this purpose, since each child would be seen twice in structured situations (both with and without medication). In addition to providing a standardized activity, the PPVT-R would also yield scores that could provide useful information about the effect of Ritalin on the quality of performance. Thus, the PPVT-R was an excellent tool for this research project.

Case Example 4

Julia was a five-year-old girl brought to a child psychiatry outpatient clinic by a social worker. Julia had reportedly been severely neglected, and possibly abused, by her family. She was now in the custody of the Department of Social Services, which was requesting psychological evaluation, including both emotional assessment and educational recommendations.

During her first session with the psychologist, Julia was mute and withdrawn. She would not respond to questions and did not play with the dolls and other toys in the room. The psychologist attempted to administer the Wechsler Preschool and Primary Scale of Intelligence, but Julia would not talk or manipulate the blocks or puzzles on the test. The psychologist therefore decided to use the PPVT-R, since the only response necessary would be pointing. Holding the little girl on her lap, the psychologist used the training plates to demonstrate pointing to a picture as a word was spoken. Julia was willing to perform this activity, since the early items were easy for her. As she touched each picture, the psychologist praised her efforts, even if her answers were incorrect. This interaction seemed to help Julia relax somewhat. Partway through the test she initiated some verbalizations, and answered simple questions about toys she liked to play with and foods she liked to eat. This suggested to the psychologist that, with time, Julia would be willing to talk about other, more serious issues. A complete PPVT-R was administered in this session, although the psychologist planned to interpret the scores with extreme caution, if they were used at all, because of the child's recent history. Nevertheless, when the standard score was computed to be in the low average range, the psychologist was fairly confident that Julia was capable of functioning at least at this level, if not higher, when environmental stresses were relieved. Furthermore, the process of testing with this nonverbal instrument seemed to make the child more willing to cooperate with the psychologist in other assessment procedures.

Case Example 5

Mr. Jones served as admissions director at a small private school. He wished to improve the image of the school, which was suffering from declining enrollment. He therefore decided that the school would advertise itself as an academy for gifted children. He had all applicants to the school tested with the PPVT-R. Those with a standard score above 120 he labeled as gifted, and admitted into the program. Applicants who scored below 85 he called borderline retarded, and declined to admit.

This was clearly an inappropriate use of the PPVT-R. In clinical situations the PPVT-R should only rarely be used in isolation. Using it for significant placement decisions is particularly inappropriate. Furthermore, Mr. Jones did not appear to understand that all test scores are influenced to some degree by chance and error, as reflected in the standard error of measurement. Thus, rigid cutoff scores are frequently misleading. Finally, although the PPVT-R correlates fairly well with tests of academic achievement and general intelligence, the test task of receptive vocabulary for single words is too narrow to measure either general academic excellence or developmental delay.

ASSETS AND LIABILITIES

The PPVT-R is a brief test that is simple to administer and score. It is normed on a large national sample, and has good reliability. The test can be used with clients of many ages and with a variety of conditions, including speech disorders, limited intelligence, and extremely withdrawn or passive behavior. The test yields several derived scores, including age equivalents and percentiles, that are easily understood by consumers of test results.

The major liability of the PPVT-R is that it is a test of one limited skill: receptive knowledge of single words. Although this skill may correlate well with other abilities, such as general intelligence and academic achievement, the PPVT-R alone cannot be substituted for more comprehensive tests of these abilities.

CONCLUSION

The PPVT-R can be an excellent assessment tool for psychologists and other professionals who understand its uses and limitations. The PPVT-R is not an intelligence test; but, as the case examples have demonstrated, it has a place in the repertoire of clinicians and researchers who work with special populations.

REFERENCES

Bracken, B. A., & Prasse, D. P. (1984). Peabody Picture Vocabulary Test—Revised: An appraisal and review. *School Psychology Review, 13,* 49–60.

D'Amato, R. C., Gray, J. W., & Dean, R. S. (1987). Concurrent validity of the PPVT-R with the K-ABC for learning problem children. *Psychology in the Schools, 24,* 35–39.

Dunn, L. M. (1959). *Peabody Picture Vocabulary Test.* Minneapolis, MN: American Guidance Service.

Dunn, L. M., & Dunn, L. M. (1981). *Peabody Picture Vocabulary Test—Revised.* Circle Pines, MN: American Guidance Service.

Index